QUETICO

QUETICO

Near to Nature's Heart

Jon Nelson

A NATURAL HERITAGE BOOK
A MEMBER OF THE DUNDURN GROUP
TORONTO

Published by Natural Heritage Books
A Member of The Dundurn Group

Cover and text design by Jennifer Scott
Editor: Jane Gibson
Copy-editor: Shannon Whibbs
Printed and bound in Canada by Transcontinental

Library and Archives Canada Cataloguing in Publication

Nelson, Jon, 1943-
    Quetico : near to nature's heart / by Jon Nelson.

Includes bibliographical references and index.
ISBN 978-1-55488-396-7

    1. Quetico Provincial Park (Ont.)--History. 2. Natural history--Ontario--Quetico Provincial Park. 3. Nelson, Jon, 1943-. I. Title.

FC3065.Q4 N44 2009   971.3'117   C2009-900291-4

1   2   3   4   5   13   12   11   10   09

Dundurn Press
3 Church Street, Suite 500
Toronto, Ontario, Canada
M5E 1M2

Gazelle Book Services Limited
White Cross Mills
High Town, Lancaster, England
LA1 4XS

Dundurn Press
2250 Military Road
Tonawanda, NY
U.S.A. 14150

Conseil des Arts du Canada   **Canada Council for the Arts**   **ONTARIO ARTS COUNCIL CONSEIL DES ARTS DE L'ONTARIO**

Canadä

We acknowledge the support of the **Canada Council for the Arts** and the **Ontario Arts Council** for our publishing program. We also acknowledge the financial support of the **Government of Canada** through the **Book Publishing Industry Development Program** and **The Association for the Export of Canadian Books** and the **Government of Canada** through the **Ontario Book Publishers Tax Credit Program** and the **Ontario Media Development Corporation**.

Care has been taken to trace the ownership of copyright material used in this book. The author and the publisher welcome any information enabling them to rectify any references or credits in subsequent editions.

J. Kirk Howard, President

Cover photos by Jon Nelson except top right photo of Billy Magee courtesy of the Oberholtzer Foundation, Excelsior, Minnesota. All other visuals are courtesy of Jon Nelson unless otherwise identified.

DEDICATION

Tom Miyata worked in his quiet, persistent, and eloquent way for over three decades to preserve and protect Quetico Park. He fought harder, longer, and more effectively than anyone I know to make Quetico a wilderness park and to ensure that it remained that way. Everyone who loves a wild Quetico owes Tom a deep debt of gratitude.

I was, and still am, inspired and motivated by Tom Miyata and his love of the outdoors, his knowledge, his enthusiasm for life, and his passion for wilderness. My family and I were blessed to have known him and his family. He is a central figure in many of my best memories of canoeing, camping, fishing, hunting and — more importantly — he was a dear friend.

This book is dedicated to Tom Miyata. A huge hole was created in the fabric of my life when he died in 2007.

CONTENTS

LIST OF MAPS

NEAR TO NATURE'S HEART: AN EXPLANATION

In 1897, William and Jennie Richardson set off on their honeymoon. They travelled by birchbark canoe into the centre of Quetico, along with their Indian guides. At the conclusion of their three-week trip, Jennie noted, "it is good to be so near to nature's heart, even if for so brief a space."[1]

This book is a series of writings about the natural and human history of a place that was set aside early enough that it still contains intact ecosystems with an aura of the past. The phrase "near to nature's heart" summarizes the feelings of those who, like myself, treasure the time they have been able to spend in Quetico.

ACKNOWLEDGEMENTS

My wife Marie and our children, Leif and Anna, have been my main support and inspiration. Marie is truly my better half and we've had the joy of watching our children grow into two independent and inquiring young adults. We are incredibly proud of them.

Tempest Benson, Tom Miyata, Bruce Curtis, Don Bowser, Bob Cary, Marie Ottertail, John Boshey, Bernice Hyatt, and Johnny Sansted are just a few of the people who are no longer with us whose enthusiasm for Quetico influenced me greatly. Numerous people, such as Shirley Peruniak, Bob Hayes, Joe and Vera Meany, Betty Powell Skoog, Dinna Madsen, Kalvin Ottertail, Don Meany, Janice Matichuk, Keith and Arlene Robinson, and John Sohigian continue to work in various ways to keep the spirit of Quetico alive.

Although I have a general knowledge of the topics covered in this book, I am not an expert in any of them. I have relied heavily on the expertise and co-operation of many people who are authorities in their fields. The chapters that relate to the retreat of the glacier through the Quetico-Superior and its effect on the landscape couldn't have been written without the valuable comments and corrections made by Brian Phillips, Phil Kor, and Matthew Boyd. They have conducted fieldwork in northwestern Ontario and have practical knowledge of the effects of glaciers on the Quetico-Superior landscape.

Even though I have conducted archaeological research in Quetico, I consulted with numerous archaeologists who have worked in the area and are very knowledgeable about the first explorers into this area. These include Bill Ross, Walt Okstad, Tony Romano, Sue Mulholland, Lee Johnson, Bill Clayton, and Mike McCloud. Their views have influenced my interpretation of the post-glacial period and how and when people moved into this area. Since almost nothing is known about the first people in the Quetico-Superior, archaeologists disagree on many particulars. We all agree, however, that Quetico's first explorers were awesome people at an awesome time.

Andrew Hinshelwood and I were very fortunate that Elders from the Lac La Croix First Nation in 1999 (John Boshey Sr., Marie Ottertail, Helen Geyshick, Robert Ottertail, Helen Jordan, and Doris Whitefish) were willing to patiently explain their views and listen to ours. We were also greatly aided by consulting with, and learning from, a variety of people with experience in trying to bridge the gap between archaeologists and Native peoples. The people who aided my understanding of matters relating to interactions between archaeologists and Anishinaabe people include Kalvin Ottertail, Scott Hamilton, Jill Taylor-Hollings, Doug Gilmore, Walt Okstad, and Dave Woodward. I am grateful to Andrew Hinshelwood, who collaborated with me in the writing of Chapter 3 dealing with archaeology and Anishinaabe spiritual beliefs.

The chapter on moose research is based, in part, on research conducted by Tim Timmermann, who also gave me a better understanding of moose biology and insights into their research. Willard Carmean is the "grand old man" of white pine research in northwestern Ontario and I relied heavily on him to provide a more complete understanding of the importance of white pine and the significance of McNiece Lake. Tim Lynham and Lisa Solomon were valuable sources of information on fire ecology and their research on white pine regeneration in Quetico. Twenty years ago, when writing my thesis, I relied heavily on Richard Ojakangas for information on the geology of the Knife Lake area and he was again helpful in my attempt to make the complex volcanic origins of the Knife Lake bedrock understandable. All of these people not only conducted important research in the Quetico-Superior, but also generously shared as much of their knowledge as I was able to absorb.

The prelude regarding Quetico's 100th anniversary was greatly aided by suggestions made by Bruce Litteljohn, who played a significant role in making Quetico a wilderness park. Others who read and commented on portions of the text include Mike Barker, Kalvin Ottertail, Jay Leather, Dave Elder, Fergy Wilson, Gerald Killan, John Soghigian, Robin Reilly, and Bill Addison. This section is my brief interpretation of Quetico's formation and evolution since it became a protected area in 1909, and it reflects, as does the rest of the book, my broad personal interests and biases. More detailed accounts of Quetico's history can be found in works by Shirley Peruniak, Gerald Killan, and George Warecki.

Others read all or parts of chapters and made constructive comments on the chapters relating to special places in Quetico and ecology sections of the book: Joe Walewski and Erica North (lichens), Jeep LaTourelle (Prairie Portage), Rick Gollat (moose research), Sally Burns (The Pines), Steve Kingston and Doug Morris (pukak), Tony Elders and Lynn Hazen (beaver), Pete Doran, Nadia Kovachis, and Caleb Hassler (aquatic ecology), Ellen Bogardus-Szymaniak (fire ecology), Lori Gregor (carnivorous plants), Paula and Andy Hill (McNiece Lake), Jamie

McMahon, Dick Hiner, Anna Nelson, and Leif Nelson read and commented on many articles. Their advice and expertise greatly added to the depth of the articles and helped me avoid many errors.

A special thanks to Shirley Peruniak, who knows more about Quetico Park than everyone else does collectively, for reading many of the articles and making many helpful suggestions. My wife Marie played a major role in this book. She was my primary editor, the person I bounced ideas off of, and who kept my spirits up when I got discouraged. She was always the person to suffer through my first drafts, make copious corrections of spelling and grammar, and tirelessly remind me to "loosen up" my writing and be less academic. Johnnie Hyde was influential in persuading me to write the early stages of this book. Heather Peden edited many of the early drafts and helped immensely to get my writing more organized and less repetitive. Phyllis Dalgleish patiently helped me overcome some of my deficiencies in computor usage. Thunder Bay's Gregg Johns of Imagetech was my guide in learning the technicalities of using digital cameras. Prior to that, the people at Primary Foto Source were helpful during the decades I used slide film.

The maps were made by Cathy Chapin from Lakehead University. While making these wonderful maps she frequently made alterations as I changed my mind as to what I wanted. Jennifer Garrett, Lise Sorenson, and Mary Lambirth used their considerable artistic talents to help illustrate the book. I am particularly indebted to Jennifer, who made two paintings — a depiction of spring and fall turnover of lakes and a Late Palaeo-Indian spear point — specifically for this book.

The John B. Ridley Research Library at the Quetico Park Interpretive Centre at French Lake, with its wealth of information on Quetico Park, was a vital source of information for this book. Andrea Allison was invaluable in locating information and photos that I required. The library is an underutilized and valuable resource of tapes, articles, photos, notes, and other materials that have been compiled by park staff for decades. The library contains a wealth of information about Quetico Park and the people who have shaped it. The Atikokan Centennial Museum was a valuable source for information on the history of the Atikokan area.

My thanks also go to Barry Penhale, publisher emeritus, and Jane Gibson, editor, of Natural Heritage/ Dundurn Press for their patient and encouraging support of my early efforts. With their help, the work has been molded into a readable book.

I've been fortunate to have many terrific people accompany me on canoe trips in Quetico. Andy Hill, in particular, spent a lot of time with me exploring various parts of the park. In recent years I have taken trips where one of the objectives was to gather information and photos for this book. Marie Nelson, Andy and Paula Hill, Dick Hiner, Leif Nelson, and Heather Sutton have been my primary companions on these outings. On archaeological research trips sponsored by the Quetico Foundation from 1996 to 1999, Frank Jordan was my usual partner with a variety of students from Lac La Croix and Atikokan also helping out. Dick Hiner, Norman Jordan, and Ralph Ottertail Jr. were research assistants on Knife Lake in the late 1980s, and James Burns and Dan Fotheringham were able assistants in the research on Knife Lake in 2001. All of these people made it possible for an insulin-dependent diabetic to continue taking extended canoe trips into Quetico. When canoeing with me they knew that low blood sugar was sometimes a bigger concern than high winds. Thanks.

This book is, to an amazing degree, a collaborative effort made possible by the assistance of many people. However, any errors or misinterpretations in any section of this work are mine alone.

INTRODUCTION

Much of my adult life has revolved around Quetico Park. For twelve summers, my wife Marie and I worked as Quetico Park rangers at Beaverhouse Lake, Cache Bay, and Prairie Portage. Those wonderful years inspired me to return to school when I was forty-five years old. After my degree was completed, we returned to northwestern Ontario and I spent six summers conducting archaeological research in Quetico Park while teaching biology and chemistry at Confederation College in Thunder Bay. I continued to teach at the college until my retirement a few years ago.

Working as a park ranger and researcher, I made numerous canoe trips into Quetico Park and a few into the Boundary Waters Canoe Area Wilderness (BWCAW). In addition, I have snowshoed and canoed extensively in the park for my own enjoyment. All of these trips provided opportunities to take photos and provided the background necessary for writing this book. The chapters were written specifically for this book, but some are substantially revised and updated from articles that appeared in the *Boundary Waters*

Journal, the *Chronicle Journal* (Thunder Bay), the *Globe and Mail* (Toronto), and *Canoesport Magazine*.

I grew up in Montevideo, a small farming community on the prairies of southern Minnesota, and went to Concordia College in Moorhead, Minnesota. After a canoe trip in the early 1960s, I became infatuated with canoeing and Quetico Park. Years later, I met Marie Pelkola, who had worked many summers at the Minnesota (now Voyageur) Outward Bound School and had taken many trips into Quetico Park and the BWCAW. Our mutual interest in canoeing and a desire to live in the north caused us to move to Atikokan, Ontario, in 1973.

We bought a small resort with Rob and Martha McManus, another couple from Minnesota, and quickly became immersed in the wonderful diversity of Atikokan. Our arrival coincided with the controversy over logging in Quetico Park and we met local people, such as Tom and Bettina Miyata, who were active and outspoken in their support for the cessation of logging in the park. We slowly lost our "Mercan" accents, adopted Canadian ways,

Cathy A. Chapin, Lakehead University Geography Department.

and learned the local vernacular. This includes: putting vinegar on our chips (french fries); wiping our faces with serviettes (paper napkins); wearing toques (stocking caps) and Sorels (winter boots) when it gets cold; catching pickerel (walleyes), lawyers (burbots), and hammer handles (small northern pike) through the ice; putting on clean gotch (underwear) in the morning before plugging in the electric kettle; and sitting on chesterfields (sofas) drinking Molson Stock Ale while watching the Habs (Montreal Canadiens) or the Leafs (Toronto Maple Leafs) on *Hockey Night in Canada*.

After a few years we sold our resort and were hired to work as rangers in Quetico Park. It was, for us, the perfect job. Bob Hayes, a Quetico Park ranger in the 1940s and a friend of Marie's parents in Winton, Minnesota, told me that when he first flew into Basswood Lake in 1943 he felt that "he was descending into the ultimate paradise." Not surprisingly, Marie and I had similar feelings when we flew into Beaverhouse Lake for the first time in 1976.

We were fortunate to have an amazing group of co-workers in Quetico Park. The other park rangers, portage crew, naturalists, and park supervisors were an extremely enthusiastic, dedicated, and diverse group of people. Joe and Vera Meany, Mike and Priscella O'Brien, Wilber and Bernice Hyatt,

MAP 1: QUETICO PARK AND SURROUNDING AREA
Ontario's Quetico Park lies adjacent to the Boundary Water Canoe Area Wilderness (BWCAW) in Minnesota.

Glen Nolan, Carrie Frechette, Janice Matichuck, Shirley Peruniak, Shan and Margie Walshe, Bob and Sally Burns, Dave Elder, Mike Barker, Gary Parker, Wayne Bourque, Lorne Morrow, Dan Romanson, and Hillary Petrus are just a few of those who greatly enriched our lives.

Mike Barker, the district manager for the Atikokan District of the Ministry of Natural Resources from 1973 to 1979, would begin the park's spring introductory staff session by reminding us that we were working in the best park in Ontario and that we were the best in the world at what we did. We all believed he was right in both assertions. From 1976 through 1987 we worked as park rangers and those years, from my biased perspective, were the "golden age" of Quetico Park.

When we began working at Beaverhouse Lake, Quetico was blessed in having Shan Walshe and Shirley Peruniak, two outstanding full-time naturalists. Doug Haddow, George Holborn, and Sally Burns also worked as naturalists at times during those years when learning more about Quetico's natural history was given a high priority. Shan Walshe motivated me, along with thousands of others, to learn more about plants and their role in the environment. He taught by example and loved the fieldwork involved in being a park naturalist. As often as possible he went on canoe trips and spent a minimum amount of time at a desk at French Lake. There are many canoeists who have fond memories of encounters with Shan on portages, in bogs or swamps, along the shorelines of lakes, or anywhere an unusual plant had caught his attention.

Shirley Peruniak's interest in the human history of Quetico, her enthusiasm, and depth of knowledge inspired me to learn more about the park's past. I was strongly influenced by Shirley's example of talking to — and more importantly, listening to — the people of Lac La Croix. From the beginning, she persistently worked with the First Nations people there, a practice that was not common in the 1970s, to gather stories and photos documenting their past. By obtaining a better understanding of the role of the Lac La Croix First Nation in Quetico's past, she helped pave the way for their having a greater say in Quetico's future.

Shirley has a special gift for getting people to talk freely about the past. She has compiled tapes of Atikokan, Lac La Croix, Ely, and Grand Marais residents, loggers, bush pilots, trappers, poachers, park rangers, and anyone else she could find with knowledge of Quetico's history. These tapes, along with a treasure trove of photos and information gathered by Shirley and other park staff, have been compiled by Andrea Allison at the John B. Ridley Research Library in the Quetico Park Information Pavilion at French Lake.

My years in the park — particularly experiencing the beauty and mystery of pictographs and seeing evidence of ancient quarry activity on Knife Lake — stimulated an interest in archaeology. I went back to school in 1986 to obtain a masters degree in anthropology at Trent University in Peterborough, Ontario. The research I conducted focused primarily on the first people to enter Quetico Park after the retreat of the glacier some thirteen thousand years ago.

Most of my research was funded by the Quetico Foundation, but my final summer's research in Quetico was made possible by the assistance of the Friends of Quetico. Marie was one of the original board members when it was formed in 1984 and I currently serve on the board. The goals of the Friends of Quetico include furthering education and supporting research in Quetico Park. A percentage of the profits from this book will go to supporting ecological research in the park, particularly fieldwork employing students from Atikokan and Lac La Croix. The future of Quetico depends on the involvement of young people, especially those from communities near the park, in its preservation.

While researching Knife Lake's stone quarries, it became apparent to me that, in order to understand various aspects of how, when, and why this particular rock type was chosen for tools by Quetico's earliest residents, I had to become familiar with more than just archaeology and geology. I found that the same type of broad approach was needed when writing chapters for this book. Understanding carnivorous plants and the bogs they grow in, for example, requires some understanding of chemistry, symbiotic relationships, plant ecology, and even the glacial history of the area. For all the chapters,

I tried to integrate information from a variety of fields of study in order to make the stories more complete and understandable.

My interest in using photography to illustrate aspects of plant and animal life led me to investigate the insides of pitcher plants, the Lilliputian world of ground lichens, and the tracks of otter sliding across the snow. Fast shutter speeds can stop a running moose dead in his tracks as he continues to run, while very long exposures of rapids and falls can reveal aspects of moving water that the eye doesn't see. The images used to highlight, clarify, and expand specific topics or items mentioned in the text are an essential ingredient of this book.

The themes of Quetico's long and varied human history, glacial effects on the landscape, symbiosis, ecological interactions, and my own experiences in Quetico Park are threads that run through and, hopefully, tie this book together. I strove to make the Native Canadian past, which is unfortunately often referred to as "pre-history," part of our shared history. Ecologists have coined the term "deep ecology" to include humans as an integral part of the environment rather than just outside observers. It is my intent that this book reflect a "deep history" of Quetico Park, where the symbiotic relationship between humans, both Native and non-Native, and the land is a primary focus.

Anthropologist Norman Hallendy quoted an Inuit shaman who told him, "From time to time, the spirits seek us out because they are in need of human warmth for a little while. This is the time to listen very carefully to what they are saying because they are trying to tell us what we are really thinking."[1] I have tried to listen carefully — to spirits that sought me out, to fellow humans that I sought out, and to the land — and then to write and photograph as accurately as possible about what I have learned.

PRELUDE

QUETICO: ONE HUNDRETH ANNIVERSARY OF A "MAGIC LAND"

In 1909, Ernest Oberholtzer, a pioneer in preserving the Quetico-Superior region, made a canoe trip in Quetico with his Ojibwa friend Billy Magee. They saw moose almost every day; they were intrigued by the pictographs they encountered; they marvelled at the beauty of Rebecca Falls and Sue Falls; and they saw large stands of old pine, including a white pine on Jean Lake that they estimated to be one-and-a-half metres in diameter. This was Oberholtzer's first extensive trip into the Quetico-Superior region and the experience inspired him to dedicate his life to preserving its wilderness character.

As Oberholtzer and Magee zigzagged across Quetico, in addition to the wondrous scenery and wildlife, they found many examples of human impact on the landscape. They saw foundations for the Hudson Bay Company post on the Pickerel Lake to Dore Lake portage, dams on the Maligne and Knife rivers, a logging camp on the Knife River, and a trading post on Basswood Lake. They also talked to rangers patrolling for poachers and putting out fires. And on numerous occasions they encountered Ojibwa people. During their journey they noticed pole structures for spearing sturgeon on the Namakan River; saw cedar strips drying for baskets and bear pelts hanging on racks at Lac La Croix; stayed on a site where birchbark canoes were made on Poohbah Lake; and came upon an Ojibwa couple in a birchbark canoe using a blanket for a sail on Kawnipi Lake.

Recalling his trip years later, Oberholtzer noted that Quetico in 1909 was such a special place that the Indians felt "that there is a spiritual power back of it all." He noted that "it was no wonder that they had traditions and felt spirits in there, it had a spirituality about its appearance, you felt you were in kind of a magic land."[1]

Native peoples have a long history in Quetico. Over twelve thousand years ago, near the end of the last ice age, Palaeo-Indians moved into the area. They were followed by a series of Native cultures culminating with the Sioux, Cree, and, finally, the Ojibwa, who inhabited the area when the first white settlers arrived. Those settlers, some of whom remained in

Quetico Park

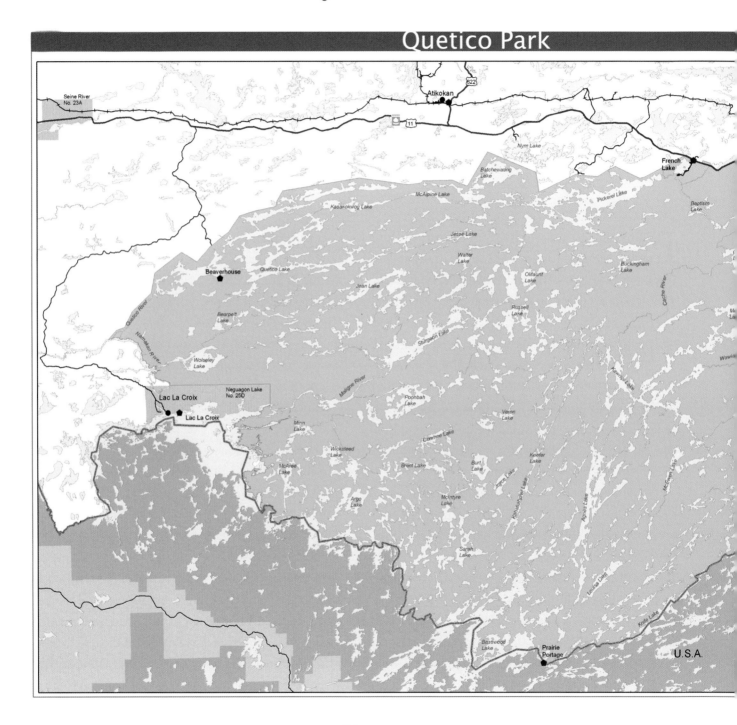

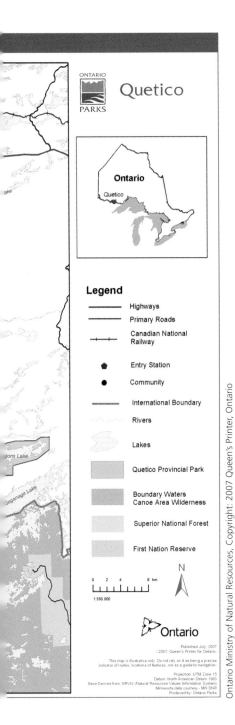

Ontario Ministry of Natural Resources, Copyright: 2007 Queen's Printer, Ontario

Courtesy of the Oberholtzer Foundation, Excelsior, Minnesota.

MAP 2: QUETICO PARK

This contemporary map of Quetico Park can be used to find most of the locations mentioned in the text.

ABOVE

Billy Magee paddles on a lake in the newly created Quetico Forest Reserve while on a canoe trip with Ernest Oberholtzer in 1909.

A golden September sunrise in the Rawn Narrows of Pickerel Lake is an indication of the magic that still exists in Quetico.

the Quetico-Superior, were part of a diverse group of people that began traversing this terrain in the 1600s: European explorers searching for the Pacific Ocean, voyageurs transporting trade goods and furs, and surveyors and geologists paving the way for settling the area west of Lake Superior. As well, Grey Nuns travelling to Winnipeg in 1844 to set up a school; the 1870 Wolseley expedition to quell the Riel Rebellion in Manitoba; settlers heading west along the Dawson Route; and trappers, park rangers, poachers, timber cruisers, loggers, and miners all comprise just a small sample of those who have moved along Quetico's waterways after the arrival of the Europeans.

One hundred years after Quetico was first set aside, we walk many of these same portages and pitch our tents on the same campsites where everyone from Palaeo-Indians to Oberholtzer and Magee spent the night. We are fortunate that Quetico was protected early enough that its combination of a glorious, mainly undisturbed, landscape and its long and varied human history still retains the magic that Oberholtzer found in 1909.

PROTECTING THE
QUETICO-SUPERIOR REGION

Although Native peoples, European explorers, and fur traders routinely traversed the Quetico-Superior region by canoe, it was very difficult to construct roads and railway lines through its maze of bedrock and water. Consequently, the Quetico-Superior was largely untouched by the industrial age until the late 1800s. When development came, however, it came with a rush.

Just south of the border, the town of Ely, Minnesota, was connected to the Duluth and Iron Range Railroad in 1888. Expansion of the railroad was triggered by the discovery of iron ore. The first iron mine opened south of Ely in Soudan, Minnesota, in 1882. Iron ore was also found near Ely and by 1890 there were ten operating or proposed mines near the town. Logging was in high gear in 1895 when the Knox Lumber Company sawmill in Winton, Minnesota, cut 20 million board feet of lumber. Just three years later, another logging company, Swallow and Hopkins, bought land on Fall Lake in Winton to build their sawmill. By 1900, logging was occurring on Basswood Lake and Swallow and Hopkins constructed the Four Mile Portage (seven kilometres) to facilitate the transport of logs from Basswood Lake to Fall Lake. Logging spread swiftly along the Minnesota side of the border lakes from Crooked Lake to Knife Lake.

North of the border, there was a flurry of mining activity. The Jackfish Mine, one of the first gold mines[2] in Ontario, was opened east of Quetico after gold was discovered in 1870 and was functioning by the 1880s. By 1895, two additional gold mines were operating, one west of Atikokan at Mine Centre and one east of Atikokan at Sapawe. In 1897, the Geological Survey of Canada found indications of iron ore just north of Atikokan beneath the water of Steep Rock Lake. This rich ore deposit would become the Steep Rock Iron Mine when the demand for iron ore soared during the Second World War. A smaller but more accessible iron ore deposit, called the Atikokan Iron Mine, was in production from 1905 to 1913. Meanwhile, prospectors found iron ore deposits along the Man Chain west of Saganaga Lake. In addition to gold and iron mines, in 1902, a copper mine was also in operation at Burchell Lake, east of the future Quetico Park.

By the turn of the century, a railway passing just north of Quetico was under construction. In 1901, a ceremonial "silver spike" was driven in at Atikokan to mark the completion of the Canadian Northern Railway linking Winnipeg and Port Arthur (now part of Thunder Bay). By that date, sawmills operating near the railway west of Atikokan at Calm Lake and Mine Centre were supplying lumber for rail-line construction and repairs, as well as lumber-camp development. Timber cruisers had laid out two timber berths in the northern part of the future Quetico Park in 1891, and, with the railway completed, there was now a means of getting logs, sawed lumber, and ore to markets in other parts of Canada.

With the rapid depletion of natural resources, private citizens and government officials in both the United States and Canada were becoming increasingly concerned about the destruction and waste that accompanied the boom in logging and mining. Shan Walshe, an outstanding Quetico Park naturalist from 1970 to 1991, noted that "After hundreds of years of regarding the wilderness as an enemy to be exploited and destroyed, some people in the United States and Canada began to have a change of heart … fearing that their natural character and strength would disappear along with the wilderness."[3]

In the Quetico-Superior region, the initial impetus for setting aside areas protected from these rapid and extensive developments seemed to come primarily from the United States. This was primarily because the resource exploitation was more extensive on that side of the border. A key figure in the preservation movement in Minnesota was Christopher C. Andrews, who had been the American ambassador to Sweden and Norway from 1872 to 1882. After seeing how tree-planting, fire suppression, and other conservation efforts in Scandinavia had improved their forests, he decided that these practices would also be beneficial for forests in Minnesota. When he became Minnesota's forestry commissioner, he instigated similar procedures. In 1900, Andrews successfully lobbied Congress to set aside the Cass Lake Forest Reserve in north-central Minnesota, the first forest in the United States to be managed by forestry principles. When he canoed from Basswood Lake to Crane Lake in 1905, he saw that the border areas also had potential for recreational activities. He urged Minnesota and Ontario to join together to create "an international forest reserve and park of very great beauty and interest."[4]

Concern over the preservation of Canadian resources was also growing as the trees, in particular, were rapidly disappearing. Clifford Sifton, Canada's minister of the Interior from 1896 to 1905, noted that Ontario and Canada were "spending their forest capital instead of living on the interest."[5] The Ontario government responded to the pressure for action by passing the Forest Reserves Act in 1898, which offered protection of timber from logging. Although governments were making progress in preserving forests, the public was more concerned that moose and other game animals were declining at an alarming rate. Moose were especially vulnerable because the numerous logging and mining camps

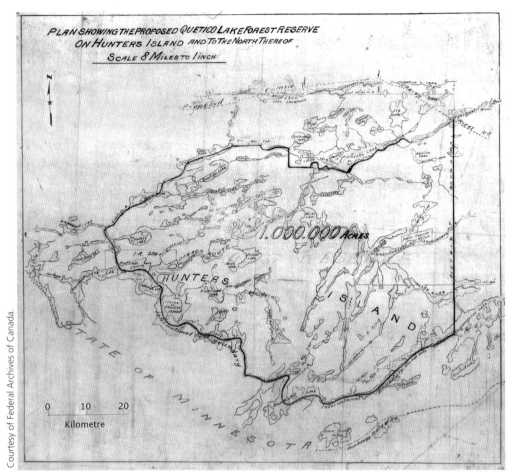

Courtesy of Federal Archives of Canada.

MAP 3: THE PROPOSED QUETICO FOREST RESERVE
From its modest beginning as a Forest Reserve, Quetico has evolved into a world-renowned wilderness park.

required great quantities of fresh meat. Professional hunters provided game for logging and mining camps; a single logging camp would consume fifty to one hundred moose — known as "pine beef" — in a winter. Trophy hunters were adding to the problem by killing moose just for their antlers.

The member of Ontario's Parliament from Fort Frances, William A. Preston, was disturbed by the effects of hunting and poaching on game populations and worked to establish a game refuge in Quetico. He found an unexpected ally in officials of the Canadian Northern Railway, who thought that the railway could benefit if the Quetico area could be promoted as a tourist destination. The combined efforts of an unlikely coalition of fish and game associations, conservationists, railway executives, and government officials, were able to successfully make their case for protection for game animals.

The interest on both sides of the border to create greater resource protection came to fruition in 1909. On February 13, 1909, the United States set aside the Superior National Forest. Minnesota followed their example and created the Superior Game Refuge to protect moose and other game animals. On April 1, 1909, just six weeks after the creation of the Superior National Forest, Ontario established the Quetico Forest Reserve. In retrospect, a remarkable degree of co-operation and foresight was shown by

Courtesy of the Oberholtzer Foundation, Excelsior, Minnesota.

Robert Readman, chief fire ranger in Quetico, cooks on a campsite in the Quetico Forest Reserve in August of 1909. That fall, he and Ephram Crawford were appointed Quetico's first park rangers.

government agencies in both countries when they established these adjacent protected areas.

The Order-in-Council that officially established the Quetico Forest Reserve declared: "In view of the large quantity of pine timber in this territory the lands therein should be withdrawn from location settlement or sale and kept in a state of nature as much as possible."[6] Although public pressure for a Quetico reserve came primarily from concerns over the plummeting number of moose, the creation of a forest reserve rather than a game reserve indicated that the desire to protect the large stands of pine was the Ontario government's main reason for preservation. Protection of moose and other game animals was secondary to preserving timber, with its considerable economic value.

In a forest reserve, timber could be withdrawn from sale, but still be available for harvesting in later years. To protect the resource, funding was concentrated on fighting fires and the remaining funds were not adequate to protect moose or other game animals. During the first few years of the forest reserve's existence, it became apparent that moose hunting and the poaching of fur-bearers was occurring on a large scale. A 1912 government report on the Quetico Forest Reserve noted: "At the present time no protection is afforded the reserve from October to May, and the very abundance of the big game and fur-bearing animals undoubtedly offers very great temptation to the hunter and trapper who is aware of this fact."[7] The report went on to note: "It is apparent that if the reserve is to fulfill its

functions and to be conserved to posterity, greater expenditures will have to be devoted to the maintenance of a more adequate staff to protect it."[8]

The Forest Reserve status provided a refuge for game animals, but in order to give more protection to them, Quetico Provincial Park was created in 1913. Quetico was the third provincial park in Ontario and the first created under the new Provincial Parks Act.[9] Park status provided stricter regulations to protect game animals and funding to enforce the regulations. However, while animals were now protected, logging, mining exploration, and commercial fishing were allowed.

Courtesy of the John B. Ridley Research Library, Quetico Park Information Pavilion.

The first ranger cabin in Quetico was built by Robert Readman and Ephram Crawford in the fall of 1909. This small but impressive building, complete with porch, rocking chair, bear-proof windows, and decorative moose antlers, was probably located on Ottawa Island on Basswood Lake.

QUETICO PARK AND FIRST NATIONS PEOPLE

Unfortunately, there was also a downside to the creation of the park. Aubrey White, the deputy minister of Lands, Forests and Mines, noted the Ontario government's position in a 1909 memorandum stating that although there were Native Reserves in the newly created park, "the Indians will not be interfered with."[10] This was not the reality of what occurred.

Two bands of Native peoples were directly affected by the creation of the Quetico Forest Reserve in 1909. Like other indigenous peoples throughout the western hemisphere, their populations had already been devastated by the onslaught of diseases introduced through European contact and now the game and fish resources they depended upon were being rapidly depleted by logging and mining camps. The Sturgeon Lake Reserve 24C was completely surrounded by the Quetico Forest Reserve. The Sturgeon Lake band was comprised of nomadic people who spent much of their time on Sturgeon Lake, but they chose Kawa Bay on Kawnipi Lake when forced to identify a single location for a reserve. When land

MAP 4: THE KAWA BAY RESERVE 24C, 1890

This 1890 map shows the location of Reserve 24C at the mouth of the Wawiag River. While it uses the Anishinaabe words for both the Wawiag River and Kawnipi Lake, the map was drawn at a time of transition and it also shows McKenzie Lake, named for the explorer Alexander Mackenzie, and Shelly (Shelley) Lake, said to be named for English poet Percy Bysshe Shelley.

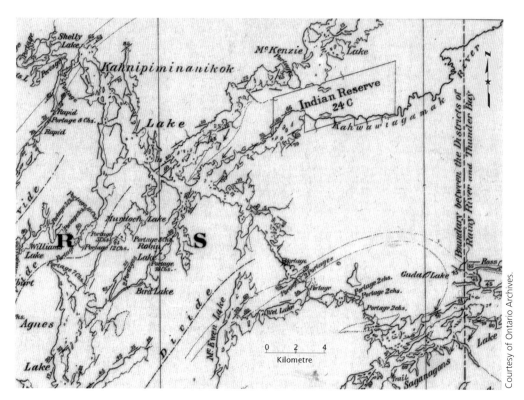

Courtesy of Ontario Archives.

for the their reserve was surveyed in 1877, there were fifty-two band members.

Although the mouth of the Wawiag River at Kawa Bay is a resource-rich area, it was not sufficient for their needs, and the band had to remain nomadic in order to take advantage of resources not on reserve land. The creation of the Quetico Forest Reserve on their traditional lands meant that their subsistence-hunting activities were now restricted, thus making their lives more tenuous. Another Native reserve, Lac La Croix Reserve 24D, was located at the southwest corner of the forest reserve. Although they were not surrounded by forest reserve land, band members were hampered in their seasonal movements and subsistence activities. In addition, their use of border lakes and other areas in Minnesota was compromised by the creation of the Superior National Forest.

As the Quetico game and fish wardens had the job of enforcing the ban on killing game animals, it was their responsibility to remove both bands from the Quetico Forest Reserve. A chance meeting between Leo Chosa, the operator of a Basswood Lake trading post, and Quetico wardens Robert Readman and Ephram Crawford led Leo to write government officials in December 1910. He was astonished and dismayed to discover that the bands were to be removed in mid-winter. Leo stated that, "I doubt very much that there exists today a civilized people under the sun that would uphold and compel its officers to enforce a law that would deprive a man of his home and throw his wife and little ones on the mercies of a northern winter to endure the tortures that the Indians in question will have to undergo if they are compelled to move from Hunter's Island this winter."[11]

Accounts vary as to whether the Natives were removed as originally planned. Most members of Kawa Bay (24C) found refuge with other bands, but primarily with the Lac La Croix band. Since government records indicate that they were still paying annuities to members of 24C until 1931, the park rangers — who undoubtedly knew many of the band members — may have "looked the other way" instead of rigorously enforcing the regulations. According to government records, by 1915 the number of people belonging to 24C had shrunk to just four people, a rapid decline from the twenty recorded four years earlier. The government dissolved the 24C Reserve in 1915 because there were so few surviving band members, but they continued to make annuity payments at Lac La Croix to 24C band members for many years.

In 1931, the Department of Indian Affairs reported that only two members of the Sturgeon Lake band were alive. They transferred them to the Lac La Croix Reserve and declared the band "extinct." Contrary to this declaration, there currently are people from both the Lac La Croix First Nation and the Seine River First Nation who claim to be descendents of people from 24C. In 1950, the government of Ontario amended Quetico's boundaries and 24C officially became park land. Although the government terminated 24C, the band never officially surrendered the land and the Lac La Croix First Nation filed a land claim in 1980. The matter is still pending.

THE EVOLUTION OF QUETICO PARK

A major threat to Quetico Park occurred in 1925 when E.W. Backus, an American businessman with large timber holdings and owner of water-power rights along the border, proposed to build a series of dams along the international border. His plan for generating electricity would have turned Basswood, Crooked, Lac La Croix, and other border lakes into huge reservoirs, flooding thousands of hectares of land.

In 1928, Ernest Oberholtzer helped to set up the Quetico-Superior Council to fight the Backus plan and deal with other issues that affected the boundary waters. The ambitious Backus plan ran into opposition on many fronts, frustrating his efforts until his death in 1934. One of the interesting spin-offs of this controversy is that the Canadian Committee of the Quetico–Superior Council evolved into the Quetico Foundation in 1954. The foundation is still very active and continues to work quietly to preserve Quetico as a wilderness area. They have funded many books, and currently support a summer student research program enabling students from Atikokan and the Lac La Croix First Nation to participate in research in Quetico. The Quetico Foundation was the driving force behind the formation of the John B. Ridley Research Library at French Lake and continues to aid in the maintenance and growth of this facility.

The Shevlin-Clark Company began extensive logging in the northern part of Quetico Park in 1917, and by 1926 timber was being cut on Pickerel, French, Batchewaung, Jesse, Oriana, and Quetico lakes. At the same time, logging was occurring in Minnesota up to Quetico's southern limit at the international boundary. Extensive logging was also taking place in the western part of Quetico in the 1930s, despite disruptions due to labour unrest. When the Ontario government announced that the old-growth pine near McNiece and Yum Yum lakes could be logged, there were so many letters of protest that the decision was reversed. This restriction resulted in protection for what is probably the largest stand of old-growth pine in Ontario.

Courtesy of Atikokan Centennial Museum, Atikokan, Ontario.

Tommy Mathieu of the J.A. Mathieu Lumber Company looks over pine logs on Lac La Croix in 1939.

Frank MacDougal was the first superintendent of Algonquin Provincial Park who was also a professional forester and a pilot. He promoted reforestation and utilized airplanes for law enforcement, fire protection, and emergencies. When he was appointed deputy minister of Lands and Forests in 1941, he began applying policies he had used in Algonquin Park to other Ontario parks. He instigated a "three hundred foot" shoreline reserve along all canoe routes in Quetico Park. Logging was already in decline and the depletion of merchantable timber resulted in the cessation of logging in the rest of Quetico in 1946. Lumbering in the park did not resume until the Jim Mathieu Lumber Company, from Fort Frances, Ontario, was issued a licence to log the northeast sector in 1961.

Public opposition to logging escalated rapidly as logging roads penetrated deeper into that portion of the park. Surprisingly, it was the Algonquin Wildlands League rather than the Quetico Foundation that would spearhead this opposition. The Quetico Foundation was comprised primarily of businessmen and professional people, a generally affluent group who were comfortable working with government agencies, but who were not at ease in confronting either them or logging companies. The Algonquin Wildlands League, on the other hand, was a group of younger businessmen, writers, teachers, and university professors who were accustomed to public confrontation. The league was formed in 1968, a time when public demonstrations were proving to often

work better than quiet diplomacy. From the beginning, the Wildlands League took a more aggressive, adversarial approach when dealing with conflicts over logging and other issues in Algonquin Park in southern Ontario. The members were very adept at using the media to express their concerns, speaking out at meetings, and questioning government policies on natural resource issues such as logging.

Bruce Litteljohn, now a widely published writer, editor, and photographer from Bracebridge, Ontario, was a member of the Quetico Park Portage Crew from 1959 to 1962. He became an outspoken advocate of maintaining the ecological integrity of Ontario's parks and was the leader in the Wildlands fight against logging in Quetico Park. His numerous articles on the negative environmental effects of logging and photographs of the roads and bridges in the northeastern part of the park helped bring the issue of logging to the public's attention. In effect, Litteljohn was the primary "spark" that kept the logging issue burning. Many Minnesota environmentalists, including Sigurd Olson and Miron Heinselman, joined Ontarians in the battle to eliminate logging in the park, emphasizing that in Quetico Park the "logging issue is at heart an ecological issue."[12]

At the same time, timber companies were working to make their case for the continuation of logging in the park. Their arguments focused on the number of jobs that would be lost if the sawmill in Sapawe — just north of Quetico Park — was shut down. However, those opposed to the continuation of logging made their case so effectively that the Ontario government decided it needed to determine the feelings of the general public about logging, as well as other issues affecting Quetico Park. This led to the formation of the Quetico Provincial Park Advisory Committee in 1971, mandated to gather public opinion and determine the future direction of Quetico.

The advisory committee received 263 written briefs and over 4,000 letters, and heard 144 oral briefs delivered at public hearings in Atikokan, Lac La Croix, Fort Frances, Thunder Bay, and Toronto. Presentations were overwhelmingly in support of stopping logging in the park, with many of the most eloquent and moving arguments coming from Atikokan canoe outfitter Charlie Erickson, Thunder Bay teachers Bill Addison and Dave Bates, and Fort Francis resident Irene Park. Addison recalled how Atikokan high school teacher Tom Miyata and his wife Bettina "made a subdued emotional plea in front of a hostile audience. When they finished, applause rocked the walls. It was apparent from the faces of the Committee members that they had been swayed."[13]

It was clear that the opposition to logging was broadly based and not solely the sentiment of urbanites and suburbanites from southern Ontario. Testimony concerning the availability of wood outside park boundaries convinced the advisory committee that a logging ban would not damage the local economy. The government accepted committee recommendations to make Quetico a "primitive park," which included a ban on logging, mining, and hunting. The committee proposed that the purpose of Quetico Park was "to preserve, in perpetuity, for the people of Ontario an area of wilderness not adversely affected by human activity and containing a natural environment of aesthetic, historical and recreational significance."[14]

Environmentalists were relieved that their long battle to stop logging came into effect in 1973 when Quetico was classified as a Primitive Park. Mike Barker, the new district manager for the Ministry of Natural Resources (MNR) in Atikokan, was aware that if there were delays in building the roads and logging camps north of the park, local jobs and support for Quetico as a wilderness area would both be lost. With his guidance, the Ontario government and the logging companies were able to work together, and the transition from logging in the park to logging north of the park went smoothly.

The 1977 Quetico Park Master Plan was the next major step in the "wilding" process. Lands and Parks supervisor Dave Elder and regional park planner Dale Smith were the authors of this important document that solidified Quetico Park as a wilderness area. They used the recommendations of the Quetico Park Advisory Committeee as a template to guide the writing of the first Quetico Park master plan. A daily visitor quota system for each entry station, the prohibition of outboard motors and snowmobiles, a can and bottle ban, a maximum group size of ten, and the introductory steps in a prescribed burn plan were all implemented by this bold and progressive document. These changes weren't undertaken in isolation. Since many of the same issues were being addressed in the Boundary Waters Canoe Area Wilderness (BWCAW), as well, the two adjacent areas not only kept each other informed, they co-operated to make their systems work more efficiently. Since the United States Forest Service was the first to implement a Visitor Distribution Program and a can and bottle ban, Quetico was able to learn from its experiences.

Fergus "Fergy" Wilson became park superintendent in 1975 after serving as a park naturalist and park planner for the region. He was involved in the early stages of the preparation of the master plan and in his role as superintendent, he was responsible for its implementation. In addition to the changes listed above, the park boundaries were also adjusted. The water of Lac La Croix was taken out of the park and Batchewaung Lake and all of Saganagons Lake were included. To complete the transformations of Quetico that occurred in the 1970s, Quetico was officially classified as a Wilderness Park in 1978.

Many issues between the Lac La Croix First Nation and Quetico Park simmered below the surface, but few received much attention until the 1970s. When motor restrictions in Quetico Park were being considered, Lac La Croix band leaders became concerned that this would stop band members from using motors while guiding fisherman in the park. Compromises were reached with park officials that allowed the use of ten-horsepower motors when guiding on designated lakes in the park. Jay Leather, Quetico Park superintendent from 1987 to 2000, worked diligently investigating ways that the band could become more involved in, and benefit from, its relationship with the park. Steve Jourdain, the chief at Lac La Croix when Jay started as park superintendent, emphasized the importance of generating opportunities for employment that were not previously considered feasible for band members.

Master Plan reviews were conducted in 1982 and 1989, but only minor "tweaking" of the 1977 Master Plan occurred. A significant change in park policies occurred in 1991 when Bud Wildman, Ontario minister of Natural Resources, made an unprecedented statement in the Ontario legislature when he apologized to the Lac La Croix First Nation for "the lack of respect that has been shown for its people and its rights."[15] The Ontario government did more than just apologize; in 1994, they signed an Agreement of Co-existence with the Lac La Croix First Nation. This agreement seeks to compensate Lac La Croix for the displacement from their traditional homeland and loss of economic opportunities that occurred when Quetico was first set aside as a forest reserve in 1909. This agreement and the Revised Park Policy brought about significant changes by recognizing the problems that the creation of Quetico Park and current park policies have caused the people of Lac la Croix.

The agreement also states: "The First Nation must be an active and full participant in the future planning, development and management of the Quetico

Chair of the Ontario Provincial Parks Council Lloyd Burridge, Lac La Croix Band Councillor Elaine Jourdain, Quetico Park historian Shirley Peruniak, Chief Leon Jourdain, and Park Superintendent Jay Leather gathered at the Lac La Croix First Nation for the signing of the Agreement of Co-existence in 1994. Leon Jourdain was Chief of the Lac La Croix First Nation and Jay Leather was Quetico Park superintendent during the negotiations for this important agreement.

area...."[16] Since the signing of the agreement, some advances have been made in making Lac La Croix a more active partner in park activities. Lac La Croix First Nation members staff the ranger stations at Lac La Croix and Beaverhouse Lake, band members have worked on interior portage crews,[17] park warden and natural heritage education positions for band members have been funded, and a work centre has been developed. Progress has been slow, but there are obvious reasons why Lac La Croix would be distrustful of government promises. It will take

time and positive actions on both sides before a more complete partnership in managing Quetico Park is reached. Finding a way to protect the wilderness character of the park and, at the same time, respecting the needs of the Lac La Croix First Nation are challenging issues that test the commitment and resolve of both parties.

Funding to implement the changes in the Master Plan and to hire additional staff in the late 1970s and early 1980s made it possible for the park not only to have full-time naturalist Shan Walshe, but supplementary naturalists, as well. The naturalist program, to Shan's delight, was based on Mike Barker's belief that "people in the field ought to be in the field. They should be in the bush and not sitting around in a bunch of offices."[18] Fieldwork for Shan's authoritative book, *Plants of Quetico and the Ontario Shield*, his weekly newspaper column "Lynx Tracks," and a substantial number of natural history pamphlets were produced during this period. In addition, Shirley Peruniak started compiling information on the history of Quetico Park that culminated in the publication of *An Illustrated History of Quetico Provincial Park* in 2000.

Shirley began gathering information on the human history of Quetico Park in the 1970s and spent time at Lac La Croix getting the First Nations side of the story. Working with band members, she compiled an impressive, multi-volume pictorial history of the Lac La Croix Reserve. Quetico Park and Lac La Croix have both benefited greatly from

Shirley Peruniak has worked with Lac La Croix Elders to document their past in Quetico and the surrounding area. Here, Shirley is talking to Roy and Amelia Burnside at Lac La Croix in 1975.

support for students working in the natural heritage program and in the John B. Ridley Research Library at French Lake.

Another Master Plan review is scheduled for completion in 2009. Important and contentious issues — the park's obligations in generating economic benefits for Atikokan residents, new access points into the interior, the role of fire, the treatment of artifacts found in the park, adjustments of park quotas, park fees, and the effects of climate change on the park — will be analyzed and decisions made on how to proceed in the ongoing quest to define Quetico's role as a wilderness park.

Shirley's efforts, and, as a result of her style and ability to reach out, she was able to establish a strong bond, probably greater than by any park staff member before or since, with individuals at Lac La Croix.

The Friends of Quetico was established in 1984, the year Quetico Park celebrated its 75th anniversary. The primary goal of the Friends is the preservation of Quetico Park as a wilderness area, which they work toward by supporting research and projects whose objectives are to increase the understanding of the value of wilderness and of the natural and human history of the park. Over the past twenty-five years, they have funded research and published numerous books about Quetico, including *An Illustrated History of Quetico Provincial Park*, *Plants of Quetico and the Ontario Shield*, and *The Birds of Quetico Park*. They also provide financial

QUETICO: THE WILDER TWIN

Since their birth in 1909, the Quetico Forest Preserve and a portion of the Superior National Forest have matured into world-class wilderness canoe areas. In spite of their obvious similarities — both born in 1909 and both attaining wilderness protection status in 1978 — Quetico Park and the BWCAW are definitely more like fraternal than identical twins. Since their arrival one hundred years ago, their inherent differences and varying outside pressures have caused them to grow and mature along distinct but parallel paths. They now behave like siblings that co-operate to a large degree, but they also compete for customers and prestige. The most obvious difference is that the Superior National Forest is a multi-use public land area with only the Boundary Waters Canoe Area Wilderness being protected as a wilderness, while all of Quetico Provincial Park enjoys wilderness status.

Atikokan and Ely, along with the economies of northwestern Ontario and northern Minnesota, have not benefitted equally from the establishment of the twin parks. This became apparent very early. In 1921, Superintendent Hugh McDonald's report for Quetico noted that access from the Canadian side was virtually impossible and "the result is that the money spent by … tourists is spent with American merchants instead of Canadians as we would desire."[19]

In sharp contrast, five years prior to that glum pronouncement on the dificulty of entering Quetico from the north, the *Ely Miner* newspaper reported, "Tourists are arriving on every train and by auto from all over the country and are enjoying the canoe trips, the camping on lakes and Burntside facilities to the utmost."[20] This trend toward more tourists entering from the south has continued and geography is the primary reason. Ely has Minneapolis, Milwaukee, Chicago, and other large metropolitan areas within a day's drive, while Atikokan is far removed from Canadian cities and a few hundred extra kilometres and a border-crossing from the American ones. A number of resorts and outfitters have aggressively marketed Ely as a destination for canoeing, fishing, and winter activies. As a result of their success, Ely is a thriving tourist destination known as "the Aspen of the North" and "The Canoe Capital of the World," while Atikokan, "The Canoe Capital of Canada," attracts far fewer tourists.

Differences in ease of access combined with the distribution of population dictates that most Quetico Park visitors are American, with relatively few Canadians using either Quetico or the BWCAW. In 1930, just six of 1,234 Quetico Park canoeists were Canadian and in 2006, only twelve percent of park visitors were Canadian. In addition, because of the dam at Prairie Portage, canoeists coming through Ely have direct towboat access to Quetico Park. It is much faster and far cheaper to reach Canada by towboat at Prairie Portage or to within a few kilometres of the Cache Bay ranger station than it is to drive around to the Canadian entry stations on the north side of the park.

Because of the preponderance of American users, Quetico has to struggle to keep its Canadian identity. Park rangers are often asked why the Canadian flag flies at the Prairie Portage and Cache Bay ranger stations. There have been times when canoeists told park rangers that their United States congressman was going to get the Quetico Park can and bottle ban and motor restrictions rescinded. Although these were simply confusions over which country the visitor was in, they also reflect the degree to which some Americans feel that Quetico is an extension of the United States.

The BWCAW is the only wilderness park in the United States east of the Rocky Mountains. The intensity of the controversies that arise over the use of this area are a testimony to its value to both the environmentalists and to those who treasure the way things were done prior to the restrictions now in place. A prosperous economy has built up around supplying and serving canoeists using the BWCAW, and the number of outfitters and others whose jobs depend on the flow of tourists puts a lot of pressure on the United States Forest Service to maintain high quotas. These intense pressures do not exist in Quetico Park, enabling Quetico to set more stringent quotas and charge higher fees without being overly concerned with the reaction of outfitters and canoeists from the United States. No latrines, no fire grates, no designated campsites and less stringently maintained portages contribute to the feeling that a truer wilderness experience can be found in Quetico than in the BWCAW.

Sometimes policies, however, have unintended effects. The trend over the last few decades to increase camping fees and the high cost associated with camping and fishing in Quetico has shifted the balance of visitors. There has been a decrease in the number of youth groups entering the park and a corresponding increase in the number of high-income people. Many people reading this book probably entered Quetico as a part of a church or youth group and these groups are now finding it more difficult to afford the park. There is a real fear that, unless this trend is reversed, Quetico will become primarily a park for the elite.

Although Quetico Park and the BWCAW have strong similarities, they are far from identical twins that happen to exist on different sides of the border. As Quetico and the BWCAW have made adaptations and changed into their current forms, Quetico has remained the "wilder" twin throughout this process.

THE NEXT HUNDRED YEARS

Quetico has undergone many changes since its beginnings as the Quetico Forest Reserve in 1909. The change in status to a provincial park in 1913 gave protection to moose and other game animals, but allowed logging to occur. Quetico's designation as a wilderness park has protected it from logging and mining and its quota system has limited the abuse caused by over-use. More gradual, insidious forces, however, are currently at work. Acid rain, air pollution, and climate change do not respect park boundaries, and, as global pollution continues to increase, the water and air quality within Quetico Park is affected, as well. Anyone who has paddled in Quetico since the 1970s has noticed that the trend is for the ice to go out earlier and for lakes to freeze up later. Quetico Park lies in the transition zone between the boreal forests to the north and the primarily hardwood forests to the south. It seems as though Quetico Park is sliding south and becoming less boreal as the years go by.

Researchers on both sides of the border have found that maples, oaks, and other southern deciduous trees are increasing, while black spruce, white birch, black ash, and northern pines are in decline. Lee Frelich, a researcher from the University of Minnesota who has studied the forest composition of the BWCAW for eighteen years, has concluded that the combination of global warming and invasive species is rapidly changing the composition of our forests. The boreal nature of Quetico-Superior forests is clearly diminishing. Due to the milder winters over the last two decades, animals that have trouble dealing with very cold conditions and deep snow are moving into the area as the weather warms and snow cover decreases. In addition to an increase in the number of white-tailed deer, in recent years raccoons, grey fox, grey squirrels, skunks, and badgers have been seen in or near the Quetico-Superior area. Reports of cougar, who may be moving into the area because of the increase in deer populations, are also increasing.

Concerns for the plummeting moose population due to hunting to supply logging, railway, and mining camps was the original impetus that led to the protection of Quetico. There is again concern over the decreasing moose population. While there are probably a number of factors causing the decline, some researchers believe it is primarily due to heat stress caused by higher temperatures, particularly during the spring calving season. In contrast to the moose population, white-tailed deer are increasing in numbers. The brain worm they carry is probably one of the causes of the reduction in moose population.

The movement of animals in response to environmental change is usually relatively slow. Anglers, however, have aided the invasion of exotic species.

New regulations have been put into place in Quetico Park to slow the introduction of new species of fish, angleworms, crayfish, and leeches that were previously brought in as bait. There is also monitoring of other exotic species, such as the spiny water flea and purple loosestrife, that may be harmful to the environment. The monitoring of introduced species will undoubtedly increase in years to come as concerns over the invasion by these species continue to grow.

Quetico and other wilderness parks will probably play a bigger role as research areas in upcoming years. Fire ecologist Miron Heinselman foresaw this years ago. He noted: "I suspect our large nature reserves and other relatively unmodified areas of the globe still hold the key to many new ecological principles. And it may be that only here can the full complexity of natural systems ever be worked out, because some processes are visible only at full ecosystem scales."[21] The existence of two adjacent wilderness areas makes Quetico Park and the BWCAW especially attractive areas for researchers. Together they form a large ecosystem where the movements of animals in protected areas can be monitored. This is already been done with radio-collared wolves and lynx, and more co-operative research is planned.

Conducting research in wilderness areas has a special appeal to those interested in field research rather than working in a lab or conducting computer analysis of someone else's work. Numerous research projects, including those in fire ecology and archaeology, are currently being conducted in the Quetico-Superior area. Quetico has had success with multi-year research projects. Two of these — a fascinating study of moose behaviour during the rut, which was conducted over six fall seasons and a ten-year study of white and red pine regeneration after forest fires — are chronicled in this book. There is a potential for much more research to be done, especially with Lakehead University in Thunder Bay and University of Minnesota-Duluth in close proximity to these wilderness areas.

Managing wilderness areas like Quetico Park and the BWCAW is a delicate balancing act between protecting the environment without depleting the economic opportunities of the people in Atikokan and Ely, who have these parks in their own backyards. Atikokan, in particular, has been hard hit the last few decades with mine and mill closures, plummeting lumber prices, and the imminent closure of its coal-fired power plant. It is understandable that people in Atikokan have questions about how Quetico Park benefits them when so little of the economic benefits have flowed in their direction. Although wilderness values have to remain paramount for the long-term viability of Quetico Park, it is imperative that Atikokan residents begin to see more economic benefits coming from having a wilderness park on their doorstep.

The Ontario definition of a wilderness park is a "substantial area where the forces of nature are permitted to function freely and where visitors travel by non-mechanized means and experience expansive solitude, challenge and personal integration with nature."[22] In the United States, the 1964 Wilderness Act defines wilderness as "an area where the earth and its community of life are untrammeled by man, where man himself is a visitor who does not remain." Both of these definitions seem to be in accord with the humorous definition of wilderness as a place "where the hand of man has never set foot." The hand of man, however, set foot in the Quetico-Superior over twelve thousand years ago and has been there ever since. Native peoples have been an integral part of the Quetico-Superior area for thousands of years. To a large extent, their stewardship was responsible for the relatively intact state of the Quetico-Superior ecosystem when the area was protected in 1909.

One of the primary reasons for the strong appeal of Quetico Park and the rest of the Quetico-Superior area is that the heavier and more destructive hand of modern man has had relatively little negative impact. The activities of fur traders, trappers, prospectors, and fishermen left relatively few scars. Visitors seem to be charmed by the reminders of logging activities from the early 1900s. The remains of wooden dams used to raise water levels can be seen in numerous locations. Saws, horseshoes, and other metal debris from logging activities are slowly rusting away. At the site of an old logging camp on the Beaverhouse Lake to Quetico Lake portage, shrubs and trees are slowly engulfing a rusting car that was driven over from Flanders, a railway stop on the Canadian National Railway. Rhubarb and chives, vestiges from the logging camp, are still growing wild seventy years after the camp was abandoned. Not long ago, abandoned ranger cabins were burned as eyesores that were out of place in a wilderness park. Now these buildings are cherished and funds are being sought to maintain the abandoned ranger cabins at Cabin 16 and King's Point on Basswood Lake.

Quetico Park is justifiably proud of its past and is attempting to correct past injustices. The recognition that the creation of Quetico a hundred years ago caused great damage to the Anishinaabe (Ojibwa) living in and adjacent to the park ultimately led to the inclusion of the Lac La Croix First Nation into park management. This reintroduction of Anishinaabe thought into decisions related to Quetico should prove beneficial to both the park and its visitors.

Over the last one hundred years, Quetico has evolved from a forest reserve visited by a few hundred people to a wilderness area that attracts thousands of canoeists from around the world. Today, it is still a magnificent merger of sculpted bedrock with water and northern pine forests. With the added attraction of timber wolves, moose, bald eagles, loons, northern lights, and lake trout in a landscape having the greatest concentration of aboriginal rock paintings in eastern North America, it is no wonder that Quetico Park is considered by many to be the finest canoeing park in the world.

The protection given Quetico in 1909 and the resolve of people who fought to make it a wilderness park allows us to paddle today in a Quetico that is very similar to what it was one hundred years ago. We can pass on a pristine Quetico to succeeding generations only if we continue fighting to maintain its wilderness character.

PART ONE

ICE AGE LEGACY OF QUETICO PARK

With the retreat of the Laurentide Glacier, the last ice age ended only twelve thousand years ago, a mere pittance in geological time. Although the work of researchers has established some baseline information about the glacier's retreat, very little is known with certainty about this critical period when glacial ice and meltwater sculpted the Quetico-Superior into the landscape we know today. Even in geographical regions that have been extensively studied, there are differing opinions and conflicting views about the timing of the glacier's retreat, its impact on the landscape and the plants and animals that first inhabited the area. Since relatively little field research has been carried out in the Quetico-Superior, there are many unanswered questions regarding this region.

"Ice Age Journey," my account of the glacier's retreat through the Quetico-Superior region, is based on extensive reading followed by talking to, corresponding with, and receiving feedback from experts in glacial movements. Having people with first-hand knowledge of glacial matters in this area as guides was a tremendous help. Since there is uncertainty about specific times for the glacier's retreat or for precise dates or locations of Lake Agassiz shorelines, my account is an attempt to find a middle ground on a complex topic. I hope my fascination and interest in this remarkable time period has allowed me to write a comprehensible account of the glacier's retreat and its effect on Quetico Park and the surrounding area.

Even though I have carried out field research relating to Palaeo-Indians in Quetico Park, my work in the second chapter, "Palaeo-Indians: First Explorers of the Quetico-Superior," relies heavily on other archaeologists in both northwestern Ontario and northern Minnesota who are very experienced and knowledgeable about the earliest inhabitants of this region. Some Palaeo-Indian sites have been found on both sides of the border, but our knowledge of the first people to occupy this region is very hazy. The topics of glacial retreat and the entrance of the first humans are stories that are deeply interwoven.

This bedrock along the shore of Sturgeon Lake was exposed by the glacier over twelve thousand years ago. Wave action and times when water levels are exceptionally high have kept it relatively free of lichens and other vegetation.

When describing events from the distant past I use names that are utilized today, such as Quetico Park, Atikokan, Pickerel Lake, Wawiag River, Lake Superior, and Prairie Portage, when referring to locations in the past. This is done because the terms used by the first people in the Quetico area are not known, and to make it easier to follow the proposed events as they unfold. I generally use the term Ojibwa when referring to this group of people in the past and Anishinaabe when referring to the people living today. In order to make it easier to relate to how long ago these events occurred, I have used calendar years, rather than radiocarbon years, throughout the book. Care has to be taken when reading about occurrences in the past since most archaeologists and geologists use radiocarbon dates and there can be a significant difference between radiocarbon years and calendar years. For example, the Clovis culture ended about eleven thousand radiocarbon years ago. This converts to thirteen thousand years ago in actual calendar years.

The third chapter, "The Future of the Past in Quetico Park: Archaeology and Anishinaabe Spiritual Beliefs," was co-written with Andrew Hinshelwood, an archaelogical review officer with the Ontario Ministry of Culture. It deals with some of the complications that have arisen in interpreting the human history of North America and how archaeologists in the Quetico-Superior are adjusting and adapting their methods in conducting research. The transition from a North America with solely Native cultures to our contemporary cultural mix has been a rocky one. Although North Americans handle cultural differences better than people in most areas of the world, we are only fooling ourselves if we think that archaeological or historical interpretations of our past, primarily written by university-trained people of European descent, are objective and balanced. Most of today's archaeologists and historians, however, are making a conscious effort to correct this.

I grew up in a small town in rural Minnesota and went to a Lutheran college in northern Minnesota. During the 1950s and early 1960s, virtually everyone in both locations was not only Caucasian, but also predominantly Scandinavian. It wasn't until my graduate-school days in Washington, D.C. that I had my first significant introduction to other cultures. I vividly remember going into a church with predominantly Afro-American worshipers and being astonished by the gospel singing and the constant verbal interaction between the minister and the congregation. The differences — between that service and the Lutheran church services that I attended in my youth — were striking.

On another occasion, in university, I recall meeting a student from India in the hallway and simply saying "Hi." He responded by solemnly placing the palms of his hands together in front of his heart, bowing and saying, *Namaste.* I had mumbled a vague word of greeting and he replied by saying "I bow to the spirit within you." The difference between the depth of his greeting and the casual simplicity of mine is quite astonishing.

The cultural gulfs between traditional Native people and people from predominantly European back-grounds in northwestern Ontario today are probably as great as those between a Minnesota Lutheran and a Hindu from India in the 1960s. When problems arose while conducting archaeological research in Quetico in 1997, I was extremely fortunate to be able to meet with Lac La Croix First Nation Elders to talk about our differences. When discussing issues relating to archaeological research with traditional Anishinaabe Elders such as Marie Ottertail and John Boshey from Lac La Croix, both Andrew Hinshelwood and I found that the cultural differences between the Elders and us were considerable. Our chapter on the background to these meetings and our attempt to reach a workable compromise is simply our interpretation of these encounters. I'm sure an account from an Elder's perspective would be very different and very enlightening.

Until these meetings took place, I regarded artifacts such as arrowheads and pottery shards simply as physical objects to be analyzed. I didn't grow up in a culture that viewed tools and other everyday objects as having spiritual aspects and this was a difficult concept to grasp. The Elders assertion that "pictographs are prayers," however, was a revelation that I could easily understand. From the first time I saw pictographs, I felt that there was an elusive quality to them that went beyond graffiti or simply relating a story.

All three of the chapters in Part One are about complex topics loaded with uncertainty. Geologists and archaeologists will slowly uncover more information that will make the story of the glacier's retreat and the peopling of the Quetico-Superior more complete. Much like the retreat of a glacier, our understanding of what method or methods allow us to interpret the past as accurately and fairly as possible will also move slowly and erratically. As we continue to share insights and interpretations, and incorporate Anishinaabe views, an interesting and very different historical landscape will reveal itself.

CHAPTER ONE

ICE AGE JOURNEY

When the last glaciers reached their maximum about twenty thousand years ago, Quetico Park and the rest of the Quetico-Superior were buried under hundreds of metres of ice. The Laurentide Ice Sheet stretched from the Atlantic Ocean to the Rocky Mountains, extended south into Iowa, covered all of Minnesota except for the southeast corner, and much of Wisconsin. Another ice sheet, known as the Cordillaran Ice Sheet, extended from the Rocky Mountains to the Pacific Ocean. These massive glaciers blanketed much of the northern half of North America and had an enormous impact on the land. Their colossal weight and slow advance greatly altered or obliterated many old landforms and created entirely new ones.[1]

As the Laurentide glacier was expanding, movement of glacial ice ground up existing deposits into a mixture of silt, sand, gravel, small rocks, and small boulders. Boulders embedded in glacial ice left scratches called glacial *striae* or a train of crescent-shaped gouges, known as *chattermarks*, in the bedrock as evidence of the glacier's passing. So much water was converted to ice that the oceans dropped over one hundred metres and the weight of the glacial ice deformed the crust by pushing down the land beneath it. Life slowly migrated south as the glacier advanced. Jack pine and black spruce retreated to central and southern United States and the deciduous forests found refuge in Florida.

THE GLACIER'S RETREAT: A NEW BEGINNING

When the climate began to warm about twenty thousand years ago, not only did the glacier stop advancing, it actually began to recede. The global warming triggered the demise of the continental glacier and marked the beginning of the end of the last ice age. The glacier's retreat initiated a series of changes that still reverberate throughout the Quetico-Superior region.

Glaciers are not just ice — they are relentlessly churning systems with silt, gravel, and boulders

MAP 5: MAXIMUM EXTENT OF GLACIER

When the Laurentide Glacier reached its maximum size, it covered all of Ontario and only a tiny portion of Canada wasn't under glacial ice. The glacier extended well south of the Quetico-Superior and only the southeastern part of Minnesota was free of ice.

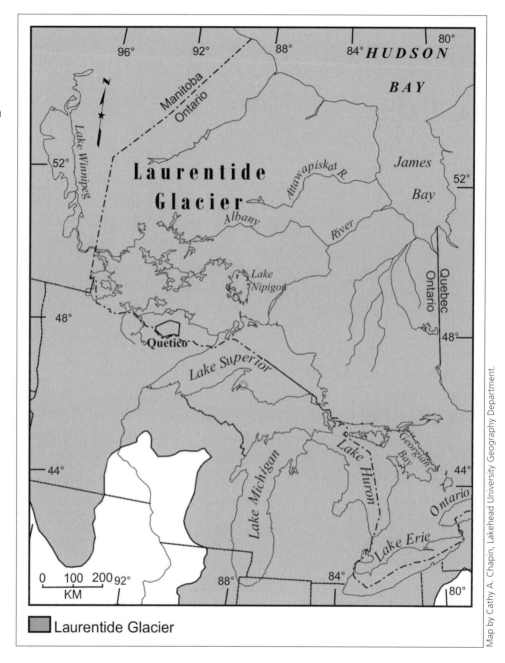

Laurentide Glacier

Map by Cathy A. Chapin, Lakehead University Geography Department.

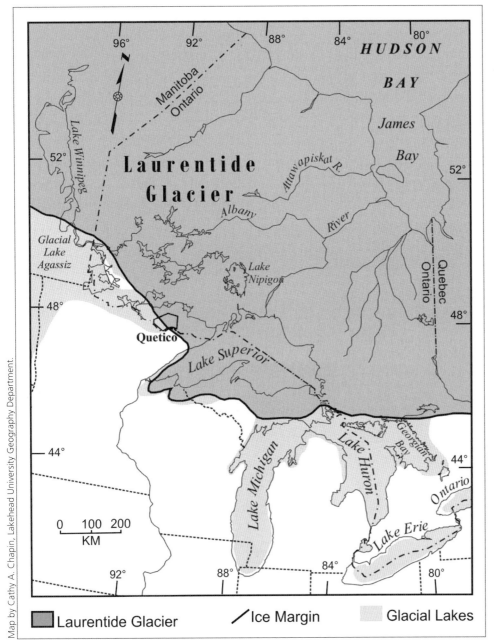

Map by Cathy A. Chapin, Lakehead University Geography Department.

MAP 6: GLACIER ALONG THE ONTARIO-MINNESOTA BORDER, NORTH OF ELY, MINNESOTA
As the glacier receded across the Minnesota-Ontario boundary, glacial Lake Agassiz continued to expand. The huge glacial lake covered much of the Quetico-Superior area as the glacier continued to recede to the northeast.

51

embedded in an icy matrix. The combination of materials caught up in the glacier — wind deposited sand and dust, pollen, bird droppings, and seeds — creates conditions where bacteria, algae, lichens, moss, and invertebrates exist amidst the debris emerging from the surface of the melting glacier. Researchers investigating glaciers in mountains in western North America discovered totally unexpected life forms. They found small worms, known as ice worms, feeding on air-transported pollen grains, fern spores, and red algae in the glacial ice. It is likely that the receding Laurentide glacier at the end of the ice age was also host to a variety of worms, lichens, algae, and other forms of life.

The demise of the continental glaciers was a relatively swift — in geological time — but erratic process that took place over the course of thousands of years. The glacier's recession was slower in the beginning, in all requiring over six thousand years to recede to the southern edge of the Quetico-Superior region. It is thought that by 13,500 years ago, the glacier had retreated north of Ely, Minnesota, while all of Quetico Park and most of the BWCAW remained beneath glacial ice. The ice continued to shrink back and decrease in thickness as the climate warmed. As the glacier receded through the Quetico-Superior area, it retreated to the northeast rather than directly to the north.

The retreat of the glacier was as dramatic and transforming as its advance. A prodigious amount of meltwater collected at the foot of the glacier and was distributed to the south via network streams. This water, melting off the glacier faster than it was being drained away, formed a huge lake south of the glacier known as glacial Lake Agassiz. During the early stages of Lake Agassiz, it drained southward down a swollen Minnesota River to the Mississippi River and on to the Gulf of Mexico.

The size and shape of the glacial lake depended on the balance between the rates at which water was flowing into and out of it. The resulting variations in Lake Agassiz created shorelines that were continuously in flux. In addition to oscillating shorelines, entire islands would appear, disappear, and reappear at a different size as the water levels changed.

With the glacier extending from the Atlantic Ocean westward to the Rocky Mountains, the water

The water melting off the retreating Laurentide glacier must have closely resembled this stream of meltwater from the Athabaska glacier in Alberta.

was prevented from flowing northward, as it does in many locations today. Because the enormous weight of the glacier depressed the crust of the earth, however, new outlets at lower elevations than the southern outlet down the Minnesota River would occasionally be uncovered as the glacier retreated. When this occurred, the levels of Lake Agassiz would drop rapidly. These outlets, such as the one that may have opened near the Minnesota-Ontario border east of Gunflint Lake about 13,200 years ago, and a series of other eastern outlets that opened later when the glacier had receded north of Quetico Park caused the water leaving Lake Agassiz to flow toward today's Lake Superior and eventually to the Atlantic Ocean rather than south to the Gulf of Mexico.

As the general warming trend continued, the glacier continued to recede through Quetico Park. There were intervals, however, when the weather became colder and the glacier would slowly advance again. When the glacier advanced, it would push a jumbled mass of sand, gravel, broken rock, boulders, and other glacial debris ahead like a giant bulldozer. When the glacier began to shrink back again, it would leave behind a long, sinuous ridge of glacial till called a *moraine*. Around thirteen thousand years ago, one of these advances formed the Steep Rock Moraine. The moraine and the accompanying wall of glacial ice that was the leading edge of the Laurentian glacier, formed a dam across what is now Pickerel Lake.

The combination of the Steep Rock Moraine and glacial ice, probably several hundred feet high, acted as a barrier that helped maintain Lake Agassiz at such high levels that most of Quetico Park and the BWCAW would have been submerged under the gigantic lake. The current shorelines of lower elevation lakes, such as Lac La Croix, would have been under more than thirty metres of water. The glacier paused for a while at the Steep Rock Moraine and then continued its erratic retreat. Due to the glacier's movement in a northeasterly direction, the French Lake area was probably the last part of Quetico Park to be free of glacial ice. The leading edge of the shrinking glacier withdrew northeast of French Lake, where it again halted and readvanced to form the Eagle-Finlayson Moraine. Geologists believe this moraine formed just a few hundred years after the Steep Rock Moraine. The northeast portion of Quetico Park is unusual in having these two moraines less than ten kilometres apart. In contrast to the close proximity of the Steep Rock and Eagle-Finlayson moraines, the next closest moraine is about one hundred kilometres to the north and the nearest prominent moraine to the south is almost a hundred and fifty kilometres away in northern Minnesota.

The sequence of events that occurred as the glacier continued its retreat northeast of the Eagle-Finlayson Moraine has more than its share of unanswered questions. Researchers believe that Lake Agassiz was still lapping near the base of the glacier when it reached the height of land located about twenty kilometres northeast of French Lake. This divide now separates water flowing to the west from water flowing east toward Lake Superior and eventually to the Atlantic Ocean. During this period of high lake levels, Lake Agassiz probably occupied most of the low-lying areas in Quetico Park and the BWCAW. Much of the area east of Basswood Lake had elevations that kept it above the water of Lake Agassiz. Higher elevations within Lake Agassiz would have been islands in the gigantic lake that extended west to the prairies, south to the Mississippi watershed, and was larger than all of today's Great Lakes combined.

As the glacier continued its retreat, the depression of the earth's crust by its weight would have substantially lowered the height of land, creating a series of outlet spillways for Lake Agassiz to flow into Lake Superior. The first of these outlets apparently opened no earlier than twelve thousand years ago. Since these spillways were lower than the outlet at the southern end of the lake, the rapid release of water would have caused a substantial drop in the Lake Agassiz water levels.

As the glacier continued to recede north of the height of land, newer outlets to Lake Superior were opened and the levels of Lake Agassiz continued to drop, causing lakes along its periphery to become separate from Lake Agassiz. At this time, just the lower areas of Quetico Park, such as Crooked Lake and Lac la Croix, may have remained under the water of Lake Agassiz. Throughout the remaining flooded parts of the Quetico-Superior area, Lake Agassiz still had a multitude of islands and great variations in depth.

As the water level of Lake Agassiz dropped, many of the landforms we recognize today in Quetico and the BWCAW made their appearance. Cliffs, like those on Quetico Lake and Kahshapiwi Lake, would have slowly emerged from the water. This may have occurred numerous times due to Lake Agassiz's oscillating water levels. As the water receded, islands became attached to the mainland, and large lakes would have divided into smaller lakes. The Falls Chain became a series of large, turbulent rapids fed by glacial meltwater flowing toward a receding Lake Agassiz. The Maligne, Basswood, Wawiag, Pickerel, French, and Namakan are some of the rivers that flowed toward the lake and became temporary spillways for water rushing into Lake Agassiz. Many of today's small creeks were substantial rivers during this time and some substantial creeks from that period have undoubtedly dried up and filled in with vegetation.

Although long, low ridges that mark former Lake Agassiz shorelines are easily seen today in the relatively flat, agricultural land of northwestern Minnesota, North Dakota, and Manitoba, definite Lake Agassiz shorelines have been extremely hard to find in the rocky, forested Quetico-Superior area. The one notable exception is the portion of the Steep Rock Moraine where The Pines is today. This was evidently the shoreline of Lake Agassiz when it temporarily stabilized near the level of today's Pickerel Lake and French Lake. Since the bedrock at the outlet of Pickerel Lake kept its water level from dropping any farther as Lake Agassiz receded, the

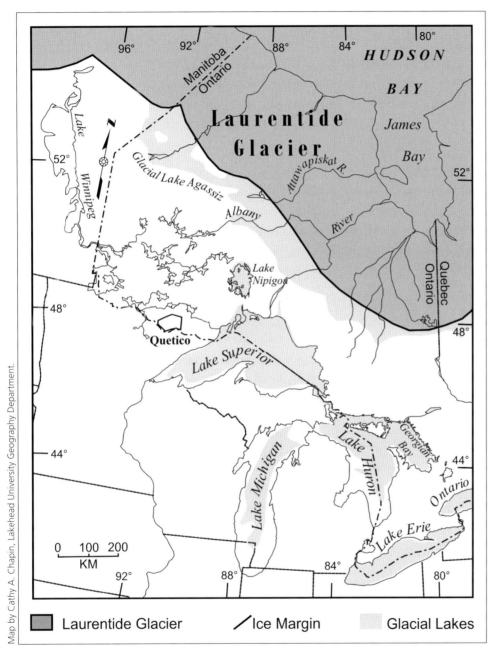

Map by Cathy A. Chapin, Lakehead University Geography Department.

MAP 7: GLACIER NORTH OF QUETICO PARK

As the glacier continued to shrink farther to the north, the water levels in Quetico dropped considerably. By about ten thousand years ago, they reached levels approximating those found today.

55

complex of lakes around Pickerel Lake are thought to be the only lakes in Quetico that have retained shorelines at, or close to, those found at the time of Lake Agassiz.

Lake Agassiz continued to get smaller and more of the Quetico-Superior region emerged from the lake surface as the glacier continued its retreat toward Hudson Bay. By eleven thousand years ago, the glacier had retreated far enough that Lake Agassiz was gone from the area and left myriad smaller lakes as its legacy. About a thousand years later, Quetico Park and the rest of the surrounding area obtained the drainage patterns and appearance that we see today.

A TRANSFORMED LANDSCAPE

The advancing Laurentide Glacier and the flooding that followed its retreat completely and dramatically transformed the Quetico-Superior area. The prodigious power of an advancing glacier stripped off the surface layer, sheared bedrock, and pulverized it into fragments that varied from huge blocks to fine sand. Rocks embedded in the ice left linear scratches (glacial striae) that are visible today on the shores of many lakes, including Saganaga, Knife, and Sturgeon. The debris, called glacial till, was plastered onto and scattered across the landscape. Some of the till was redistributed along the changing shorelines of Lake Agassiz and to low-lying areas by rivers flowing toward the lake.

The high cliffs on Quetico, Kahshapiwi, Ottertrack, Lac La Croix, and Agnes lakes are clear evidence of the glacier's power. The glacier not only sheared bedrock and created walls of stone, it also transported large hunks of bedrock, known as glacial erratics, varying distances. Some of these massive boulders were transported over a thousand kilometres from their point of origin. As a result, glacial erratics are scattered throughout the Quetico-Superior landscape. The large granite sentinel in the water at the entrance to Fred Lake is the most dramatic example of a glacial erratic that I have encountered. The glacier left behind a landscape as variable below the current water levels as it is above. Deep lakes such as Agnes, Saganaga, and Beaverhouse were formed where weaker or fractured rock was deeply gouged by the ice. Lake bottoms in Quetico Park vary from the large boulders visible in Argo and Plough lakes to the silty sand carried in by large post-glacial rivers on French, Sturgeon, Beaverhouse, and Kawnipi lakes.

The fast-moving rivers created by meltwater from the retreating glacier deposited large amounts of sand and silt into Lake Agassiz. When the lakes shrank to their present size, the shallow bays where silt was deposited were usually left above the present lake levels. These areas, once part of Lake Agassiz, were transformed into flat, boggy, or swampy areas adjacent to rivers that are shrunken remnants of their post-glacial predecessor. The best example of this in Quetico is the flat, boggy area east of Kawnipi Lake's Kawa Bay (see Chapter 5). The Wawiag River

This cliff on Quetico Lake, formed by the glacier and first exposed when the water of Lake Agassiz receded, has been altered by thousands of years of erosion.

This large, glacial erratic is found on an island campsite on Pickerel Lake.

now winds through silt and sand that were deposited by a large, post-glacial Wawiag River into a shallow bay of Lake Agassiz.

Glaciers left behind two types of long, winding gravel ridges. When the glacier margins advanced or remained stable in one location for an extended time period, a moraine marks the position of the edge of the glacier. Numerous moraines are found in Minnesota south of the BWCAW and two, the previously mentioned Steep Rock and Eagle-Finlayson moraines, cross the northeast corner of Quetico. In addition to moraines, sinuous *eskers*, originally the elevated beds of rivers flowing under the ice, can also be found winding through the landscape. Because eskers are flowing out from under the retreating glacier, they are usually oriented at right angles to the moraines.

Thousands of years of erosion and a blanket of vegetation make moraines and eskers difficult to distinguish from other topography. What separates them from other landforms is their relatively uniform height and linear morphology. A few eskers have been identified in the Quetico-Superior landscape. A string of three islands made up of sand and gravel in the south arm of Knife Lake is likely the eroded remains of an esker. A geological report from the 1800s identifies the low ridge between Birch Lake and Polaris Lake as an esker. Recent mapping of natural heritage features by the Ontario Ministry of Natural Resources identified a small esker at the south end of Agnes Lake in Quetico Provincial Park. Since very little research has been carried out in the Quetico-Superior, less specific information is known about glacial features than in most other areas.

In addition to the changes left by moving ice, large chunks of glacial ice left behind by the receding glacier melted in place, leaving circular depressions called *kettles*. These are scattered about the landscape as potholes or small lakes often surrounded by a slightly elevated rim.

The landscape is still recovering from the massive weight of the glacier. As the glacier melted and most of the water drained away, the earth's crust began to rise back up. This recovery, known as glacial rebound, occurred rapidly over the first few hundred years and then slowed. Although the distance that the crust has rebounded varies from place to place, it has been found that the land north of Lake Superior has risen about two hundred metres since the glaciers retreat. The recovery is still occurring and the crust north of Lake Superior is still rising 0.4 centimetres per year. Although this seems like a minuscule amount, at this rate the land will raise over two metres in the next five hundred years.

CHANGES IN FLORA AND FAUNA AFTER GLACIAL RETREAT

The work of pollen specialists, glaciologists, ecologists, and palaeontologists has helped pry the postglacial landscape and its megafauna loose from the anonymity of the past. The warm temperatures over the last few decades have provided ecologists the opportunity to study plant succession in the wake of the retreat of alpine glaciers. They have found that lichens usually appear within the first year, pioneer plants within three years and shrubs and small trees within seventy years. It is reasonable to assume that a similar succession of lichens and hardy arctic plants grew in the wake of the retreating Laurentide glacier at the end of the last ice age.

Fortunately, there is a way to test these assumptions the rate of vegetation change after the glacier's retreat. A record of the past plant communities that succeeded the retreat of the continental glacier can be found in the bottom of lakes and ponds. Although no detailed pollen studies have been done from lakes in Quetico Park, Lake of the Clouds, a small lake in the BWCAW, just south of Ottertrack Lake, has had pollen from its lake sediments analyzed. Wind-blown pollen settles on lakes and ponds and sinks to the bottom, where it is incorporated into the growing sedimentary record. Since pollen from most species of plants can be identified by their distinctive shapes and sizes, sediment cores can be taken from lakes and ponds and the analysis of the pollen at various depths gives a good overview of past plant communities.

With the bottom layer of pollen representing the first plants after the glacial retreat and the top layer representing plants from more recent years, the stratified layers of pollen represent the history of plant succession. There are complicating factors, however, in this scenario. Some plants, especially coniferous trees, produce large amounts of pollen that can be carried hundreds of kilometres by the wind, while other plants produce very little pollen or pollen that is not transported very far. Consequently, analysis of pollen cores gives a picture, although somewhat fuzzy, of the vegetation changes in a particular area. Since the vegetation is the main factor that determines what animals were present at any given time in an area, inferences can be made about the animals present based on the vegetation.

The pollen analyzed from Lake of the Clouds and from other lakes within a few hundred kilometres of the Quetico-Superior area all show a very similar pattern of vegetation changes over time. The pollen from the oldest zone indicates sparse vegetation composed mainly of lichens, sedges, grasses, herbs, and spruce trees. This mixture of cold-adapted vegetation, known as tundra, comes from the Finnish word *tunturi*, meaning "treeless plain." The mixture of tundra vegetation with a scattering of trees indicated by the pollen studies has been called "tundra-like," "woodland — prairie — tundra," and "open boreal forest" by various researchers. Dale Guthrie, a prominent Alaskan biologist, called similar vegetation that followed the glacier's retreat in Alaska the "mammoth steppe." He believes that this environment, named after the woolly mammoths that thrived on the vegetation, was more productive than today's tundra and is the primary reason for the size of the ice age mammals that fed on it.

Up until about thirteen thousand years ago, the land south of the glacier was home to a staggering array of large mammals known as the ice age megafauna. They included woolly mammoths, mastodons, sabre-toothed tigers, camels, horses, and giant sloths. Some of these animals were extremely large; 220-kilogram beavers, giant sloths that were four metres feet tall standing upright, and five-tonne woolly mammoths. Most of the megafauna adapted well to cold conditions and they fed on the tundra-like vegetation and grasses as the glacier receded.

The predators of megafauna were also huge. Dire wolves, cousins of today's timber wolf, weighed eighty kilograms. Skeletal remains of these megafauna are found throughout much of North America. In areas with warm, dry climates, such as much of the American Southwest, there are numerous well-preserved remains of ice age mammals. The La Brea Tar Pits in Los Angeles contain thousands of skeletons from this time period, especially of carnivores such as dire wolves, sabre-tooth tigers, and the American lion. In addition to the preservation in hot, dry areas, virtually intact woolly mammoths have been recovered from permafrost in Siberia and Alaska. In 1901, a Russian scientist came across a woolly mammoth eroding out of the ice in northern Siberia. His dog team ate portions of a woolly mammoth that had been frozen for twenty thousand years — no mention of freezer burn — and suffered no ill effects. In addition to preservation in extreme climates, the bones of woolly mammoths have been recovered in southern Minnesota, Wisconsin, South Dakota, southern Ontario, and Manitoba. Recently, the bones of a mastodon, an elephant slightly smaller than the woolly mammoth that fed on spruce needles, were recovered in southern Wisconsin.

By thirteen thousand years ago, when all of the Quetico-Superior area except for the northeastern corner of Quetico Park was free of glacial ice, many of the large ice age mammals were extinct or on the way to extinction. Apparently there was a period of less than one thousand years when the southern part of Quetico-Superior could have been home to ice age megafauna and they may not have even seen the northern part of Quetico Park. Evidence for their existence has not yet been found to confirm their presence anywhere in Quetico-Superior — not a single bone, tusk, or tooth.

A possible reason for the lack of evidence is that the acidic soils of the Canadian Shield are very hard on bone and antlers, and only in unusual situations do they last a decade, let alone thousands of years. Moose bones and antlers just two or three years old are usually heavily chewed by rodents and covered with fungus, moss, and bacteria that recycle the valuable nutrients. Only unlikely circumstances, such as remains settling into a peat bog or being quickly covered with silt at the bottom of a lake, allow for long-term preservation of organic material such as antler and bone in our environment.

In spite of these constraints, the remains of an animal at least 6,500 years old have been recovered near Quetico Park. A skull of an extinct form of bison was found while peat was being dredged on the edge of a bog near Kenora, Ontario. The large, bison skull with the protruding horns was picked up intact by a backhoe operator who joked, "I told my friends that I dug up the Devil himself."[2] The presence of a bison associated with grasslands north of Lake of the Woods was a shock, but analysis of pollen from the site indicated that the bison was living in a mixed forest and grassland environment that had succeeded the earlier tundra. This environment would have been similar to where bison now live in Wood Buffalo National Park.

The warming of the climate that ended the last ice age caused a slow but steady replacement of the rich tundra-like environment, which provided a wide variety of nutritious food for the megafauna, with a forested landscape. The loss of the tundra and the extinction of the megafauna near the end of the last ice age left North America without any really large grazing mammals. This niche remains empty to this day everywhere in the world except in parts of Africa.

THE STEEP ROCK CARIBOU ANTLER

Not all of the prominent mammals at the end of the last ice age were megafauna; caribou also flourished in the Quetico-Superior region during this time period. Direct proof of their existence at this early time period came from the recovery and analysis of a large caribou antler from deep in the silt at the bottom of Steep Rock Lake just north of Atikokan, Ontario.

Charlie Brooks and Dick Kaemingk admire the caribou antler they found eroded from silt near the bottom of the pit at Steep Rock Lake.

Due to the combination of high demand and dwindling iron ore reserves in the United States and Canada during the Second World War, the decision was made to drain Steep Rock Lake to get at the iron ore at the bottom of the lake. Once the Seine River was diverted around the lake and the draining began in 1943, huge dredges were brought in to pump the silt from the bottom of the main body of the lake into the river. The silt left exposed along the lakeshore had to be washed into the rapidly draining lake using high-pressure hoses. On April 16, 1957, Charlie Brooks and Dick Kaemingk were monitoring the area along the shore when they noticed a large antler in the silt, dug it out, and set it aside. They estimated that the antler was located beneath twenty to thirty metres of silt and clay.

The caribou antler they recovered was not a solitary find. Charlie Brooks remembered seeing other antlers on top of the barges, presumably put there by other workers and later discarded. It is not surprising that the presence of caribou antlers at the bottom of Steep Rock Lake was not considered unusual since woodland caribou were common in the area until the 1930s. It is extremely fortunate that Brooks had the curiosity and foresight to set aside the antler that he and Kaemingk recovered from the bottom of the lake and to donate it to the Atikokan Centennial Museum.

It is ironic that the caribou antler was found near Atikokan since *atikokan* means "caribou bones" in Ojibwa.[3] There are other references to caribou in the immediate area with the Atikokan River flowing through the town and Caribus Lake and Caribus Creek just south of Atikokan. Since so little is known about mammals from the past in northwestern Ontario, the age of the antler so deeply buried in the silt was eagerly anticipated. When tested, the antler was found to be 9,940 +/-120 radiocarbon years — which converts to about 11,500 calendar years. This means the antler came from a caribou living fairly close to the retreating glacier near the end of the ice age.

The antler was originally thought to be from a woodland caribou, but experts now believe that it is probably from a male barren-ground caribou. The presence of barren-ground caribou — animals that now live in the tundra of northern Canada and Alaska and migrate south to forested lands for the winter — on Steep Rock Lake may seem surprising. Their occurrence just north of Quetico Park not long after the glacier had retreated to the north, however, is consistent with evidence from pollen studies that indicate the area was primarily tundra with some spruce and birch at that time.

Barren-ground caribou migrate in large herds and shed their antlers in early winter after the completion of the rut in the fall. The recovered antler was shed by a barren-ground caribou bull on the ice of Steep Rock Lake after it spent the summer somewhere north of Atikokan. The bull probably continued on its journey with the rest of the migrating herd to its winter range farther south. A herd of barren-ground caribou would have been a major resource for any Palaeo-Indians living in the area. Caribou are hunted during the fall migration for both their hides and for food. However, the location of these ancient migration routes in the Atikokan area, or anywhere in the Quetico-Superior region, remains a mystery.

Other evidence for the presence of caribou in Quetico is found in rock paintings. In the winter of 1983, Phil Sawdo, an Atikokan trapper, discovered rock paintings on a creek-side cliff north of Montgomery Lake. These paintings are the only known ones in Quetico that are not located on a navigable body of water. Phil found two sets of paintings about fifty metres apart. One set contains an outline of a caribou with antlers that extend the length of the body with faded unidentified drawings below it. The other, located many yards away, has a bow-legged human figure beneath a large mammal with tall, branching antlers reminiscent of a caribou but with a body that seems more moose-like. No wonder this painting has been identified as both a moose and a caribou. Just north of the paintings are two small valleys that could have funnelled caribou migrating down from Buckingham Lake and the Pickerel Lake into the narrows with the pictograph cliff on one side and a high hill directly opposite. Phil Sawdo thought that the pictographs depicted a location where caribou were ambushed during their spring and fall migrations.

The spring after the pictographs were discovered, Dick Hiner and I paddled as close as we could get north of the paintings and walked the rest of the way.

When standing at the site, it was easy to understand Phil's conjecture that this is a natural ambush site. It isn't known how old the Montgomery Lake rock paintings are and, because of the similarity between barren-ground caribou and woodland caribou that were present in Quetico until the 1930s, the paintings could be depicting either one. Other pictographs, such as those on Agnes and Quetico lakes, have been identified by some observers as depicting caribou, but they are considered to be woodland rather than barren-ground caribou. Since there are no rock paintings that are definitely known to date back to Palaeo-Indian times, all of the paintings that resemble caribou are likely woodland caribou from the more recent past. Nevertheless, it is certainly possible that migrating barren-ground caribou were ambushed at the narrows north of Montgomery Lake by Palaeo-Indians.

There is other evidence that caribou were in the Quetico-Superior region during the Palaeo-Indian period. The Cummins site, a large, Late Palaeo-Indian site near Thunder Bay, produced fragments of bone that have been identified as caribou. Archaeologists have suggested that this location, as well as other sites from the same time period, provide evidence of caribou hunting by bands of Palaeo-Indians along the north shore of Lake Superior. The antler from Steep Rock Lake is an indication that these early explorers probably were also hunting caribou herds in the rest of the area.

FLORA AND FAUNA CHANGES SINCE THE MEGAFAUNA EXTINCTION

The tundra-like conditions that sustained the megafauna, caribou, and other grazing animals lasted for approximately one thousand years in the Quetico-Superior region. The transition from tundra with small trees into a mixed forest dominated by white birch and black spruce began approximately twelve thousand years ago in the southern part of Quetico-Superior, and the change moved north as the glacier retreated. The white birch-black spruce forest was dominant for about two or three thousand years and it slowly evolved into a mixed pine-spruce forest. About a thousand years later, the mixed conifer-hardwood forest, similar to that found in the Quetico-Superior landscape, became the primary forest type.

The alterations in vegetation inevitably led to changes in animal populations. Tundra vegetation supporting barren-ground caribou, gave way to forests supporting woodland caribou. These animals slowly disappeared over the last hundred years as a combination of logging and vegetation changes made conditions better for moose and white-tailed deer. Because of the lack of bone preservation, there are many unknowns regarding the time of arrival of the woodland caribou, moose, and white-tailed deer, and the possible role of elk in the area.

A RICH MOSAIC

Many of us probably wish we could have seen woolly mammoths, longhorn bison, mastodons, and barren-ground caribou grazing on the tundra-like landscape that once existed in the Quetico-Superior region. The sight of a beaver as large as a black bear and a wolf almost twice as large as those that live today would probably leave us speechless. The British zoologist Alfred Russel Wallace was referring to the extinction of these ice age megafauna when he noted: "We live in a zoologically impoverished world, from which all the largest, the fiercest, and strongest forms have disappeared."[4] It's obvious that much was lost in the millennia since the glacier retreated but much has also been gained.

The moose, white-tailed deer, timber wolves, black bear, lynx, martin, fisher, bald eagle, osprey, and loons that inhabit the Quetico-Superior region today are as impressive, in their own way, as the creatures that came before them. The glacier left behind a mangled mix of deep lakes, boulder-strewn shorelines, expanses of bedrock covered to varying degrees with rock debris, gravelly beaches, and rock-strewn streams and rivers. This seemingly inhospitable mixture of rock and water has weathered and evolved from tundra into the rich mosaic of plants and animals that we now call the Quetico-Superior.

CHAPTER TWO

PALAEO-INDIANS:
FIRST EXPLORERS OF THE QUETICO-SUPERIOR

The first people to enter the Quetico-Superior area encountered a landscape rubbed raw by glacial ice, witnessed glaciers calving into an inland sea, and crossed a landscape devoid of trees.[1] The earth was recovering from an ice age and a massive continental glacier was melting and receding northward. These first explorers, known as Palaeo-Indians, entered a landscape that had recently been populated by vigorous, cold-adapted plants and animals. They were following herds of barren-ground caribou that grazed on succulent tundra plants. In the southern part of the Quetico-Superior area, woolly mammoths and mastodons may also have been prey for these highly mobile big-game hunters who had the technology and skills to thrive in a changing and often hostile, environment.

Since the continental glacier was receding, much of the area was flooded by glacial meltwater that formed glacial Lake Agassiz. The first people to enter the Quetico-Superior region probably came into the higher elevation areas in the eastern part of the BWCAW and moved north into the eastern part of Quetico Park. As the glacier continued to recede and the water level of Lake Agassiz dropped, they then moved into the rest of the area.

The Palaeo-Indians entered this new land as members of small groups that were essentially extended families. Because their prey was mobile, they had to move quickly and often. They also had to find plants for food and medicine, build shelters, make and repair clothing, find stone for tools, and care for the young, the sick, and the elderly as they travelled. Since they were the first explorers of this region, there were no maps, no guides, and no one to ask for advice as to what lay ahead. They experienced the joys and terrors of entering a fresh, new, unexplored land. The information they needed was carried in their heads and they relied on their companions and their collective know-how for survival. They were intrepid explorers of the first magnitude, but neither their names nor the time of their arrival is known.

DISCOVERY OF THE AMERICAS

The people who first entered the Quetico-Superior area were the descendents of people who arrived in the Americas hundreds, thousands, or even tens of thousand of years earlier. Little is known about these earliest inhabitants of North America, but evidence about their existence is gradually accumulating. A big breakthrough occurred in 1929 when unusual, fluted spear points were found associated with mammoth bones near Clovis, New Mexico[2]. Fluted spear points were soon found in various other North American locations from the foothills of the Rockies, to the east coast, and south into northern Mexico. Fluted points have long vertical flakes (flutes) removed from both sides of the base in order to produce grooves. These flutes apparently made it easier to attach a wooden shaft to the spearpoint. Since fluted points have only been found in the Americas, they have been called the first American invention.

These early Palaeo-Indians were given the name the Clovis culture and all of the sites have been] dated to between 13,300 years ago to 12,800 years ago (11,300–10,800 radiocarbon years). For decades nothing irrefutably older was found and — most archaeologists believed — and many still do — that the Clovis people were the first inhabitants of the Americas. The distinctive fluted Clovis points have been found embedded in the rib cages of mammoths, mastodons, and other ice age mammals these early Palaeo-Indians hunted for food. Their tool kit, which included large knives, choppers, and scrapers, in addition to fluted spear points, indicated they were hunters of large game.

Another tool they probably possessed was a deceptively simple, but remarkably effective, throwing stick called an atlatl. The atlatl allowed them to throw two-metre-long spears tipped with large spear points with enough force to kill a mammoth from a distance of up to two hundred metres. Because the atlatl allowed the killing of large, dangerous, protein-rich animals from a safe distance, it is understandable that it has been called one of the most important inventions of all time.

Since little is known about Clovis people except for their stone tools, important questions about the clothes they wore, the type of dwellings they lived in, and their modes of transportation are still unanswered. Some of these mysteries are unravelling as technological advances and new research techniques allow a more complete recovery of material and more thorough analysis of small bones and plant remains from archaeological sites. Results from these detailed investigations have led archaeologists to believe that the first impression of Clovis people as just hunters of big game is too simplistic. Excavations in dry caves and rock shelters where preservation of organic material is superior to that in open sites indicate that, in addition to being big-game hunters, the Clovis people also consumed a wide variety of small game and plants. They also used plant fibres to make sandals, baskets, textiles, and nets to ensnare animals and fish. Some archaeologists have even speculated that Clovis people were primarily scavengers who obtained most of their food by driving predators away from animals they had killed.

The Clovis people inhabited a substantial portion of North America south of the glacier during the time of the ice age megafauna. As the woolly mammoth, mastodon, woodland musk ox, horse, camel, stag moose, giant beaver, and other megafauna were decreasing in numbers, and probably not by coincidence, the Clovis period was also coming to an end. The decline and eventual extinction of the megafauna has been attributed to over-hunting by the Clovis people, but two other possible reasons — climate change and disease — have also been proposed.

A new spear point, smaller and with flutes well over half the length of the point, replaced the Clovis spear point. The people using these points were known as the Folsum culture.[3] They primarily hunted a species of bison, larger than those that live today, that persisted after most other ice age mammals had died off. The Clovis and Folsum people were subsequently replaced by, evolved into, or merged with other groups entering the Americas to create a succession of cultural groups that comprise the Late Palaeo-Indian period.

With the demise of the ice age megafauna near the end of the Folsum period, the distinctive fluted points made by Clovis and Folsum hunters were replaced by long, lanceolate spear points that were not fluted. The people who made them, known as Late Palaeo-Indians, are primarily identified by their unfluted spear points that varied greatly in size and shape from one area to another. These spear points — given names such as Agate Basin, Scottsbluff, Eden, and Hell Gap by archaeologists — were named after the location where the first evidence of their existence was uncovered. The distribution of Late Palaeo-Indian sites indicates that they did not have sharply defined boundaries, but moved as the climate, their prey, and competing groups fluctuated over time. In spite of differences among the three Palaeo-Indian groups — Clovis, Folsum, and their regional Late Palaeo-Indian descendents — they all used large spear points to hunt caribou and other large animals, and utilized a variety of small game and local plants.

There is growing evidence, however, that Palaeo-Indians may not have been the first inhabitants of the Americas. The "Clovis first" hypothesis is now being seriously challenged. Until about thirty years ago, the vast majority of archaeologists believed that America's first inhabitants came across the Bering Land Bridge about fifteen thousand years ago, travelled down an ice-free corridor along the foothills of the Rocky Mountains, and rapidly spread throughout the Americas south of the glacier. Since the 1970s, a few archaeological sites have been found, containing stone tools that are distinctively different from those used by Clovis people and appear to be older than those on Clovis sites. Some of these pre-Clovis sites — all of them at least somewhat controversial — are thought to be over forty thousand years old. These earlier people appear to have used a variety of relatively unsophisticated stone tools, but nothing as well made or distinctive as the Clovis fluted point has been found on pre-Clovis sites. Since one of the most prominent pre-Clovis sites is in Chile near the southern tip of South America and others are in the southeastern United States, the northern entry over the Bering Land Bridge is now seriously questioned.

New controversies are arising as to who these people were and where they came from. The Bering Land Bridge theory is now just one of many possibilities. A variety of other theories for the origin and mode of transportation of the first people in the Americas — from northern Asia by boat along the Pacific coast, from Europe across the North Atlantic, and from Polynesia across the South Pacific — have been hypothesized. New technologies, especially DNA analysis, should help to unravel the mystery of who arrived here first and where they came from.

PALAEO-INDIANS: FIRST EXPLORERS OF THE QUETICO-SUPERIOR AREA

It is not known for certain when people first entered the Quetico-Superior region. Although no artifacts have been recovered, it is possible that pre-Clovis people did live here prior to the last glaciation. If they were, the glacier would have moved and altered or buried evidence of their existence. Finding evidence of pre-glacial inhabitants of Quetico-Superior would be harder than finding a needle in a haystack since, in this case, a huge glacier not only demolished the haystack, but it also pushed both the needle and the hay hundreds of kilometres to the south and buried them under glacial debris. Therefore, it is generally accepted that the first human inhabitants of the Quetico-Superior were nomadic Palaeo-Indian hunters moving north in the wake of the retreating glacier.

By 13,500 years ago, the area south of Ely, Minnesota, was free of glacial ice, even though ice still occupied part of northwestern Minnesota and a glacial lobe occupied the Lake Superior basin. Animals adapted to sub-Arctic conditions followed the tundra vegetation that grew as the glacier retreated. The initial movement of animals into the Quetico-Superior area would have been dependent on vegetation appearing in sufficient quantities to support the megafauna that the Clovis people hunted. Although it is not known how quickly the region reached this level of vegetation growth, pollen studies provide evidence that a maximum of a few hundred years was all that was required for the presence of sufficient tundra plants to attract and sustain animal occupation. However, fluctuations in the levels of Lake Agassiz would have alternately flooded and exposed some areas numerous times, thus delaying substantial plant growth.

Although the Quetico-Superior landscape, with its abundance of bedrock and lakes, wouldn't have had a strong appeal for grazing animals, it undoubtedly had patches of tempting vegetation and the attraction of cooler temperatures for cold-adapted animals in a warming environment. It is intriguing to think that at least some of the portages in the Quetico-Superior area may have originated even before the arrival of the first humans. Loren Eiseley, an American anthropologist and writer, once speculated that humans first moved across and explored the Americas by following the trails of the animals they hunted. "In every major continent to which the great herbivores have penetrated, there once ran a series of game trails beaten into the landscape by millions of feet. The trails led to everything that man desired. They ran to water, they ran to salt licks and they found their way across the lowest divide … Certain it is that he must have marched on many a well-worn trail left for him where, ironically, no human foot had ever trod."[4] The heavy feet of ice age mammals might have created trails that were simply transformed by Palaeo-Indian hunters into portages. Some of these portages may still be in use today.

Humans followed their prey as they moved into the land rich in new growth. Although no bones of ice age mammals have been found in the Quetico-Superior region, remains of woolly mammoths have been recovered from southern Minnesota, southern and central Wisconsin, South Dakota, and southern Manitoba. Some of them, such as the 14,500-year-old woolly mammoth skeleton that was excavated near Kenosha, in southeastern Wisconsin, contained cut marks and were found in association with stone tools.[5] In addition, a partial mastodon skeleton that may have had a Clovis point associated with it was found in southwestern Wisconsin in 1897. The skull of an extinct form of bison was found northwest of the Quetico-Superior near Kenora, Ontario. However, no evidence of human activity was found associated with it. In addition, an 11,500-year-old antler from a barren-ground caribou was found north of Atikokan, Ontario (see Chapter 1 for more detail). This is a significant discovery because these caribou were such an important resource for Late Palaeo-Indians.

In addition to the megafauna, the Quetico-Superior region had another resource that was essential for the survival of the first explorers — stone that could be used for tools. Fine-grained lithic (stone) material that can be flaked into spear points, knives, scrapers, and other essential implements is a rare commodity in the predominantly granitic area. Surprisingly, the eastern Quetico-Superior has three glassy lithic materials that flake with a sharp edge and are ideal for making stone tools.

The first is Knife Lake siltstone, a fine-grained, silica-rich component of the metamorphosed volcanic rock found along the shorelines of Knife Lake. Palaeo-Indians quickly discovered that this distinctive black or grey rock was terrific for making the durable knives and spear points they required.

The other two materials were jasper taconite and Gunflint silica. These tough, chert-like lithic materials are found in the Gunflint Formation, a band of silica-rich rocks that runs from Gunflint Lake to the north shore of Lake Superior. Boulders and cobbles of these three materials were pushed south by the glacier and Palaeo-Indians undoubtedly encountered and used them for making stone tools before they found the "motherlode" of Knife Lake siltstone on Knife Lake and outcrops of Gunflint silica and jasper taconite near Gunflint Lake and North Lake. The vast majority of their tools were made from these three "weapons grade" materials because strong durable tools were needed to hunt and butcher large mammals. Native people from later time periods primarily used stone, such as Hudson Bay Lowland chert, that was easier to flake and made sharper tools, but wasn't nearly as durable as Knife Lake siltstone.

Fluted spear points from the Clovis and Folsum periods have been found in Minnesota, Wisconsin, North Dakota, and southern Manitoba. Three Clovis spear points, a complete point made from Knife Lake siltstone and two broken bases, were found in the Reservoir Lakes area north of Duluth, Minnesota. The Reservoir Lakes are located just one hundred kilometres south of the BWCAW. In addition, a possible Clovis spear point, a broken and highly contested artifact, has been found on the edge of BWCAW east of Quetico Park. Due to the fluctuating levels of Lake Agassiz, geologists have found clear evidence of its shorelines in Quetico only at "The Pines" on Pickerel Lake. Since Palaeo-Indians of the Clovis and Folsum cultures would have probably camped along the shores of Lake Agassiz, not knowing the locations of those shorelines has hindered finding their campsites.

As the glacier shrunk back north of Quetico Park at the conclusion of the Clovis period, Lake Agassiz was also getting smaller. In many cases, Palaeo-Indians arriving after the Clovis and Folsum cultures would have camped on the same campsites as those used today. This makes finding Late Palaeo-Indian sites in Quetico-Superior easier to find and numerous spear points attributed to this period have been found throughout northern Minnesota, the BWCAW, and Quetico Park. The term "Late" in this case is misleading; they arrived over twelve thousand years ago and persisted for at least another two or three thousand years.

A large number of Late Palaeo-Indian points have been found on the Reservoir Lakes, many recovered by the late Elaine Redepenning[6], and at other locations in northern Minnesota outside of the BWCAW. In the Boundary Waters area, Late Palaeo-Indian points have been found on a variety of lakes, including Moose Lake, Saganaga Lake, Knife Lake, South Fowl Lake, Rose Lake, Fall Lake, Basswood Lake, and Hungry Jack Lake.

Virtually the only artifacts that have survived from these early time periods are stone tools — very large and skillfully made unfluted spear points, knives, and

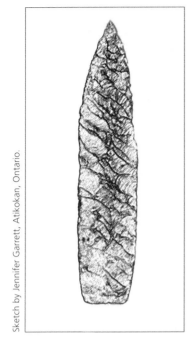

Generally thought to have been made between 11,500 and 10,000 calendar years ago, this type of long, thin, Late Palaeo-Indian spear point, known as an Eden point, was found in Quetico Park. This ten-centimetre-(four-inch-) long point is made from Knife River Flint from North Dakota.

snowshoes, sleds, or canoes. Since they successfully adapted to an environment that was covered in deep snow for half the year, and was as much water as land the rest of the year, it seems safe to assume that the first explorers in the Quetico-Superior had both snowshoes and some sort of watercraft.

QUETICO'S FIRST EXPLORERS: SAVING THE BEST FOR LAST

The glacier continued its slow and erratic retreat and the northern part of Quetico Park became free of glacial ice about 12,500 years ago. It wasn't until about twelve thousand years ago that the water of Lake Agassiz dropped to the level of Pickerel Lake. By this time, most of the ice age megafauna is thought to have been extinct. Thus, it seems unlikely they lived in the northern part of Quetico for very long, if at all. On the other hand, it seems highly likely that ice age megafauna, although their populations were already declining, would have inhabited the southern part of Quetico. If animals were following fairly closely behind the glacier, then people hunting them could have entered the southern part of Quetico Park near the end of the Clovis period. This is definitely possible since archaeologists from Maine to Alberta, including Mike McLeod, working east of Quetico Park just north of the Minnesota border, have speculated that Palaeo-Indians were living within thirty kilometres of the glacier.[7]

scrapers. The spear points, probably thrown by an atlatl, are usually about the same size as Clovis and much larger than anything made in later time periods. Due to a combination of time and the nature of our environment — acidic soils, wet conditions, and freeze-thaw cycles — almost nothing organic remains from the Palaeo-Indian periods. As a result, no radiocarbon dates for Palaeo-Indians in the Quetico-Superior area are available. Archaeologists have about the same degree of understanding — very little — of the Late Palaeo-Indians (from here on just called Palaeo-Indians) who occupied the Quetico-Superior region as they do about their Clovis predecessors. It currently isn't even known if Palaeo-Indians had

So far, no megafauna remains — not even a tooth — have been found in Quetico Park, nor have Clovis points been found in the park or anywhere else in northwestern Ontario. This lack of evidence may reflect that there never were megafauna or Palaeo-Indians from the Clovis period in this area. Or — as I believe — we simply haven't looked long enough or hard enough. Palaeo-Indians, whether they were Clovis, Folsum, or Late Palaeo-Indians, were entering a glacier–scoured landscape that no human had ever seen and were Quetico's first true explorers. They would have been well adapted to a landscape of tundra, bedrock, and water since prior to entering the area they had travelled through northern Minnesota and the BWCAW. In this case, they were literally saving the best for last.

People probably first entered Quetico Park somewhere east of Basswood Lake since the lower elevations west of there were under Lake Agassiz. The lakes in the southeastern part of Quetico would have had shorelines similar to or somewhat higher than those that exist today. Palaeo-Indians were the first to see Silver Falls, the first to stand on the shores of Knife and Saganagons lakes, the first to paddle Ottertrack and McEwen lakes, and the first to portage into Blackstone and Other Man lakes. They would have seen these places when the water levels were higher and the rivers wider, deeper, and faster-flowing than they are today.

When the water is high, the Falls Chain can be a challenging place to canoe. Imagine what it would have been like if the amount of flow was increased manyfold by runoff from the melting glacier. The tremendous flow of cold water must have made the trips taken by the Palaeo-Indians down the Falls Chain into Lake Agassiz very treacherous and very exciting. Today's portages would have been underwater, so they would have probably used very long portages to avoid the fast, dangerous sections.

When Palaeo-Indians first entered Quetico Park, Lake Agassiz must have looked much like Wicksteed Lake does today — a lake with numerous islands and many shallow areas. Only the tops of today's cliffs and hills would have protruded from the water. Lakes such as Beaverhouse, Crooked, and Argo were probably under more than thirty metres of water and the higher elevations would have been islands in the lake. What are now rapids on the Maligne, Quetico, and Namakan rivers were calm places in the depths of the giant lake.

During the earliest stages of Lake Agassiz's existence, it drained south toward the Gulf of Mexico. As the glacier retreated north of Quetico Park, however, an outlet opened that allowed the lake to drain east toward Lake Superior, causing lake levels in the Quetico-Superior to drop. It is generally believed that the water in glacial Lake Agassiz temporarily stabilized at today's level of Pickerel Lake approximately twelve thousand years ago or shortly thereafter. At that time, Pickerel Lake would have been situated along the eastern edge of Lake Agassiz. The three intact Late Palaeo-Indian points that have

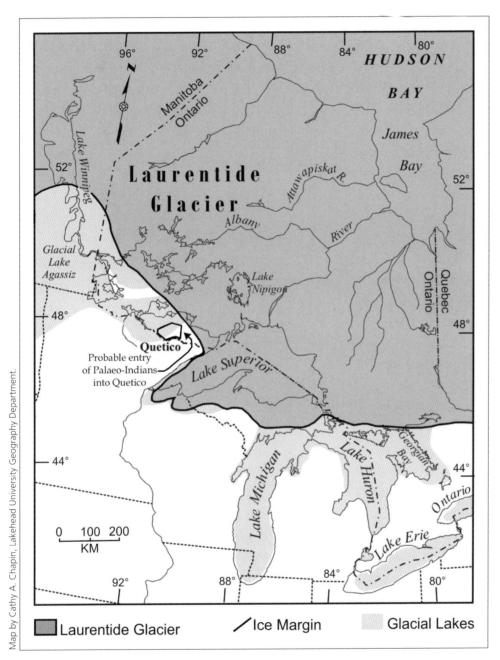

Map by Cathy A. Chapin, Lakehead University Geography Department.

Quetico
Probable entry
of Palaeo-Indians
into Quetico

■ Laurentide Glacier   / Ice Margin   Glacial Lakes

MAP 8: PROBABLE ROUTE OF ENTRY OF PALAEO-INDIANS INTO QUETICO

Palaeo-Indians followed the retreating caribou and ice age mammals that fed on the vegetation growing in the wake of the glacier's retreat. People probably entered in the southeast part of today's Quetico since Lake Agassiz covered the land to the west and the glacier occupied much of the land to the north and east.

been found on Pickerel Lake campsites are indications that Late Palaeo-Indians lived along the shore of this glacial lake.

One of these spear points was made from Knife Lake siltstone. Because quarries of this high-quality material were located on Knife Lake, the lake would have had a special appeal to these people. The unusual number of Late Palaeo-Indian points found on both the Ontario and Minnesota sides of Knife Lake attest to its importance. As the glacier continued to retreat north of Quetico, new outlets were opened and the levels of Lake Agassiz may have dropped to levels close to what they are today by as early as ten thousand years ago. Late Palaeo-Indian points have also been found on Basswood Lake and Sturgeon Lake, lakes that were under Lake Agassiz in earlier Palaeo-Indian time periods. Palaeo-Indians sites in Quetico are difficult to find because the shorelines that they would have camped on are now, in many instances, above the current shorelines and heavily covered with vegetation.

The Palaeo-Indians who first entered Quetico probably hunted caribou and a declining population of ice age megafauna. Over the course of many generations, they witnessed the further decline and eventual extinction of many of the animals they depended on for food. While the loss of sources of food would have been difficult, these early inhabitants were probably relieved to note the demise of large predators like the short-faced bear and dire wolves that may occasionally have made humans their prey. The era of the Palaeo-Indians encompassed major environmental changes during their time in the Quetico-Superior. They lived in an era that spanned the extinction of megafauna and the replacement of megafauna by animals that could live in a forested landscape.

EXPLORATION AND IMAGINATION

Douglas Preston, an American author who has written extensively about North America's past, has noted:

Sometime during the last Ice Age, a seemingly trivial event took place, one that would change human history forever: a human being first set foot in the new world. We do not know where this person came from, or why, or where the first footfall landed on the New World. Unlike the first man to walk on the moon, the unknown pioneer who made this giant step for mankind was probably not aware of doing anything significant at all, perhaps just taking one more weary stride on a long tramp across the frozen tundra, searching for game. But in that moment, a Garden of Eden of vastness and splendor fell to our species. It would be the last inhabitable area of earth to be occupied by human beings. Not until we colonize the stars will an event of comparable significance take place.[8]

The first people to enter the Quetico-Superior area were a continuation of the exploration of a part of North America just released from the glacier. Since we don't know the time, the location, or the names of the first explorers of this magnificent part of North America, there is a tendency to minimize the significance of what they did or even ignore them completely. While we rightly celebrate the accomplishments of Pierre Radisson, Jacques de Noyon, Sieur de la Vérendrye, Alexander Mackenzie, Simon Fraser, David Thompson, and other Europeans who explored a land new to them, but one that had been inhabited for thousands of years, we overlook those who came first.

I find it exhilarating to be able to travel over portages and sleep on campsites that were used by the first people to enter this area. When paddling on Pickerel Lake, imagine what it would have been like when Lake Agassiz stretched all the way to the prairies and tundra grasses grew in abundance along the shore. Curlews were flying overhead and barren-ground caribou travelled along a moraine where red pine and Jack pine now flourish. Palaeo-Indians gathered around a small campfire, eating arctic hare and cattail stew seasoned with wild ginger while retelling their grandfathers' stories of woolly mammoths and huge wolves.

For thousands of years, the descendents of these Palaeo-Indians called the Quetico-Superior region home and sought plants for their medicinal value; caribou, berries, whitefish, moose, and wild rice for food; stone outcrops for tools; wood for dwellings, atlatls, and arrow shafts; and birchbark for containers and canoes. Although twelve thousand years of Native people living off the land ensures that there aren't many places where no one has been, Quetico is still a land that invites exploration.

The joy is in having such a magnificent place to explore. It is always exciting to see a moose feeding in the shallows, discover an osprey nest on a seldom-visited lake, find a Calypso orchid, or gaze in wonder at pictographs that hint of an earlier and strikingly different time. Every portage leads to new possibilities. For over forty years I have marvelled at discovering places and objects in Quetico that have been seen by many others — but are new to me.

CHAPTER THREE

THE FUTURE OF THE PAST IN QUETICO PARK: ARCHAEOLOGY AND ANISHINAABE SPIRITUAL BELIEFS[1]

It seems strange that the history of North America's indigenous peoples has been told with so little input from the descendents of the people whose lives are being chronicled. Most of the material evidence of their long and varied past has been obtained by archaeological investigations conducted by non-Native archaeologists. But their scientific investigations of physical objects reveal only part of the story. The views of contemporary Native peoples and the ideas expressed in their oral history have usually been disregarded or thought to be of secondary importance. Not surprisingly, they have expressed concerns that their past has primarily been interpreted by others.

Lakota author Luther Standing Bear recalled that:

> We went to school to copy, to imitate; not to exchange language and ideas, and not to develop the best traits that had come out of uncountable experiences of hundreds and thousands of years living upon this continent.

Our annals, all-happenings of human import, were stored in our song and dance rituals, our history differing in that it was not stored in books, but in the living memory. So, while white people had much to teach us, we had much to teach them, and what a school could have been established upon that idea.[2]

What a school indeed! Unfortunately, this mutual exchange of ideas and language hasn't occurred to any extent in schools in either Canada or the United States. This has resulted in a very one-sided view of the past. Author and urban activist Jane Jacobs has concluded that North Americans "… live in a grave-yard of lost aboriginal cultures, many of which were decisively finished off by mass amnesia in which even the memory of what was lost was also lost."[3]

There are more than twelve thousand years of human history in the Quetico-Superior and the first 97 percent is the story of the Native peoples who have lived in this region. It is unfortunate that most accounts of the past are by people, like the writer of this chapter, whose ancestors only shared the last 3 percent of this history, while very little attention has been paid to Native peoples' interpretation of their own past.

TRADITIONAL ARCHAEOLOGY AND THE PAST

Archaeology is the scientific analysis of the material remains that previous cultures left behind. As archaeologists working in Quetico Park and surrounding areas, we have searched for and analyzed these material remains and drawn conclusions about the past based on this evidence. Since organic material breaks down very quickly in our boreal environment, archaeological studies have typically been confined to non-perishable items that survive hundreds or thousands of years. Stone flakes from tool manufacture and sharpening, fragments of clay cooking vessels, the occasional intact or broken arrowhead, spear point or scraper, and copper fragments or trade items from the fur-trade era make up the vast majority of items collected. Thousands of these artifacts have been catalogued and are now stored at the Quetico Park Information Pavilion at French Lake.

Ongoing changes in Quetico-Superior's environment required changes in technologies and lifestyle of those living here. These adaptations are reflected in the change from large spear points to smaller arrowheads, the size and design of hide scrapers and stone axes, and the shift from stone tools to copper tools. Pottery, which was apparently introduced from the south about 2,500 years ago, may have been used to store wild rice. These durable material remains — broken arrowheads, worn-out scrapers, and pottery fragments — are primarily associated with food procurement or subsistence, which would have been only a part of life in the past. However, it is this limited range of non-perishable material that archaeologists use to reconstruct history.

There are many ways to view the world, based on what it is one chooses to see. Archaeologists have usually minimized, or even ignored, the viewpoints of the people whose ancestors they are studying. By doing this they have chosen to see the past through a European filter. Michael Budak, author of *Grand Mound*, an excellent booklet about the history of the boundary waters along the Rainy River, wrote: "Ultimately, the picture archaeologists draw of the past is only a shadowy outline of what went on."[4] The incorporation of interpretations by Native people today — many of which will be in sharp contrast to those drawn by archaeologists — will help shed some light into the shadows of the past.

ALTERNATE VIEWS OF THE PAST

N. Scott Momaday, an anthropologist who is also Native American, clearly expressed his thoughts on why Native people should have a greater voice in interpreting the past in North America. "My forebears have been in North America for many thousands of years. In my blood I have a real sense of that occupation. It is worth something to me, as indeed that long, unbroken tenure is worth something to every Native American."[5]

To an increasing extent, archaeologists are accepting the idea that Native people should be involved in the planning and execution of research projects. Most have come to recognize and respect the knowledge that resides within Native communities. Increasingly, anthropologists and archaeologists are realizing "… it is important to recognize that oral traditions and archaeology represent two separate but overlapping ways of knowing the past. There is no doubt that a real history is embedded in Native American oral traditions, and that this is the same history archaeologists study."[6]

Many anthropologists are creatively combining oral tradition and archaeological concepts to obtain a more inclusive interpretation of the past. Based on what these researchers have found throughout the Americas, the oral history of Native peoples often differs greatly from what is found in archaeological reports, magazine articles, and textbooks, and this is undoubtedly true in the Quetico-Superior area

also. Although still in the minority, a growing number of archaeologists are actively involving local Native people in their work, looking to them for advice and guidance rather than simply as sources of information or, as is too often the case, possible roadblocks to their research.

Ruth Gotthardt is an archaeologist in the Yukon who works with Native communities to organize archaeological projects, trains people to do the work, and then lets the community take control of the project. She told us: "Our work with First Nations is done as a partnership, with opportunities for First Nation students to gain some experience in archaeology and for elders to participate in the projects to provide information on the past for both the archaeologists and the students."[7] Using this co-operative approach, significant contributions have been made to the understanding of the Yukon's past. With increasing frequency, northwestern Ontario and northern Minnesota archaeologists, such as those at Lakehead University in Thunder Bay, those working for the Superior National Forest, and many private consultants on both sides of the border are now making strong efforts to involve local First Nations people in archaeological projects.

A prime example of working with First Nations in Ontario is the work of Jill Taylor-Hollings and Scott Hamilton, archaeologists from Lakehead University. They have consulted and worked alongside Elders and band members whose traditional lands overlap with Woodland Caribou Provincial Park in northwestern Ontario. A number of band members have taken trips into the park with Jill and Scott and have participated in archaeological surveys and excavations. Park superintendent Doug Gilmore has noted, "It seems that the communities or Elders that have worked with the park and archaeologists together on a project are as willing to learn from us as we are from them. I think that is the key to our partnership so far, we are both learning from each other and are walking forward together."[8] In a similar fashion, Dave Woodward, an archaeologist for the 1854 Treaty Authority, and the Superior National Forest Heritage Resource Group are working with members of the Bois Fort band to identify, monitor, and, if necessary, restrict use of sites of significant cultural importance in the Superior National Forest in northern Minnesota. At one such culturally sensitive site on a border lake island, a meeting between Bois Fort band members and Forest Service personnel was held in 2007 and a drum ceremony was conducted in 2008. These activities were followed by campsite closure and rehabilitation. It seems apparent that this type of active and co-operative involvement is increasing. The participation of Native people in the design and execution of archaeological research and the writing of archaeological reports — as many archaeologists are now encouraging — will result in a more complete and accurate view of the past.

WORKING WITH LAC LA CROIX ELDERS: THE SPIRITUAL DIMENSION OF ARCHAEOLOGY

Over the past few decades, Quetico Park managers have sought the active involvement of Lac La Croix First Nation in setting policy objectives and standards of practice for the park. Shirley Peruniak began her discussions with Lac La Croix Elders in the 1970s in her ongoing quest to learn more about the history of the park. The Quetico Park management seemed to follow Shirley's lead of strengthening this communication and since then agreements have been reached with the Lac La Croix First Nation on a number of issues.

In 1995, Quetico Park began working toward a comprehensive plan for the management of cultural resources within the park. As part of the process, Andrew Hinshelwood, archaeologist for the Ministry of Civilization and Culture, talked with Lac La Croix Elders, and information on their traditional history and traditional lands was collected. The knowledge of these Elders, coming from interviews conducted with Henry Geyshick, Helen Geyshick, Bob Geyshick, Frank Jordan Sr., and Bob Ottertail, provided both invaluable guidance in the process of learning about and preserving the archaeological, cultural, and spiritual sites within the park, and was also an excellent opportunity to broaden the park's managerial outlook.

It quickly became obvious that the Elders viewed the landscape in ways very different from Andrew's understanding of the term. The primary difference seemed to be the Elders' belief — prevalent among a variety of Native-American groups — in the presence of the spiritual in the landscape. From the viewpoint of the Lac La Croix Elders, all archaeological sites and the objects found within them possess a resonance derived from a spiritual dimension. In *Searching for the Lost Arrow: Physical and Spiritual Ecology in the Hunters World*, Richard K. Nelson describes how "Animals, plants, rocks and other elements of the physical world, possess qualities that are both natural and supernatural. The environment is inhabited by watchful and potent beings who feel, who can be offended, and who should be treated with respect."[9]

Even more significant from an archaeological point of view, the Anishinaabe Elders did not acknowledge the distinction between the archaeological "past" and the modern "present." They stated that all archaeological sites and the objects found within them continue to have a spiritual resonance derived from past use, and that this spiritual dimension, existing in the present, makes the sites places of contemporary cultural importance. In other words, archaeological sites are contemporary places, not just places of archaeological interest. In fact, as one Lac La Croix Elder observed, these places cannot be used for archaeological purposes because they are already *in use* by Anishinaabe people in stories, songs, memories, and religious practice.

The "spirits" that inhabit the Anishinaabe landscape make the landscape alive in a different sense than is perceived by most Euro-Canadians. This concept of "spirits" in plants, animals, and other objects is a recurring one in Anishinaabe thought. Pictographs were of particular concern to the Elders because they are the most visible and overtly spiritual of the cultural sites in the park. They are the clearest representation of the Elders' belief that cultural heritage sites and artifacts are physical traces of past and ongoing spiritual practices. From their perspective, pictographs are prayers that reflect the myths and legends that bind the culture together.

The connection to the past for contemporary Lac La Croix members is both personal and collective: how one individual acts toward the spirits of the past holds consequence for all members. In drumming and songs, past supplications of ancestors to the deities are recalled as evidence of a longstanding connection between the physical world of humans, the natural world, the present, and the past. These actions connect people to the spirit world and provide benefit to the current and future generations of Anishinaabe people. These beliefs are echoed by Anishinaabe author Louise Erdrich, from Minnesota, who noted that pictographs "reflect a spiritual geography, and are meant to provide teaching and dream guides to generations of Anishinaabeg."[10]

The knowledge that these sites hold a strong spiritual value to traditional Anishinaabe leads to a better understanding of the ongoing concern that the Elders have in seeing pictograph images reproduced on mugs, T-shirts, and as logos on commercial enterprises that don't reflect a sacred nature. They strongly advocate making park visitors aware of the Anishnaabe belief in the spiritual nature of the pictographs and of the need to treat them accordingly. Pictographs should be approached with the same level of respect we extend to a religious site or memorial. The Elders see taking photos of pictographs as merely "taking" from the site, without making any sort of positive contribution. Sketching or drawing the pictograph images, however, is regarded as creating something anew and adding to the creative energy of the original. In their view, these are worthwhile means of recording an image as a keepsake from a canoe trip. The Elders' primary objective, however, is to have canoeists treat pictographs with the respect they deserve.

ELDERS AND ARCHAEOLOGY

During Andrew's discussions with the Elders in 1995, specific questions arose concerning how archaeological surveys were being conducted in Quetico Park. He found that there were concerns about digging on sites their ancestors used. To the Elders, the bigger concern was the removal of artifacts from archaeological sites and their storage in Quetico Park Interpretive Centre at French Lake.

In 1999, Andrew and I received a grant to explore the cultural context of the Elders' beliefs in order to better manage Quetico Park's cultural resources.

Another series of meetings with Lac La Croix Elders ensued in August and September, involving the following elders: John Boshey, Marie Ottertail, Helen Geyshick, Robert Ottertail, Helen Jordan, and Doris Whitefish. The discussions, conducted with the use of both the Ojibwa and English languages, were wide-ranging and covered differing concepts of the sacred nature of landscapes, the passing of traditional beliefs to young people, the importance of artifacts, missionaries, pictographs, and many other topics. As a result of this co-operative work, policies for conducting archaeological research and for the handling of artifacts in Quetico Park were developed. The first set, developed in 1995, and later refined during the 1999 meetings with Elders, were followed when we conducted research in Quetico Park from 1996 to 2001.

To the Elders, archaeological sites are places of spiritual importance and the artifacts represent spiritual offerings. They proposed that the Anishinaabe term *ah-son-ji-goh-nun*, which translates as "something that is left to be returned to,"[11] accurately describes all of the material objects referred to as artifacts by archaeologists. The phrase "returned to" may simply mean that a useful implement was left for the next occupant of the site, or that the objects were left to symbolize the sacred in the broader world. The spiritual value of so many seemingly mundane objects is derived from their spiritual value in the Anishinaabe worldview. In making a spear point, for example, knappers act to the best of their skill to

Courtesy of Roy Thomas, Ahnisnabae Art Gallery. Roy Thomas, Roy Thomas Estate, http://www.ahnisnabae-art.com.

"Wisdom of Elders"

Anishinaabe artist Roy Thomas, now deceased, was a member of the Long Lake First Nation near Long Lac, Ontario (northeast of Thunder Bay), and lived in Thunder Bay for many years. He painted *Wisdom of Elders* to attest to the high level of respect First Nations people have for the knowledge of Elders.

create the object. In their work, they are aware that they are not just making a point, but are hoping to have success in hunting. Beyond this, they are also engaged in supplication to the Creator to favour their efforts — in the creation of the point, in the hunt, in the survival of their family. Produced in this environment of spiritual awareness, even the least interesting artifact, such as a flake from retouching a spear-point edge, will be imbued with spiritual power unseen by the archaeologist. Thus, Elders believe that these "mere artifacts" also represent an actual link between this world and another dimension. The removal of artifacts from sites breaks a spiritual link between the supplicant and Creator, and destroys the hope of continuing benefit from this offering.

In their view, the removal of objects from sites, site destruction, and fading pictographs all work toward the disappearance of the sites from the natural world. When these offerings to the Creator are displaced or destroyed, the connection to the ancestors and the well-being that derives from the *ah-son-ji-goh-nun* offerings through time also disappears.

ARCHAEOLOGICAL RESEARCH USING ELDERS GUIDELINES

The involvement of the Elders led to fundamental changes in archaeological research from 1996 to 2001. Acknowledging *ah-son-ji-goh-nun* in Quetico Park cultural resource management was an attempt to balance the interests of the Elders of Lac La Croix First Nation, with the interests of other concerned groups, such as archaeologists and an interested public. The first priority of the Elders was to protect the integrity and spiritual nature of the sites and the artifacts they contain. They did not exclude research as long as the guiding principle of respect was upheld. As a sign of respect, they requested that tobacco be placed on sites where artifacts are found. The belief in "a spiritual landscape within the physical landscape" led to two fundamental changes in the way research in Quetico Park was conducted: 1) Surveys were conducted so that no disturbances occur to the site. Consequently, no shovel tests, test pits, or excavations were allowed. 2) All artifacts were left on the site where they were found. The objective of the archaeological survey shifted from "collecting" to "recording."

Initially, this "no collecting" policy was seen as impeding archaeological research in the park, but we found that this is clearly not the case. The standard archaeological procedures of drawing site maps, and describing and photographing artifacts were still followed. The Elders' restrictions on not digging or otherwise disturbing the site were followed, and information about artifacts was collected in the field, but the artifacts themselves were left at the site. This system of finding artifacts and leaving them on the site became affectionately known as "catch and release archaeology."

1995 was Quetico's year of fire; more acres burned that summer than in the previous sixty years combined. These large, intense forest fires greatly increased ground visibility and provided a superb opportunity to complete an archaeological survey while working within the guidelines developed with the Lac La Croix Elders. Andrew Hinshelwood's 1996 post-fire survey, centred on Kawnipi Lake, found that ceremonial activities were evident in the pattern and nature of artifacts present at some of the sites, lending considerable objective support to the Elders' statements about the spiritual nature of the sites.

In 1997, Frank Jordan (from the Lac La Croix First Nation) and I conducted archaeological surveys in other areas of the park that had burned in 1995. Although it was the second summer after the fire, we were still able to take advantage of the resulting increased ground visibility. The following two summers, we, along with students from Lac La Croix and Atikokan, searched the shorelines of French Lake, Pickerel Lake, Rawn Lake, and Batchewaung Lake. These lakes — we refer to them as the Pickerel Lake Complex — can be considered as one water body since no portages, even in low water conditions, are required to go from one lake to another. Although the advantages created by the 1995 fire were minimal after three years of regrowth, the very low water levels in 1998 made it much easier to find artifacts along the shoreline. All of these assessments found evidence of an extensive occupation from the immediate post-glacial times through to the fur-trade era.

In 1988, prior to the agreement with the Elders, I led a team that searched the Canadian side of the Knife Lake to determine the location of quarries used to obtain Knife Lake siltstone, a lithic material used in the making of stone tools. Two subsequent events, an extensive blowdown that occurred during the storm of July 4, 1999, and the subsequent prescribed burn on the Canadian side of the lake in October 2000, created ideal conditions for conducting a survey in the summer of 2001 using the Elders' guidelines. The diminished ground vegetation led to the discovery of new quarry sites and four workshops (sites where stone tools were made). During both surveys, I worked with crews from Atikokan and the Lac La Croix First Nation.

Although the guidelines we worked out with the Elders didn't allow digging in the surveys conducted from 1996 to 2001, we found that much more ground could be covered since time-consuming activities such as shovel-testing were not allowed. We were able to investigate places such as shorelines and islands without any campsites that are not usually examined in archaeological surveys. This resulted in the discovery of many unexpected, interesting sites that we otherwise would not have found.

During our meetings with the Lac La Croix Elders, we encountered a few difficulties in bridging the considerable cultural gaps between us. While discussing the results of the 1999 survey, I was asked if I had followed the guidelines on not disturbing sites and leaving artifacts on the sites. I explained that all the guidelines were followed except on the one trip when no one from Lac La Croix was present.

On that occasion the artifacts were placed back on the site without conducting the tobacco ceremony.

Seeing the surprised looks on the Elders' faces, I quickly explained that since I felt uncomfortable performing the Anishinaabe ceremony, I had simply placed the artifacts back on the site. Elder John Boshey became very upset and spoke in length in Ojibwa while vigorously tapping his cane for emphasis. Marie Ottertail, knowing that his displeasure was obvious and did not require translation, simply told us that John was very displeased with this seeming lack of respect. Further discussions with the Elders made it clear that they all felt the same way — I had promised to do something and had failed to do it. They explained that a detailed understanding of Anishinaabe spirituality isn't required since the ceremony is performed to show respect for the artifacts and the people who used them. John Boshey's immediate reaction to my failure to perform the ceremony and the subsequent explanation of the Elders' concern was identical to how the researchers' European ancestors and their descendents, parents included, would have felt if someone had failed to deliver on a promise. Their reaction to a failure to perform the ceremony easily jumped the cultural barriers between us. After this exchange, the significance of the tobacco ceremony was better understood, and consequently was performed on all subsequent trips.

The policies for archaeological research developed with the Elders from 1995 to 1999 and implemented from 1996 to 2001 have yet to be approved by either the Ministry of Natural Resources or the Lac La Croix First Nation. At the time, these policies were implemented in the spirit of continued co-operation and communication, but the process seems to have stalled. The future of archaeology in Quetico Park depends on the policy path that is followed in the near future. While the changes in how Native artifacts are dealt with proposed by the Elders seem to be a radical departure from past archaeological practices, they are actually an extension of the way historical artifacts have been treated. Park personnel have long requested visitors to leave in place any evidence of Quetico Park's recent past that they find in the park.

When Marie and I were park rangers in Quetico in the 1970s and 1980s, we constantly reminded people that they could not take crosscut saws, horseshoes, and other artifacts from the logging days in Quetico Park home with them. These items, remnants of logging with horses that occurred just a generation ago in Quetico, commonly have just a temporary fascination and many will inevitably end up in the dump. But, left in Quetico they will remind people of the park's recent past. In a similar manner, if arrowheads, scrapers, spear points, pottery shards, beads, and voyageur pipes are left on sites, they will remind generations of people of Quetico Park's long and varied history.

Should you find an artifact in Quetico Park, first consider whether it is in danger of damage by your actions or those of others. If it is not — leave it. If it is in danger, place it in a safer location accompanied by a small amount of tobacco or some other way of showing your respect. When you complete your trip, stop at a ranger station or contact the Quetico Park office to tell them the location of the site and what you chose to do. Providing a map, sketches, or photos would also be helpful. To record a pictograph, take the advice of Elders and make a sketch rather than taking a photograph. Above all, please remember that the Elders believe that "pictographs are prayers," and treat them with the respect they deserve.

THE PAST'S FUTURE: "WE WILL GO THERE TOGETHER"

Twelve thousand years of Native habitation resulted in very little long-term alteration or damage to the environment. The natural environment that is now found in the Quetico-Superior region is primarily the result of thousands of years of stewardship by the Native people who preceded today's visitors. Over the last hundred years, Quetico Park and the Boundary Waters Canoe Area Wilderness have been placed under increasingly stringent protection to preserve and protect the area. Pictographs, clear-water lakes, campsites used by Palaeo-Indians and voyageurs, and old-growth forests have made this area the planet's premier canoeing destination. The Quetico-Superior area, the exclusive domain of Native peoples for thousands of years, is now shared with canoeists from around the world.

Kevlar canoes are now pulled up in the same places where birchbark canoes used to sit, and nylon tents are erected where hide or bark wigwams used to perch. Freeze-dried stroganoff and Kraft Dinner have replaced moose stew and wild rice — a strong reminder that not all changes are for the better. The portages and campsites contain stone tools and pieces of pottery, and some of the vertical cliffs in the area feature pictographs that are visual evidence of a long history of Native people. While the background and beliefs of today's visitors vary from those of the Lac La Croix Elders, it is incumbent upon visitors to respect and honour the Elders' beliefs in how these locations, and the artifacts they contain, should be treated.

Doug Gilmore, who has worked closely with Native people as the superintendent of Woodland Caribou Provincial Park, has noted: "We don't know just where our relationship is heading but wherever it goes we will go there together."[12] It was in this spirit that the meetings with Lac La Croix Elders were held and the way archaeological research was carried out in Quetico Park from 1996 to 2001.

Modern canoeists in the Quetico-Superior can help preserve the spiritual values of the area's archaeological sites, and enhance their own experiences by observing a simple guiding principle — *respect and honour the spiritual connection between the objects of the past and the traditional spiritual beliefs of the Ashininaabe people.*

PART TWO

SPECIAL PLACES IN QUETICO PARK

Canoeing through Quetico has left me with indelible memories of places that return to me again and again. The Emerald to Plough portage has a portion that winds past some white cedars, much larger than I thought could possibly exist in the North. I was even more surprised when we located a solitary, even larger cedar on the Minnesota side of Basswood Lake that is truly "awe"-some. This ancient, gnarled cedar is over 1,100 years old — three times as old as old-growth red and white pine. There are also trees that seem out of place and are interesting because of their location rather than their size or age. The bur oaks along Have-A-Smoke Portage and the silver maples and American elms along the levees of the Wawiag are delightfully unexpected and eccentric.

Lakes with cliffs have always held a particular fascination for me. The cliffs on Ottertrack, Crooked, Agnes, Beaverhouse, and Quetico lakes are as different as the lakes they are found on. Each cliff supports a different mix of lichens and there is always a chance that pictographs may be present. The Ottertrack Lake cliff that is across from Benny Ambrose's homestead is a rock edifice that, even after numerous trips, still evokes wonder.

It is also exciting to make small discoveries. While paddling the shoreline of Cache Bay after a few days of heavy rain, Marie and I were surprised to hear the sound of falling water in a small cove where we knew there shouldn't be a waterfall. To our surprise, the rainfall had transformed the small creek that normally just seeped down a rocky cliff into a beautiful waterfall. We named this unexpected find Platinum Falls as an homage to Silver Falls at the far end of Cache Bay.

The five chapters that follow are about areas that, for various reasons, have had a particularly significant impact on me. The chapter on McNiece Lake reflects my obsession with big trees, mature forests, and the ecosystems that have evolved in these islands of old growth. Relatively little of Hunter Island has ever been

A massive greenstone cliff on Ottertrack Lake stands directly across from the former home of Benny Ambrose.

logged and the vegetation in this part of the park clearly reflects that heritage. The McNiece Lake area, in particular, is an exceptional example of what much of the Quetico-Superior area was like before the impact of logging dramatically altered the vegetation.

The imprint of the last glacier and the power of the movement of the water released from the melting glacier are deeply etched into the Quetico-Superior landscape. This glacial legacy is evident throughout, but comes especially alive in two locations — at the levees along the Wawiag River and at The Pines on Pickerel Lake. For both places, awareness of their ice age legacy significantly enhances what is found there today.

I went to Knife Lake to carry out research on quarries where stone was obtained to make spear points, arrowheads, scrapers, and, of course, knives. I was surprised to find that the bedrock had fascinating volcanic origins and that the quarry activity went back to the time when Palaeo-Indians were entering the area. In addition, I was delighted to discover that the few people inhabiting the lake in the 1980s were as intriguing as their early predecessors.

For a site in a wilderness park, it is ironic that Prairie Portage is of particular interest because of — not in spite of — its long record of human use and habitation. Excavations on both sides of the border have documented that people have used the portage and camped at Prairie Portage for the entire span of human occupation of Quetico Park — from Palaeo-Indians to park rangers. Prairie Portage is the busiest entry station in Quetico and thousands of canoeists cross the portage on the Canadian side every summer. Twentieth-century construction — a dam, buildings on both sides of the river, and a truck portage on the American side — have had significant impacts on the landscape. Now that the extent of the significance of this site is known, the areas that were heavily used by people in the past need to be identified and treated with care so that the present doesn't obliterate the past.

Quetico Park is a wonderful mix of landscape, wildlife, and human history. Prairie Portage and The Pines are prime examples of places of known archaeological, biological, and cultural significance that we have to diligently protect to ensure that our rich inheritance is not lost.

CHAPTER FOUR

"THE PINES": ANCIENT CAMPSITE ON PICKEREL LAKE

The Pines is a campsite that approaches perfection for canoeists. The long, sandy beach is ideal for landing canoes and swimming, large trees provide shade, the camping areas are carpeted with pine needles, the prevailing west wind minimizes insects, and excellent fishing is close by. It is not surprising that people have been camping here since the site emerged from below the water of Lake Agassiz twelve thousand years ago. This striking combination of red and white pines and sand at the east end of Pickerel Lake is the result of a combination of glacial activity, the power of water to alter the landscape, and the slow succession of vegetation from tundra to pines.

GLACIAL RETREAT, FLUCTUATING SHORELINES, AND SILTY RIVERS

With the glacier's retreat to the northeast, Pickerel Lake was one of the last lakes in Quetico Park to be released from glacial ice. Although the glacier was continuing its slow retreat, begun thousands of years earlier near the Iowa-Minnesota border, there were occasional re-advances when the climate cooled and the glacier grew again. One of these created the Steep Rock Moraine, which crosses Pickerel Lake at the current location of The Pines. The glacial ice front acted as a dam that held back the water of Lake Agassiz, and most of Quetico Park, except for its southeast portion, would have been under the water of this gigantic glacial lake. When the glacier began retreating again, it stopped less than ten kilometres from the Steep Rock Moraine and formed the Eagle-Finlayson Moraine.

As the glacier continued to shrink farther north of Quetico Park, a series of outlets were opened that allowed Lake Agassiz to flow east toward Lake Superior and on to the Atlantic Ocean. Prior to the opening of these eastern outlets that caused a lowering of the level of Lake Agassiz, the water of the lake was probably over the tops of much of the Eagle-Finlayson and Steep Rock moraines. With the subsequent lowering of Lake Agassiz, long

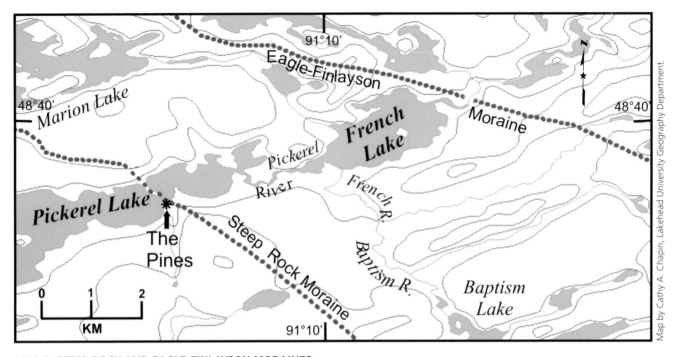

MAP 9: STEEP ROCK AND EAGLE-FINLAYSON MORAINES
The Pines is located on the west side of the Steep Rock Moraine where it crosses Pickerel Lake. The receding waters of glacial Lake Agassiz eroded both the Steep Rock and Eagle-Finlayson moraines. The Pickerel and French rivers now flow through openings in the Eagle-Finlayson Moraine, while The Pines is located just south of the gap in the Steep Rock Moraine.

portions of the two moraines would have acted as dams. Lower or weaker sections of the Eagle-Finlayson Moraine were eroded until water broke through these sections.

At this time, the French and Pickerel rivers were large rivers carrying an enormous load of gravel, sand, and silt created by the glacier's pulverization of the landscape. Boulders and large rocks were not transported far by the glacial meltwater, but the silt

and sand were carried some distance and deposited where the rivers entered the calmer waters of what is now known as French Lake. As a result, today, virtually the entire east and south shores of French Lake (the areas where the two rivers enter the lake) are sand beaches.

The two-kilometre stretch between French Lake and Pickerel Lake would have been a cold, wide, fast-flowing, river-like section of Lake Agassiz carrying the silt, sand, and other glacial debris not deposited in French Lake. This remaining suspended sediment was deposited when the river entered the main body of Lake Agassiz or what is now the east end of Pickerel Lake. As a result, this end of the lake also has a large number of sand beaches.

When the water of Lake Agassiz dropped enough that the top of the Steep Rock Moraine slowly appeared, some water would have still flowed over the lower portions of the moraine. As the water level dropped farther, erosion of the moraine continued until the water flowed through just a single location.

A canoe rests on the ancient beach at The Pines on Pickerel Lake.

The beach that formed from the sand and silt that swept through this opening is now known as The Pines. Large boulders — that were left behind when part of the Steep Rock Moraine eroded — are visible today on land and in the water on both sides of the opening into the main part of Pickerel Lake. A portion of the moraine forms the low hill behind The Pines. The moraine can also be seen on the north side of Pickerel Lake.

Most of the sand at The Pines probably came from locations well to the northeast of French Lake, but some undoubtedly came from the glacial debris in the Steep Rock and Eagle-Finlayson moraines. The amount of sand deposited into the lake decreased as the distance increased from where the glacial-debris laden rivers entered Lake Agassiz. Proceeding west on Pickerel Lake, both the size and the frequency of beaches noticeably decline with the middle section of the lake having a few small beaches while the western third has very few and none of any size.

OUTFLOW BEDROCK,
AND STABLE BEACHES

About twelve thousand years ago, the levels of Lake Agassiz reached the same level as Pickerel Lake is today. For a few hundred years, and possibly longer, The Pines would have been along the eastern edge of Lake Agassiz. At that time it would have been possible to launch a canoe from the beach and paddle west to Manitoba and southwest to southern Minnesota without any portages. Unfortunately, it is not known if there were people on Pickerel Lake at that time, or even if Palaeo-Indians had watercraft capable of being used for such a journey.

When the level of Lake Agassiz continued to drop, the bedrock at the outlet of Pickerel Lake kept the water level from dropping any further. Consequently, the water levels of the four waterway-connected lakes — French Lake, Pickerel Lake, Rawn Lake, and Batchewaung Lake — that make up what I call the Pickerel Lake Complex have remained fairly constant since then.

This is in sharp contrast to much of the western part of Quetico, where shorelines fluctuated as the land was slowly released from under the water

An aerial photo shows the interesting landscape at the east end of Pickerel Lake.

of Lake Agassiz. The current shorelines in the lower areas of the park, such as around Lac la Croix (approximately fifty metres lower than Pickerel Lake), were the last to stabilize approximately ten thousand years ago.

FROM PALAEO-INDIANS TO OJIBWA

Moraines in the tundra today are used as transportation corridors by caribou, wolves, and fox because they are elevated above the generally soggy surrounding terrain and the wind usually keeps them more insect-free than lower-lying areas. The Steep Rock and Eagle-Finlayson moraines were undoubtedly used by both barren-ground caribou and the Palaeo-Indians who hunted them.

After the retreat of the glacier when the landscape was tundra or a mixture of tundra and small trees, large herds of barren-ground caribou probably thrived on the nutritious grasses and herbs that would have dominated the Quetico-Superior landscape for hundreds of years. Using the Steep Rock Moraine as a transportation corridor would have taken the caribou and those who hunted them to the long, sand beach that ended at a narrow part of Lake Agassiz that today we call The Pines.

It isn't known with any certainty when the first people reached the northeast corner of Quetico Park, but spear points and other stone tools from the Late Palaeo-Indian period have been found at The Pines and a nearby beach. The Late Palaeo-Indian period lasted for thousands of years and it is not known if these artifacts are close to twelve thousand years old or as recent as nine thousand years.

Archaeologists have found evidence of Native use on over one hundred campsites in the Pickerel Lake Complex. As the water levels on Pickerel, French, Rawn, and Batchewaung lakes have been fairly stable for thousands of years, artifacts from all the main Native cultural time periods — Palaeo-Indian, Archaic, and Woodland cultures — have firmly established about twelve thousand years of Native Canadian habitation on these lakes. The Ojibwa were the last in a series of Native peoples living on Pickerel Lake when the major influx of Europeans arrived in the 1700s. They have used The Pines for hundreds of years and undoubtedly have many stories and legends based on significant events that occurred there.

Sigurd Olsen recorded one such story in his book *Listening Point*:

> One moonlight night I was camped there, and it was then that I heard the story of how long ago an Ottertail of the Chippewas had carried the body of his son through miles of wilderness and laid him to rest in the most beautiful spot he knew. There among towering red pines he buried the youth who would have

been the poet of his tribe, the boy who would have someday put into songs the longing and legends of his people. When death swooped down on the Indian village at the mouth of the Snake River and took him away, the father knew he must find a spot where the spirit would be at peace and, because the boy loved great trees and a song was always in his heart, chose the cathedral pines on Pickerel Lake. Two days by canoe from the village, he laid the body to rest in a shallow grave at the very end of a tremendous colonnade of Norway pines. Over the grave he built the traditional shelter of birch-bark and cedar, leaving an opening at one end so the spirit could come and go at will. Legend has it that on nights when the moon is full and birds are wakeful with its light, the spirit of young Ottertail leaves its resting place and walks among the pines down to the sand beach on the west shore of Pickerel Point. There it stands and grazes toward the village of Lac La Croix.[1]

The Ottertail family is still a large and influential part of the Lac La Croix First Nation. They have played, and continue to play, a significant part in the community as influential Elders and band councillors, and by serving in other important roles in community affairs.

EUROPEAN EXPLORERS AND VOYAGEURS

Jacques de Noyon, the first European known to travel through Quetico Park, is thought to have passed through Pickerel Lake in 1688. He was followed by other explorers, trappers, and voyageurs carrying trade goods west and retuning with fur to Montreal. The Pines, with its long sand beach and large camping area, was undoubtedly used by voyageurs since it had attributes that were ideal for them. They probably slept well in spite of finding themselves between the French Portage to the east, described by George Simpson of the Hudson's Bay Company in 1841 as "the very worst in this part of the country"[2] and Pine Portage to the west, which was known as *portage des mortes* (portage of the dead), due to the number of voyageurs who had died there.

In 1823 at the waning of the voyageur era, the American geologist William Keating, on a return trip from Lac La Croix as part of an expedition to investigate the contested boundary area west of Lake Superior, recorded his impressions in his journal after paddling the Pickerel River from Pickerel Lake to French Lake:

This stream has a narrow and smooth channel which winds through an alluvial region. Its course is so meandering that our compass frequently ranged through upwards of two-thirds of its circumference in a space of half a mile. The scene was such as a painter might have selected to depict a perfect calm of nature; the great depth of the stream, as well as its narrow bed and crooked channel, contributed to it a darker hue than is usually observed in water; and its reflection of the trees and other objects on its banks exceeded in intensity all that we had yet seen; the beautiful pembina [high bush cranberry] bushes, loaded with their neat little crimson berry, were reflected as though by a mirror; it was about sunset when we ascended this short but romantic stream. With the exception of the few individuals that composed our party, not an animated being was in sight; it really seemed as if we had passed beyond the limits of the inhabited world.[3]

When Europeans came to North America, they brought many items — metal tools, cookware, guns, horses, etc. — that were eagerly sought after by Native Americans. Europeans, however, also brought diseases such as influenza, measles, and smallpox, which devastated Native populations. The degree to which disease had diminished the numbers of Ojibwa in the Quetico-Superior is reflected in William Keating's feeling that he had passed beyond "the limits of the inhabited world" while paddling down a river that Native peoples had heavily used for thousands of years.

Keating was entering a depopulated land rather than an unpopulated one. Only scattered fragments of a people who were thriving when Europeans arrived in North America, were still living in the Quetico-Superior region when he passed through in 1823. An entire continent, and the Quetico-Superior area was no exception, had lost most of its Native population to disease. The Pines were probably a much-used site until disease greatly diminished the number of Native people in the late 1600s and early 1700s.

Prior to Quetico being set aside in 1909, geologists, trappers, timber cruisers, and the occasional recreational canoeist also stayed at The Pines. With the establishment of the forest reserve and then the provincial park, park rangers also utilized the site. Today, The Pines is one of Quetico Park's most heavily used campsites. Over the last few decades, there have been relatively few summer nights when someone wasn't camped there.

Jess Valley, a former Quetico Park ranger, cooks a meal at The Pines in the late 1930s or early 1940s.

RECENT THREATS TO THE PINES

At first glance, the red and white pines that The Pines are named after appear to be aging gracefully. Extensive use of the site has eliminated most of the undergrowth and beneath the pines is a pleasant combination of sand and pine needles. However, everywhere one looks there are signs of overuse and abuse. Many trees have lower limbs cut off, nails are protruding from many large trees and one large pine recently had a rectangular section of bark removed and names inscribed. Axe marks, the results of too many axe-throwing contests, are visible on the trunks of many trees. A dam was placed at the outlet of Pickerel Lake in 1922. The resulting elevated water levels have caused erosion to the roots of the trees nearest the water, exposing portions of the roots and causing some of the trees to lean precariously toward the lake.

The current damage caused by overuse and erosion, however, is minor compared to the three major threats to the magnificent trees' survival in the last one hundred years. When they were threatened by logging in the 1920s, Quetico Park superintendent John Jamieson decided to protect this beautiful stand of trees and managed to convince the Ontario government to exempt these red and white pines from logging. Thirty years later, another threat emerged when a major power line was being constructed between Thunder Bay and Fort Frances in the late 1950s. Surveyors had decided on a route that had the power line crossing Pickerel Lake at the narrows where The Pines is located. Once again, someone stepped in to stop the destruction of The Pines. This time it was M.S. "Pop" Fotheringham, the president of Steep Rock Iron Mines in Atikokan and a strong advocate for Quetico Park. He used his influence, along with that of Quetico Park superintendent Ross Williams, to convince the Ontario government to reroute the power line so that it now runs north of French and Pickerel lakes.

The trees blown down by strong winds in 2003 are visible on the Steep Rock Moraine through the thin stand of pines left standing.

The stand of pines, twice saved from non-natural forces, was devastated by a natural force when a severe storm swept through the site late in the afternoon on July 6, 2003. A hot, humid stretch of weather came to an end when a small, but powerful swath of wind, known as a microburst, came out of the north, accompanied by driving rain and hail. This powerful wind, which uprooted large trees and in some cases snapped them off, felled approximately five hundred hectares of trees. The damage from the wind was only a few hundred metres wide when it went through The Pines. What was once a stand of large trees, many of them over half a metre in diameter, was reduced to a thin strand of large, red pines along the beach.

In order to reduce the fire hazard created by downed trees behind the heavily used campsites at The Pines, a small, prescribed burn was carried out by the Ministry of Natural Resources on October 12, 2004. Growth rings on downed trees showed that these trees were 215 years old. Since most of the pines are of similar size, this stand was probably the result of regrowth after a forest fire in the late 1780s. A lightning strike or a campfire left smouldering are possible causes of the fire.

The narrow band of pines left in the wake of the 2003 storm is slowly succumbing to the winds coming off the lake. Prior to the storm, there was a continuous stand of trees from the beach extending up the moraine that runs at the back of the site. The blowdown levelled the pines behind the narrow band along the beach, leaving these trees no longer protected and buffered by trees behind them. The prevailing westerly winds coming off the lake have caused some trees to lean and the tops of many are dying.

ALWAYS AND NEVER THE SAME

The site now known simply as The Pines was created along the ice-front during a temporary standstill of the retreating glacier at a time when the nearest pines were hundreds of kilometres to the south. When the beach at The Pines was formed, the glacier was directly behind it and it faced a glacial lake that extended all the way to the prairies. Change is the common element in all landscapes. Looking out over Pickerel Lake from the beach at The Pines, however, I always get a feeling of timelessness. In spite of twelve thousand years of change, The Pines is the epitome of a site that is both transitory and permanent — it is both never and always the same. Quetico Park, like other wilderness parks, is cherished because it protects areas of significance and beauty from extensive human intrusion and degradation. For Pickerel Lake and the complex of interconnected lakes in the northeast corner of Quetico Park, the wilderness designation also protects the ancient shorelines where barren-ground caribou roamed and where humans have camped from the end of the Palaeo-Indian period to today. Far more than just trees and a beach — The Pines is a place where Quetico's human history merges with its glacial past.

CHAPTER FIVE

THE WAWIAG: RIVER WITH A PAST

As the glacier retreated through the northern part of Quetico, a tumultuous river transporting ice and glacial debris flowed into the park halfway up its eastern boundary. The river's progress was halted when it flowed into glacial Lake Agassiz, which, at that time, covered most of the park. The vast quantities of clay particles, silt, sand, and gravel transported by the river were deposited into a gigantic lake whose size was constantly changing. During much of Lake Agassiz's existence, the levels of the lake were substantially higher than that of most of the lakes in Quetico today. As the glacier retreated north of the park about twelve thousand years ago, the levels of the huge lake dropped and the mouth of the Wawiag River kept moving farther west. As Lake Agassiz continued to shrink, it was transformed from one mammoth lake into numerous smaller ones.

The lake that eventually formed where the glacial river entered Lake Agassiz is now known as Kawnipi Lake. Since it has substantially lower water levels than that of Lake Agassiz, most of the glacial debris transported by the river and deposited in Lake Agassiz is now on land east of Kawnipi's Kawa Bay. The last few kilometres of today's Wawiag River wind through the flat landscape underlain by the fine silt, sand, and clay, originally deposited in Lake Agassiz. The river that originated as a massive torrent of icy water, loaded with material freshly created by the glacier, is now a small, lethargic river, stained a tea colour by the organic material in the surrounding bogs and forests. A roaring river that originated as glacial meltwater is now a small river fed by creeks draining a few lakes, swamps, and bogs.

The present Wawiag River, although greatly diminished in size from its big, brawny ice age predecessor, is an intriguing reminder of what it used to be. In spite of its size, the Wawiag River, and its immediate surroundings form one of the most unusual physical and ecological settings in the Quetico-Superior landscape.

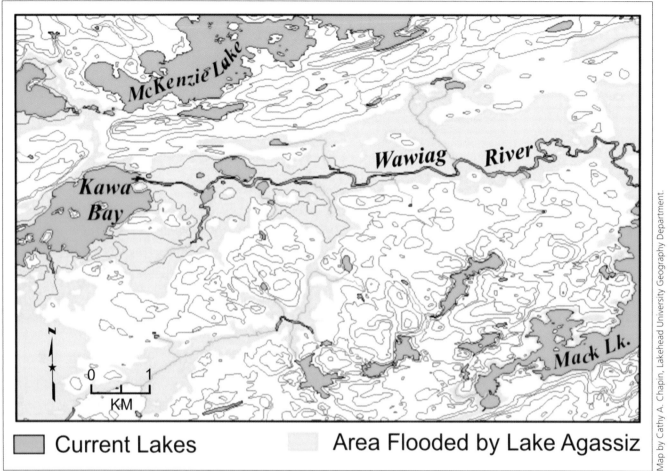

Current Lakes   Area Flooded by Lake Agassiz

Map by Cathy A. Chapin, Lakehead University Geography Department.

MAP 10: THE WAWIAG RIVER AND THE MINIMUM EXTENT OF SEDIMENT DEPOSITED IN GLACIAL LAKE AGASSIZ
The large river carrying glacial debris that flowed into Lake Agassiz has dwindled into a smaller Wawiag River that slowly twists through that glacial sediment on its way to Kawnipi Lake, a remnant of Lake Agassiz.

LINEAR DECIDUOUS FORESTS

The upper part of the Wawiag River flows through a landscape of bedrock and glacial till that supports a boreal forest dominated by spruce and Jack pine. Downstream, the dominant coniferous forest slowly gives way to the unexpected. A linear

A "linear forest" grows on the levees along the lower part of the Wawiag River. Bogs occupy the land where the river's glacial predecessor deposited silt and sand into Lake Agassiz.

deciduous forest, something found nowhere else in the Quetico-Superior, lines both sides of the river for the last few kilometres before it empties into Kawa Bay.

The Wawiag is the only river in the Quetico-Superior, to my knowledge, to have pronounced levees. Levees form when the coarser sediment carried by the river is deposited on the riverbanks when floodwaters spill over the banks. The river's levees are enriched with new sediment and organic material whenever the river floods. These narrow river levees support a veneer of trees with a lush understory and a bog lying just beyond.

Shan Walshe, a former Quetico Park naturalist, wrote a description of the plant community on these levees. He noted that, "The diversity of the flora here is extraordinary. Several of the species are southern and western strangers, which are close to, if not at, the geographical limit of their range."[1] American elm, red ash, and silver maple, trees that are rare in Quetico, dominate these levees. Boxelder (Manitoba maple) also grows on these levees, the only known location of this tree in Quetico. Paddling below these levees, canoeists feel as if they are hundreds, or even thousands, of kilometres to the south. On a hot, humid, July day, a person can almost envisage flamingos in the water and alligators slithering down the banks.

In addition to deciduous trees, botanists have found a wide variety of unusual plants on the levees. The periodic deposition of the river's sediments

Courtesy of John B. Ridley Research Library, Quetico Park Information Pavilion. Photo by Shan Walshe.

Hops, plants native to Europe and western Asia and used in the production of beer, unexpectedly grow on the Wawiag River levees. The levees are the only known place in Quetico where these plants are found.

provides a nutrient-rich base that supports lush plant growth. Finding hops, the European species used for making beer, in large tangles in the understory was totally unexpected. Other unusual species include wild ginger and carrion flower, whose flowers give off the odour of rotting flesh to attract flies to pollinate the plant. Many species of edible berries, including raspberries and blueberries, grow along the banks of the river. Chokecherry and nannyberry, two species not often found in Quetico, are present, and highbush cranberry is fairly common along the lower part of the river. The word Kawnipi is a shortened form of the Ojibwa name, *Kanipinanikok* or *Kahnipiminanikok*, which mean "where there are cranberries."

Although southern species dominate the levee communities, there are smaller variants of these communities farther upstream. Almost one kilometre east of where Mack Creek enters the Wawiag, Shan Walshe found a plant community where American elm formed 60 percent of the tree canopy and red ash 40 percent. These species are usually found only in small, isolated pockets in Quetico Park, and it is not common to find large numbers of either of these trees in one location.

Not surprisingly, the rich alluvial sediment at the mouth of the Wawiag River also supports an abundance of aquatic vegetation, including three species of water lilies. In addition to the common species of white and yellow water lilies, Shan found red-disked yellow water lily. This unusual species is a hybrid found only where both of the parents — yellow water lily and small yellow water lily — are present. The abundance of water lilies and other aquatic vegetation makes the mouth of the Wawiag River a prime moose feeding area, especially in late summer.

Shan Walshe had a particular love for bogs and the plants associated with them.

BOGS BEHIND THE LEVEES

From 1971 to 1975, Bill Muir was the staff botanist at the Associated Colleges of the Midwest (ACM) Wilderness Field Station on Basswood Lake. For those five summers, Muir, a biology professor at Carleton College, taught a field course in botany. During this time he journeyed over three thousand kilometres with his students in the BWCAW and Quetico. Although he travelled extensively through-out the Quetico-Superior area, Bill Muir didn't see any of it. He had slowly lost his sight from compli-cations from diabetes and was totally blind by 1968. He would listen to verbal descriptions of a plant, ask pertinent questions and use his senses of touch, smell, and taste to identify it. This remarkable man didn't visit the Quetico-Superior area before he became blind and therefore never saw the border country that he grew to love.

Bill's wife Libby acted as his eyes. She constantly related details of the environment they were mov-ing through. When navigating difficult terrain, Bill walked with his hand on Libby's shoulder and he listened to the small bells she wore on her belt. She walked ahead of him describing the boulders, deadfalls, low branches, and other obstacles that were coming up. Using this technique, they were able to traverse most of the habitats in the Quetico-Superior area.

Bill had a special love of bogs and he scheduled his trips so that his students could spend as much time as possible in them. He used a long wooden pole called his "cudgel" as a probe to test the bog's surface. The Wawiag River region, which contains some of Quetico Park's largest and most diverse

Bill Muir, a botanist from Carleton College in Northfield, Minnesota, loved Quetico and led university students on trips into the Quetico-Superior in spite of being legally blind.

Courtesy of Elizabeth Muir, Grand Rapids, Minnesota.

bogs, was a particular favourite of his. Because of the sediment, especially clay, that was deposited as the glacier retreated, the area near the river has a particularly high number of bogs. Since clay is relatively impermeable to the downward movement of water, the slow drainage through clay has led to most of the flat areas east of Kawa Bay becoming wetlands.

It was along the Wawiag that Bill Muir met Shan Walshe, another botanist who had a strong affinity for bogs. George Wittler, a student of Bill's and now a biology professor at Ripon College in Wisconsin, recalled the first meeting of Bill and Shan:

> We were camped in Kawa Bay near the mouth of the Wawiag River. On our first morning we paddled as a class up the river for group exploration. A small creek seemed interesting so we paddled up about half a mile. While looking at a small spruce bog and examining the unusual vegetation from the canoes, we heard a rustling in the bog forest. Expecting a moose or similar beast to emerge, we waited very quietly in our canoes. Who should pop out right by us but this strange man with his hat pulled down over his eyes.[2]

In addition to Shan and Bill, many other botanists have explored the levees and surrounding bogs for plants, but there is still much to be learned about the other inhabitants of these unusual habitats. Numerous species of atypical birds, small mammals, insects, fungus, and lichens are also undoubtedly lurking in these rich, intriguing and relatively unexplored environments.

WAWIAG WILDLIFE

Moose, attracted by the rich vegetation growing along the banks and in the shallow waters of the Wawiag River, are commonly encountered both in the river and along the two creeks, Mack and Greenwood, that flow into the Wawiag. When Marie and I were rangers at Cache Bay we often heard stories about close encounters with moose on these waterways.

Other wildlife is also encountered in this region. Once, a group of canoeists told us they had seen a cougar along the river. We excitedly wrote down details about this unexpected sighting and were eager to pass this unexpected information on to others who would be canoeing in the area. This group then continued on with their story, telling us they had also seen wild burros near the mouth of the Wawiag. They had probably seen moose calves, which have a resemblance to burros, but that certainly gave less credence to their cougar sighting. Unusual mammals are occasionally encountered in this relatively inaccessible part of Quetico. In 1999, a wolverine was trapped outside of the park just east of the Wawiag River. This was an extremely surprising occurrence since wolverines are normally found in the Hudson Bay Lowlands, hundreds of kilometres to the north.

The concentration of fur-bearing animals in this area made it an area that was heavily exploited by poachers in the past. Jack Wells, a Quetico Park ranger in 1927, told Shirley Peruniak that an old Native route up the Wawiag River leading to Shebandowan Lake became known as "the poachers' trail." People trapping illegally used this route extensively during the Depression in the 1930s to get their furs out of Quetico to lakes east of the park where transportation by roads or float planes could get their harvest to market.

The Wawiag also has unusual fish species. Writing in *Quetico Fishes*, E.J. Crossman states that the only record for the mooneye in Quetico is from the Wawiag River.[3] This fish is closely related to the goldeye, which is a fish that is smoked and sold as "Winnipeg goldeye" in Canadian stores. Canoeists on the Wawiag River have also seen many birds that are not common in the Quetico-Superior region. Eastern kingbirds, tree swallows, white-winged crossbills, rose-breasted and evening grosbeaks, Cape May warblers, great grey owls, and hawk owls have all been spotted along the river.

HUMAN HISTORY OF THE WAWIAG

Native peoples have lived near the mouth of the Wawiag River for thousands of years. Palaeo-Indians probably walked along the shores of Lake Agassiz near the mouth of the Wawiag River, and, over many generations, witnessed the shorelines slowly receding to the present level of Kawnipi Lake. They hunted barren-ground caribou when the area was tundra and woodland caribou, white-tailed deer, and moose when the area became forested. The faded pictographs on both sides of the entrance to Kawa Bay are reminders of the particular significance of Kawa Bay and the Wawiag River.

The name Wawiag is a shortened form of the Ojibwa name for the river; maps from 1890 and 1898 have the name "Kahwawiagamak." Burchell Lake is one of the lakes that drain into the Wawiag River and on early maps it is called Round Lake or Wawiagama, which means "round lake" in Ojibwa. The Wawiag enters Kawnipi Lake at Kawa Bay and Kawa is likely a shortened form of the Ojibwa name for the Wawiag River.

The concentration of natural resources near the confluence of the Wawiag River and Kawnipi Lake was a magnet that attracted Native people. The variety and abundance of wild game and edible plants found there could be matched by few places in the Quetico-Superior landscape. Moose and wildfowl were plentiful, wild rice grew in the river, and in some of the nearby bogs a variety of edible berries and medicinal plants could be gathered. Whitefish, suckers, and pickerel (walleye) could be netted in the mouth of the river, red maple and silver maple were available for tapping for maple syrup, and the levees provided soil for gardens.

When government policies forced the nomadic Ojibwa to stipulate a single small area as their official residence, it isn't surprising that the people living primarily in the eastern half of what is now Quetico Park chose the mouth of the Wawiag as their reserve. (See Map 4 of Reserve 24C on page 32) The Ontario government officially surveyed and established a reserve, called the Sturgeon Lake Indian Reserve 24C, at the mouth of the Wawiag River on Kawa Bay in 1877. Although the mouth of the river is rich in resources, in order to survive, the band remained nomadic to take advantage of other resources in a wider area.

According to government records, the population of the Kawa Bay Reserve continued to decline after it was established. The number of people registered at Reserve 24C shrank from fifty-two in 1876 to nineteen in 1909 when the Quetico Forest Reserve was created, and to just four when the 24C was dissolved in 1915. There were a variety of reasons for these population declines — jobs were available at the nearby Jackfish Gold Mine and some band members moved to other reserves — but diseases such as smallpox, influenza, and measles undoubtedly played a major role.

Robert Readman, who later became chief ranger of the Quetico Forest Reserve, recalled that, in 1906, only three or four families were living at a temporary camp at the site of the former Native village on Kawa Bay. He stated that the village had been abandoned earlier because "smallpox had decimated the population."[4] The Ojibwa on Kawa Bay were hit especially hard by this outbreak and their population never recovered.

Bill Magie's account of Chief Blackstone's snowshoe journey to Winton, Minnesota, in 1918 to inform the Ontario government about an influenza outbreak[5] cannot be verified by any other records or accounts. Chief Blackstone died in 1885 so someone else — possibly his son-in-law, who was chief of Kawa Bay in 1918 — must have made the journey. Although the 1918 influenza outbreak at 24C was evidently not as dramatic as Magie's account made it seem, it may well have been the final event in the decline of a band whose population had shrunk to just a few families due to earlier outbreaks of disease. When the government terminated Reserve 24C in 1915, the long history of Anishinaabe people making the resource-rich mouth of the Wawiag River their home came to an official end.

AN ECHO OF THE GLACIAL PAST

The deposition of vast amounts of silt and sand into Lake Agassiz by the glacial Wawiag River, followed by the lowering of the water level to that of Kawnipi Lake, created an area that is unique in the

Quetico-Superior region. Most of the sediments carried by this glacial river are now found on land. They determine the flow and characteristics of the lower part of today's Wawiag River and underlie the many rich and varied bogs that now dot this region. These sediments that now provide nutrients for the unusual mixture of southern and western species of plants inhabiting the levees were bedrock and boulders before tons of glacial ice pulverized them into silt and sand.

The area surrounding the lower part of the Wawiag River clearly demonstrates that Quetico Park's glacial legacy isn't simply part of the distant past. Today's Wawiag is a shrunken remnant of its glacial ancestor. This small and seemingly delicate river slowly twists and turns through sediment laid down by its predecessor. Echoes of ice and distant voices still infuse this region with a singular significance. They reminds us how strongly the past is linked to the present.

CHAPTER SIX

KNIFE LAKE:
VOLCANIC ROCKS AND REMARKABLE PEOPLE

My first canoe trip into the Quetico-Superior was with a group of friends just after graduating from high school in 1961. We rented canoes in Ely, put in at Moose Lake and travelled along the international border toward Saganaga Lake. To this day, I remember how the combination of bedrock, clear water, and towering pines stood in sharp contrast to the black soil, muddy rivers, and deciduous trees in the farm country of southern Minnesota where I grew up. It was a revelation to see a landscape stripped of its soil by glacial ice, leaving bedrock exposed on the surface.

The predominant bedrock material for most of Quetico and the rest of Quetico-Superior is granite. This igneous rock began the slow journey to its present form as a molten rock that cooled slowly and solidified underground. A combination of movements of the earth's crust and erosion slowly brought the granite to the surface. This gradual, erratic process can take millions or even billions of years and much of the exposed granite in the Quetico-Superior region is over two-and-half billion years old.

There are also bands, usually just a few kilometres wide, of rocks with volcanic origins in the Quetico-Superior area. These bands are indicators of volcanic activity that occurred billions of years ago. Richard Ojakangas, professor emeritus of geology at the University of Minnesota-Duluth, spent many summers in the 1970s and 1980s with graduate students analyzing and classifying rocks in the bands of volcanic material along the Ontario-Minnesota border. He has described how this material reveals a fascinating story of what the region was like 2.7 billion years ago when "explosive volcanoes rose out of a practically lifeless sea to dominate the landscape."[1]

Although much of the volcanic material appears to be the product of explosive volcanism, the presence of "pillow lava" indicates that the more iron- and magnesium-rich basaltic lava emerged more slowly and cooled underwater. These structures form when molten lava is squeezed out like toothpaste through cracks under the water and quickly solidifies as irregular, tongue-like protrusions. An

MAP 11: KNIFE LAKE AND SURROUNDING AREA

The bedrock that surrounds Knife Lake is composed of metamorphosed volcanic sediment; a type of rock seldom encountered in the rest of the Quetico-Superior.

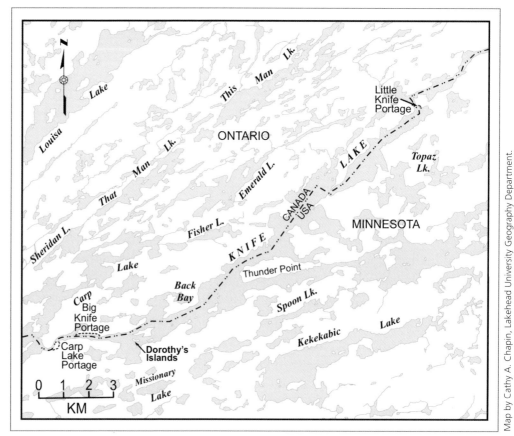

Map by Cathy A. Chapin, Lakehead University Geography Department.

easily accessible outcrop of Ely greenstone containing pillow lava is found in Ely, Minnesota, just a few blocks northeast of downtown, and can also be found in road cuts both east and west of town. Pillow lava can also be seen in the dramatic greenstone cliff on the north side of Ottertrack Lake.

The portion of the volcanic belt centred around Knife Lake is known, not surprisingly, as the Knife Lake Group. This material was formed when volcanic islands slowly eroded into gravel, sand, and silt that settled to the bottom of an inland sea and was compacted into rock by the growing weight of the deposits above. For millions of years these rocks were subjected to a variety of forces that folded, compacted, and heated them into a complex amalgam. In 1912, a geologist, struck by the complexity of the folding in the Knife Lake Group, wrote: "Superimposed upon folds of the first order are those of the second order; on these are those of the third order, and so on indefinitely."[2]

Sand-sized particles of volcanic rock known as *greywacke* comprise the predominant rock in the Knife Lake Group. The relatively coarse-grained greywacke is the non-descript grey rock found around most of Knife Lake. Between beds of greywacke, beds of mud were deposited, and these were metamorphosed into slate. The most distinctive bedrock material, however, is the very fine-grained rock known as Knife Lake siltstone. This material was formed when silt-sized particles in the volcanic sediment were transformed into a glassy rock that resembles chert. Much of it is coal-black, some is grey, and some has a greenish tint but it develops a light grey coating, or patina, on the exposed surface.

Fine-grained Knife Lake siltstone, like that found in this outcrop, was utilized for making knives and other stone tools.

Archaeologists have shown that Native peoples in the area used the fine-grained Knife Lake siltstone to make tools for about twelve thousand years, the bedrock around Knife Lake being the primary source of the material. The rock is very durable and especially suited for making knives, although it can be flaked to make sharp-edged stone tools of many kinds. Tools such as knives, spear points, scrapers, drills, arrowheads, and adzes made from this material have been found throughout Quetico-Superior and the surrounding area. Palaeo-Indians had a particular fondness for this material and used it extensively.

The Ojibwa name for Knife Lake is *Mookomaan Zaaga'igan*. Lac La Croix Elders translated the name as the "lake where rock used to make knives is found."[3] Since the earliest European explorers in the Quetico-Superior were dependent on Native people to guide them, it is not surprising that they adapted many of the Native names for the lakes, rivers, and portages they were traversing. The Ojibwa names were simply translated into French or English.

Numerous journals of the early explorers and fur traders, such as those of Alexander MacKenzie in 1785 and Alexander Henry the Younger in 1800, refer to the lake as Lac des Couteaux, the French equivalent of *Mookomaan Zaaga'igan*. English-speaking travellers called it Little Knife Rock Lake and Knife Stone Lake, names that were eventually shortened to Knife Lake. Thus, over the last four hundred years, the lake has been called Knife Lake in three different

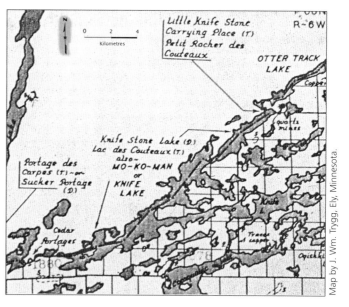

Map by J. Wm. Trygg, Ely, Minnesota.

MAP 12: DETAIL OF A 1966 MAP SHOWING SOME TERMS USED ON EARLY MAPS OF KNIFE LAKE

This 1966 map is a compilation of some of the terms that were used for Knife Lake and the portages on both ends of the lake. The terms Mo-ko-mon, Lac des Couteaux, Knife Stone Lake, and Little Knife Stone Carrying Place all refer to the earlier use of the lake as a source of stone for tools.

LEFT

This small creek flows parallel to the Little Knife Portage that connects Knife Lake to Ottertrack Lake.

languages and it is highly likely that some form of that name was used for the thousands of years stone was quarried to make knives and other tools. The Canadian explorer and mapmaker David Thompson referred to the portage at the east end of the lake as Little Knife Stone Carrying Place, a name that accurately reflects the original use of this portage.

The earliest geological explorations of the Knife Lake area were conducted by the Geological Survey of Canada and the Minnesota Geological Survey in the 1870s and 1880s. Although the origins of the name Knife Lake became less well known with time, its significance was not lost on some of the first geologists who visited the lake. N.H. Winchell, on a geological survey in 1879, described the rock on the shores of Knife Lake as "a blue-black, fine-grained siliceous rock, approaching flint in hardness and compactness. It is this sharp edged rock that gave name to Knife Lake."[4]

People coming from the west would have gone through Carp Lake on their way to Knife Lake. Carp Lake was referred to as "Pseudo-Messer Lake" in some of the journals and maps from the late 1800s. *Messer* means knife in German and *pseudo-messer* means "false knife." The name may have been translated from the Ojibwa name for the lake and be a reminder to the traveller looking for quarries that they had not yet reached Knife Lake. It is a mystery why Carp Lake had a German name for a while, but it is also strange that it is now named after a fish that isn't found in the lake.

Anyone traversing the border between Carp Lake and Ottertrack, would probably agree with the geologist of the early 1900s who wrote that the rocks on these portages "with their sharp knife-like edges, cause a great deal of inconvenience to the moccasined traveller, and even to him with thick boots."[5] A good thing to keep in mind when camping on Knife Lake — this rock that cuts through moccasins can seriously damage boots and will also slice open bare feet on campsites or in shallow water along the shore.

FIRES, LOGGING, AND WIND

Geological reports from the 1800s and early 1900s are interesting since the authors do not restrict themselves to geology. Although primarily looking for iron ore in formations that resembled those in the Mesabi Iron Range to the south, the geologists took a refreshingly wide-ranging view of the area. In sharp contrast to most narrowly focused contemporary scientific reports, these early ones comment on the species of fish caught, compare the difficulties and conditions of portages, and describe winter travel routes as well as the vegetation and fire history.

Geologists travelling along the border described a large fire in 1880, and a huge 1936 fire, the biggest ever recorded in Quetico Park, which burned part of the Knife Lake region. Over the years, forest fires have left a mosaic of forest at different stages of maturity on both the Canadian and American sides of the lake. However, due to active fire suppression, relatively few wildfires have burned around Knife Lake since the 1936 fire.

On July 4, 1999, a storm with straight-line winds of 140 kilometres per hour moved along the southern boundary of Quetico Park from Basswood Lake to Saganaga Lake. The storm devastated parts of the BWCAW, where an estimated seventeen to twenty-five million trees were blown down, but the winds touched relatively little of Quetico. One of the exceptions was Knife Lake, where the western end of the lake was hit hard by the storm. In response to the fire danger resulting from the downed trees, the Ontario Ministry of Natural Resources performed a prescribed burn in October 2000. Five years later, the United States Forest Service conducted prescribed burns in the extensive blow-down area on the American side. The burns on both sides of the border were successful with many of the downed trees being burned and the potential for future fires diminished.

Forest fires have been the primary force determining the makeup of the forests in the Knife Lake area, except for a brief period when logging occurred. Swallow and Hopkins, a logging company with a sawmill in Winton, Minnesota, logged the American side of Knife Lake in the early 1900s, but the Canadian side has never been harvested. While a few isolated stands of old-growth white pine, red pine, black spruce, white spruce, and white cedar still exist on the Canadian side of the lake, the bigger stands of very large, old pines that are characteristic of other parts of Quetico Park do not appear to be there. Yet some of the most impressive trees in the Quetico-Superior are found in this area. Huge white cedars that have never been cored, but give the impression of great age, grow on the Emerald-Plough portage just a few kilometres north of Knife Lake.

SEARCHING FOR KNIFE LAKE SILTSTONE

I spent the summer of 1988 with Dick Hiner from Atikokan and Ralph Ottertail Jr. and Norman Jordan from Lac La Croix exploring the length of the Canadian side of Knife Lake. We were looking for evidence of old quarry activity in the fine-grained Knife Lake siltstone found in portions of the bedrock around the lake. In the spring of 2001, I returned to look for sites where stone tools were made from the quarried material. By following the guidelines for archaeological research reached with the Lac La Croix Elders and taking advantage of the increased visibility created by the prescribed burn, we had the opportunity to find quarry and workshop evidence without disturbing the sites.

For thousands of years, beginning with the Palaeo-Indians, Native peoples obtained the rock and began the process of making stone tools along the shores of Knife Lake. Although we found numerous quarries, quarry activity was not easy to locate since only a small portion of the bedrock on Knife Lake is the fine-grained material required for making stone tools. It was a hot summer and walking through blackened, burned-over terrain was hot and dirty work. Our group often searched for days without finding any clear evidence of quarry activity. The Palaeo-Indians, and those who followed them, were good geologists. They found rocks suitable for stone tools in many scattered locations and we were unable to find any new outcrops of high-quality material that they had missed.

One of the joys of conducting research in Quetico Park was the opportunity to encounter items of interest that are outside the realm of the research. We found rundown trapping cabins, old dumps, caches of rusty traps, and animal bones, as well as a variety of plants and animals. The discovery of rare orchids and prairie flowers near the rocky shoreline of Knife Lake, however, was totally unexpected. At the top of a cliff near the narrows to Little Knife Lake, I stumbled across a Ram's-Head Lady's-slipper orchid, a plant on the Ontario Endangered Species List. Wood lilies, the provincial flower for Saskatchewan, but rarely seen in the Quetico-Superior landscape, grew in profusion in an open area across from Thunder Point in the 1980s but were hard to find on subsequent trips. In addition to these isolated finds, the warm and moist microclimate created by the Knife River paralleling Big Knife portage at the west end of the lake is responsible for a number of unexpected plants such as thimbleberry, big-toothed aspen, and red oak.

During our survey, we often encountered large glacial erratics, boulders deposited by the last glacier. Undoubtedly the most well known of these on Knife Lake is the "ribbon rock." This metre-wide boulder with red, white, and grey bands is located in shallow water along the north shore of the lake about half a kilometre from the Big Knife Portage. The origin of ribbon rock is a mystery, but, in the spring of 2008, we located bedrock appearing to be a banded rock similar to the ribbon rock on a hillside on Jasper Lake, about sixteen kilometres northeast of Knife Lake. Since glacial striations on the bedrock indicate that the last glacier moved from the

northeast to the southwest, the Knife Lake ribbon rock probably originated on Jasper Lake or from another bedrock source in that vicinity. A smaller boulder of ribbon rock was found somewhere on Knife Lake and brought to Dorothy Molter as a gift. Since Dorothy came to personify the Boundary Waters to a generation of canoeists, it is understandable that people brought her presents and a big hunk of ribbon rock was a unique and wonderful gift.

DOROTHY, PETE, AND BENNY

For any canoeist who visited Knife Lake between 1948 and 1986, a visit to see Dorothy Molter and drink a bottle of her homemade root beer was probably the first priority. Dorothy's island with the root beer stand was a busy place in the summer, and her brother Bud put a parking meter at the canoe landing as a humorous acknowledgement of how congested the landing had become. If every canoeist who stopped at Dorothy's had put money in the parking meter, Dorothy would have made a good living on her island.

It was a rite of passage for canoe groups who visited Dorothy's island to donate a paddle, signed by the members of the group, for the fence that lined the path up to Dorothy's summer tent. The Quetico Park portage crew was just one of many groups, clubs, and organizations proud to have one of their signed paddles alongside others from around the world.

Leif and Anna Nelson get to drink root beer and chat with Dorothy Molter in 1985. We saw Dorothy occasionally during the first year we were rangers at Prairie Portage.

Because Dorothy was depicted as a woman who lived on her own in the wilderness, she became a focus for numerous articles. Some of the articles about her were very misleading. An article in the *Saturday Evening Post* in 1952 was titled "The Loneliest Woman In America," although Dorothy estimated that three thousand people had stopped at her island over the summer when the article was written. One day, when she had at least thirty or forty people on her island — all wanting to talk to her even more than they wanted a cold root beer — she told me that her favourite time of year was winter. During the winter, she said, friends would often visit but she could also spend some time by herself.

Dorothy grew up in Chicago, Illinois, and was in the final stages of completing a nursing degree when she took a canoe trip to a resort on the Isle of Pines on Knife Lake with her parents in 1930. She immediately became infatuated with the Quetico-Superior region and its inhabitants, and came back to Knife Lake to stay in 1934. There, she lived with her companion Bill Berglund until his death in 1948. Bill, who had been a lumberjack, trapper, and game warden in the area, had purchased Isle of Pines and made it into a wilderness fishing camp. When Bill's health rapidly declined in his later years, Dorothy devoted herself to being his nurse.

After his death, Dorothy inherited the property and she continued to run the resort. The news that Dorothy was a nurse spread rapidly through the Quetico-Superior, and canoeists and others travelling through the area sought her out when medical help was needed. She was justifiably proud of the decades of medical assistance that she provided to wilderness travellers and left a notice in her will that she wanted her headstone to read "Nightingale of the Wilderness," an inscription that can be seen today on her grave next to her mother's in Pennsylvania.

Dorothy was known for her toughness and her capacity to perform hard physical labour. Although she usually had family members and friends who were willing to give her a hand getting supplies over the five portages along the Knife River and up to her cabin, living on her islands became more difficult after Bill Berglund's death. An informal group of northern Minnesota residents known as "Dorothy's Angels" made it possible for her to remain on Knife Lake. They helped cut and split firewood, and also cut and hauled the ice she needed for the summer up to her icehouse. They also helped haul the endless supplies of duck food, Snickers candy bars, root beer supplies, and propane that Dorothy required during her last few years on the island. In 1996, Bob Cary, a good friend of Dorothy's, wrote *Root Beer Lady,* a book that accurately chronicles Dorothy's life on Knife Lake.[6]

The presence of Dorothy on Knife Lake and Benny Ambrose on Ottertrack Lake became a headache for the United States Forest Service after the passage of the Wilderness Act in 1978. Benny Ambrose came to northern Minnesota after being discharged from the American Army in the aftermath of the First World War. He homesteaded on Ottertrack Lake, just one lake east of Knife Lake, and made a living by guiding, trapping, and prospecting. Although the Wilderness Act called for their removal and for their buildings to be burned, public opinion was strongly behind allowing Dorothy and Benny to stay on Knife and Ottertrack lakes. People vigorously protested the proposed government actions and the government gave in to public pressure. They were allowed to live out their lives in their wilderness homes.

Benny Ambrose died at his homestead on Ottertrack Lake in 1982. A memorial service was held on the lake and his ashes were scattered over the water by his two daughters, who spent their early years on Ottertrack Lake. In December 1986, the woman known to thousands of canoeists simply as Dorothy, died carrying wood into the cabin on the lake that she had called home for over fifty years.

Pete Cosme, whom everyone called Knife Lake Pete, spent the summers of 1939 to 1991 camped on Knife Lake, except for the years from 1942 to 1945 when he was a soldier in the Second World War. His stay on Knife Lake began when it was legal to use outboard motors in both the Boundary Waters and Quetico Park and there were no restrictions on the length of time a person could stay on a campsite. Once the motor and camping limitations came into effect, Pete managed to "fly under the radar" and continued to use a motorized canoe and stay on his campsite for most of the summer, although necessity required Pete to change residence from time to time. Well-known for his cooking and baking skills and his willingness to share them with others, he sometimes stopped at the Prairie Portage ranger station to drop off doughnuts for us. He must have heard that we primarily ate whole-grained foods, so he made ours with whole wheat. Realizing they were heavier and denser than most doughnuts, he told me that I should use any uneaten doughnuts as anchors. Pete Cosme, born and raised in Chicago, kept returning to Knife Lake as long as his health allowed. Pete died in 2002 at the age of ninety-one.

Marie and I were privileged to become acquainted with Dorothy Molter and Knife Lake Pete when we were park rangers at Prairie Portage in the mid-1980s, and, prior to that, we met Benny Ambrose when we were at Cache Bay. Although they were our closest "neighbours," we did not see them very often. It is ironic that, even though Benny and Pete tried to avoid public attention, it was the very loud public outcry over Dorothy that forced the government to bend the rules and allow all three to stay.

BONES OF THE EARTH

The bedrock, the "bones of the earth," is exposed and on display throughout the Quetico-Superior landscape. Years ago, a writer for *Backpacker Magazine* wrote that the Quetico-Superior is "a land expressed in stone, jagged and rounded, gouged and smoothed — a vocabulary of hard granite spoken eloquently in the almost forgotten idiom of ancient ice."[7] In a land that is expressed primarily in a "vocabulary of hard granite," Knife Lake speaks to us with a pronounced and exotic volcanic accent.

The rock composed of fine-grained volcanic sediment was an important source for tools needed for everyday life for thousands of years. Prior to the arrival of Europeans, people went to Knife Lake to work. They quarried the black, cherty rock and made knives and other stone tools. The portages were used to transport heavy packs full of tools required for the upcoming months or years. Canoeists now come to Knife Lake to forget about work and carry home memories of time spent on a beautiful lake.

CHAPTER SEVEN

McNIECE LAKE:
HEART OF QUETICO PARK OLD-GROWTH

The old-growth pines in the McNiece Lake area are simply astonishing. Nowhere else in the Quetico-Superior region is there such a concentration of huge pines. I first saw them about twenty-five years ago when Marie and I were rangers at Prairie Portage. Having heard accounts of their existence, I eagerly took the opportunity to go on a canoe trip to see these pines and to familiarize myself with that area north of Prairie Portage.

There are many places in Quetico with large pines, but I was astonished to find that one could go ashore almost anywhere around McNiece Lake and walk just a short distance to white pines almost a metre in diameter. The decades-old memory of an entire lake surrounded by huge white and red pines was etched into my brain. I wanted to return to see these trees again.

Fortunately, this desire to see old-growth pines was shared by my wife and our good friends Andy and Paula Hill, and we decided to make the remarkable stand of old-growth pines at McNiece Lake the focus of an August canoe trip in 2004. It was a strange feeling for Marie and I to stand in line at the Prairie Portage ranger station where we had been rangers almost two decades earlier. We bought our camping permit, had a short chat with the current ranger, Carrie Frechette, and then started paddling to McNiece Lake.

Most canoe trips are a quest for walleyes, smallmouth bass, or moose, but old-growth pines have sometimes left such a lasting and indelible impression on Quetico Park canoeists that they have sought them out on their trips. Although there are some who regard old-growth as nothing more than over-mature trees, to many they are a powerful attraction. From my perspective, this trip was simply a quest of an over-mature man to experience over-mature trees. Old growth looking for old-growth.

Even though less than 8 percent of the forests in Quetico are dominated by red and white pine, canoeists paddling through the park get the impression that these large trees are more common because many of them are found along the

Early morning fog creates a mysterious atmosphere along the white-pine–bordered shore of McNiece Lake.

shorelines of lakes. This is primarily due to the protection from forest fires that lakes give to trees along the shoreline, while the areas farther back from the shore burn. Consequently, most canoeists equate the highly visible large white and red pines along the shores of lakes with Quetico Park and BWCAW canoe trips.

McNIECE LAKE: CENTRE OF QUETICO PARK OLD-GROWTH

White and red pines used to be very common in eastern Canada, but both the number and the size of the pines are decreasing due to logging and extensive land development spurred by population growth. Dr. Willard Carmean, professor emeritus

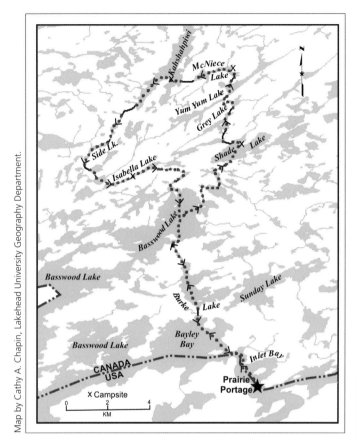

Map by Cathy A. Chapin, Lakehead University Geography Department.

MAP 13: ROUTE OF CANOE TRIP TO MCNIECE LAKE
Our canoe trip to McNiece Lake in 2004 took us into the heart of Quetico's old-growth red and white pines. Although, two summers later, a fire burned some of these pines, most are still standing and undoubtedly many of the oldest and biggest pines in Quetico are growing in locations well back from lakes and are yet to be discovered.

RIGHT
The furrowed trunks of large white pines are part of a forest cathedral on the north shore of McNiece Lake.

of Forestry at Lakehead University in Thunder Bay, stated: "In the early 1800s, someone could have travelled from the St. Lawrence Valley in eastern Canada all the way to the centre of the continent and virtually never been out of sight of magnificent old pines."[1] As you approach McNiece Lake it seems like the number of large pines steadily increases.

Clifford Ahlgren, ecologist and researcher with the Associated Colleges of the Midwest research station on Basswood Lake, found that this is not an illusion, and the stand around McNiece is what remains of a much larger population of pines. "By 1890, most of the state's remaining tall pines were limited to the Arrowhead region of northeastern Minnesota, including the border lakes country. The tall pines extended in an irregular band north, east and west of Duluth. One large finger of tall pine reached into the central portion of the present BWCAW, with the fingertip ending in the Quetico, less than ten kilometres north of Basswood Lake."[2] The fingertip, which extends a few miles north of McNiece Lake, remains unlogged, but parts of it have burned in a variety of small fires.

A combination of geography and luck saved the old-growth pines on Hunter Island. The border was an obstacle for the logging companies in northern Minnesota who had easier access to the pines than Canadian companies. Photos from the early 1900s along the Minnesota shore of Basswood and Knife lakes show a denuded lanscape. The production of the sawmills in Winton, Minnesota, peaked in 1909, a time when many of the trees were coming from the border lakes. It wasn't until the 1920s and 1930s that logging was seriously encroaching onto Hunter Island from both the north and south. By then, greater restrictions were being enforced and there was a growing sentiment that some of the forests should be given greater protection. Quetico was a provincial park and the combination of park status

and public pressure was enough to stop logging before it reached McNiece Lake.

Approaching McNiece Lake, we saw many large white pines on Grey, Armin, and Yum Yum lakes, but on Shan Walshe Lake these trees dominate the forest. It is fitting that plants — not waterfalls, pictographs or fishing — are the main attraction on this lake. After Shan's death, the lake was named in remembrance of the former Quetico Park naturalist, botanist, and champion of wilderness values.[3] Shan loved plants and found old-growth irresistible. But, as much as he loved mature forests and the plants they contain, he had an even greater love of wet, boggy places. There simply have to be interesting swamps and bogs nestled in behind the pines on the lake named after Shan. Another trip seems to be in order to confirm my suspicions.

The third and fourth days of our trip were spent wandering through the forests surrounding McNiece Lake, where white pines well over a metre in diameter are common. Many of the white pines are so big that when two people stand on opposite sides of a tree and wrap their arms around the trunk, just hands overlap. Although no record of anyone coring the old-growth on McNiece Lake could be found, based on ages of white pines obtained from other coring data, the larger white pines on McNiece must be well over three hundred years old.

Walking through old-growth pines always makes me feel I am in the presence of something fundamentally exceptional and extraordinary. Old-growth

Paula Hill stands next to an old-growth white pine along the McNiece-to-Kahshahpiwi portage.

somehow feels "different." Professor Willard Carmean has noted that old-growth pines create a "humbling atmosphere with the large pine trunks acting as pillars and the spreading crowns of the tall pines resembling the vaulted ceilings of a cathedral."[4] It was a pleasant surprise to find white and red pines of various ages, including seedlings, growing under the mature pines and to see the young mixed in with the middle-aged and the old. The mature white and red pines seem to be aging gracefully and many young pines are in position to replace them. There were also, however, many balsam and spruce growing in the shadows of the giant pines. The forest around McNiece Lake is gradually becoming more diverse as the number of balsam, spruce, and varieties of shrubs increases. What is shocking is the scarcity of deciduous trees. Poplar and birch, common in most of the Quetico-Superior area, are few and far between around McNiece Lake.

On our second morning on the lake, we were extremely fortunate to wake up to thick fog. It was a thrill for us to paddle around the lake and take photos of giant pines appearing out of the mist in the early morning light. Hundreds of years ago, much of northern Minnesota and Ontario was covered with large pines, and on this misty morning we had the

Andy Hill relaxes and reflects next to a campfire on a cool evening.

when it comes to fishing, but for Andy and Paula it is a passion, and with all four of us loving to eat fish, we had many wonderful meals of walleye and smallmouth bass. Andy and Paula are high-energy, inquisitive people that are a joy as companions. Three glorious, bug-free August evenings were spent on McNiece Lake drinking "Quetico cocktails," watching the sunset and solving major world problems. Not surprisingly, old-growth and old friends are a terrific combination.

OLD-GROWTH'S DISTINCTIVE ENVIRONMENTS

Old-growth is more than just big trees. Researchers around the world have studied a variety of old-growth forests and have consistently found that these ecosystems support a variety of flora and fauna very different from that of younger forests. The combination of the dominant white and red pine canopy; a lower canopy of pines, spruce and balsam fir; a shrub layer; and an herb-rich forest floor creates numerous ecological niches that are not found in younger forests. Investigations of the canopies of large trees in the Amazon rainforest and in the mature conifers in California, Washington, Oregon, and British Columbia continue to yield surprising findings. Researchers have found distinctive ecological communities that contain new species of insects, birds, fungi, and lichens thriving in the old-growth canopies.

feeling that we were seeing the past through a fog filter. The fog slowly lifted to reveal that the giant pines weren't an illusion but, remarkably, a remnant of the pine forests that once dominated the Quetico-Superior region.

While on McNiece Lake, we didn't just look at trees. We also went swimming, caught fish and simply relaxed. Marie and I have short attention spans

In *The Wild Trees*, a fascinating book about old-growth redwood trees and the people who conduct research in their canopies, Richard Preston describes some of their findings. They found many species of trees, shrubs, and ferns growing in pockets of soil that had accumulated where branches joined the trunk far above the ground. They described trees resembling bonsai suspended far above the forest floor.[5] They even ate huckleberries from shrubs growing ninety metres above the ground. When Preston climbed old-growth Caledonia pines in Scotland, he also found bonsai Caledonia pines in the canopy as well as a variety of lichens and mosses. Blaeberries, related to the huckleberries found in the redwood canopies and to our blueberries, were also growing in the canopies of these three-hundred-year-old pines. In addition to plants, researchers also found earthworms in the pockets of canopy soil, and beetles, salamanders, and the red tree vole living high above the forest floor.

The canopies of old-growth pine in the Quetico-Superior region also have great research potential. While they won't have the diversity of species found in the much larger conifers in the Pacific northwest, it is inevitable that fascinating discoveries await future researchers in the canopies of northern forest trees. Salamanders and voles may live in the midst of new species of beetles, moss, and lichens. Who knows, they may even find bonsai white pines and snack on blueberries — just as researchers in California ate huckleberries and those in Scotland ate blaeberries — growing in the old-growth white pine canopies.

Studies in northern Minnesota have shown that mature white and red pines play significant and diverse roles in the local ecology. Researchers observing black bears in northern Minnesota found that, if possible, female black bears commonly leave the cubs within a few metres of an old white pine when they go off to forage. Evidently, the deeply fissured bark of a large white pine is the easiest for the cubs to climb if they need to avoid predators. A study in the Superior National Forest found that approximately 80 percent of both bald eagles and ospreys build their nests in the crowns of old white pines. They obviously seek out these old pines since researchers have found that only a small percentage of the mature trees in the Superior National Forest are pines.

Occasionally, unexpected creatures, such as black bears and raccoons, hibernate in eagles' nests. Researchers in the Chippewa Flowage in northeastern Wisconsin have found both of these animals hibernating in nests. It seems especially strange that a bear would winter far above the ground in an eagle's nest. Mike Gappa, a retired Wisconsin bear ecologist, speculated that maybe "this animal in the past had some disturbance on the ground"[6] and chose to be safer, but undoubtedly colder, hibernating in a tree. Even standing and downed dead trees play an important role in the environment, serving as nesting sites for a variety of cavity-nesting birds

Trees, such as this dead pine near McNiece Lake, provide habitats for a variety of creatures.

growing in the mid-to-late 1600s and early 1700s when European explorers and voyageurs were entering the Quetico-Superior area. Some of the oldest trees were already substantial trees when Jacques de Noyon, the first-known European to pass through the area, arrived in 1688. Voracious logging and land clearing have resulted in few old-growth white or red pines surviving until today. Even in protected areas, natural forces — disease, fire, wind, and other hazards — have greatly reduced their numbers. The lives of the oldest pines encompass the entire span of time that non-Native people have lived in the Quetico-Superior region.

FIRE AND FUTURE OLD-GROWTH

We ended our stay on McNiece Lake greatly impressed with what we had seen, but also wondered how much longer the giant pines would dominate this part of Quetico. Logging was halted in the southern part of the park before it reached McNiece Lake, thus leaving much of the old-growth to flourish with only a relatively small percentage having been burned. The old-growth around McNiece Lake and in the rest of Quetico Park is protected from logging and will not be lost to the chainsaw. The trees will, however, eventually succumb to fire and the slow ravages of time.

The inevitable occurred just two years after our visit. In late July 2006, lightning ignited forest fires

and habitats for a variety of insects that are important sources of food for woodpeckers and other birds.

Based on estimates of the age of the pines, most of the old-growth around McNiece Lake started in the central part of Quetico Park and a substantial amount of the old-growth around McNiece Lake and Shan Walshe Lake burned. Since old-growth is such a valuable commodity, this is a significant loss. Quetico now has a policy of letting natural wildfires burn unless they threaten areas outside the park, and this fire was carefully monitored but allowed to burn. Canoeists passing through the burn a month after the fire noticed that, in some areas, a substantial number of the old-growth pines had been consumed along with the smaller trees and the undergrowth, while other areas were untouched. The fire left a patchwork of extensively burned, lightly burned, and unburned areas. Where there were sufficient standing red and white pines to act as seed trees, a young forest dominated by red and white pines should spring up.

Fire can obviously destroy large stands of mature pines, but it is also the force that is responsible for the success of white, red, and Jack pine forests. Miron Heinselman has noted: "White pine and red pine can persist without fire for up to 350 and possibly even 400 years for occasional individuals, but without a fire that creates favourable conditions for stand renewal, most stands will eventually be replaced by balsam and spruce as the old pines die."[7]

A much larger and generally hotter fire burned an extensive area in the eastern part of Quetico Park in 1995. I remember portaging up a long hill on the southern shore of Mack Lake on the way to Munro Lake in the eastern part of the park in 1996

and being amazed at how few trees had survived that fire. The fire had raced up the hill through a forest containing many old-growth white pines, burning almost everything in its path. (See photo of blackened base of white pine on page 216.) The only trees that survived the fire were some of the large, old-growth white pine. The survivors were blackened and had fire scars along their bases, but were still alive because of their thick, fire-resistant bark and the branches that remained above the fire. I haven't been back to Mack Lake since, but these trees undoubtedly acted as sources of seeds to the open, nutrient-rich ground below. Stands of old-growth pines are usually the result of fire. Prolonged fire suppression, on the other hand, leads to a mixed forest of balsam fir, spruce, aspen, and white birch, accompanied by a decrease in pine.

In order to ensure that Quetico Park has old-growth pines in the future to match or exceed what it has now, it is essential to think about future old-growth. Dr. Willard Carmean has noted:

> Old-growth pine forest management involves more than merely reserving scattered old-growth forest stands. For white and red pine we must also be concerned with regenerating new pine forests, and with the recognition and protection of mid-age pine forests. These newly regenerated areas, and these mid-age forests, thus can

become the old-growth forests of the future that will inevitably be naturally harvested by insects, disease and fire.[8]

Future old-growth is just seed, seedlings, and saplings now. McNiece Lake is not just a powerful reminder of what Quetico-Superior forests were like just over a century ago; it can also be an inspiration for the future. There is a hope that we can learn from these diminishing fragments of old-growth pine. If we just knew what questions to ask, these "pine elders" could teach us a lot.

CHAPTER EIGHT

PRAIRIE PORTAGE:
BOUNDARY WATERS CROSSROADS

Prairie Portage is part of a major travel route established by Native peoples thousands of years ago and utilized ever since. When you walk the portage, you are walking in the twelve-thousand-year-old footsteps of Palaeo-Indians, the 250-year-old footsteps of voyageurs, and in the recent footsteps of famed author Sigurd Olson.[1]

The portage was a place where people from different cultures and different lifestyles met, exchanged ideas and came to know one another. Prairie Portage is still an important crossroads and, on any given day during the canoeing season, it is probably the busiest place in Quetico Park. Located at the centre of the combined Quetico Park and Boundary Waters Canoe Area Wilderness (BWCAW), it functions as the primary location where canoeists pass back and forth between the United States and Canada, as well as a portage for canoeists staying in the BWCAW. In addition to the canoe portage on the Canadian side of the river, a truck portage on the Minnesota side of the border is permitted by the United States Forest Service.

A utility vehicle pulling a trailer transports motorboats back and forth between Sucker Lake and Basswood Lake.

CONTINUOUS NATIVE HABITATION FROM PALAEO-INDIANS TO THE OJIBWA

Recent excavations conducted by United States Forest Service archaeologists near the Basswood Lake end of the truck portage found evidence of human activity that extends all the way back to the Late Palaeo-Indian period. The melting of the glacier, which receded through the southern part of Quetico Park over thirteen thousand years ago, released enough water to submerge much of the Quetico-Superior under the waters of Lake Agassiz. It may have taken a thousand years for Lake Agassiz to drop to the level of Basswood Lake and make campsites there accessible. The first inhabitants of the Prairie Portage area were descendents of earlier Palaeo-Indian people who entered the

MAP 14: SATELLITE IMAGE OF PRAIRIE PORTAGE
Prairie Portage crosses a narrow strip of land that separates Sucker Lake from Basswood Lake. The portage, probably close to where the canoe portage lies today, was first used by Palaeo-Indians and the current portage is now the busiest one in Quetico Park.

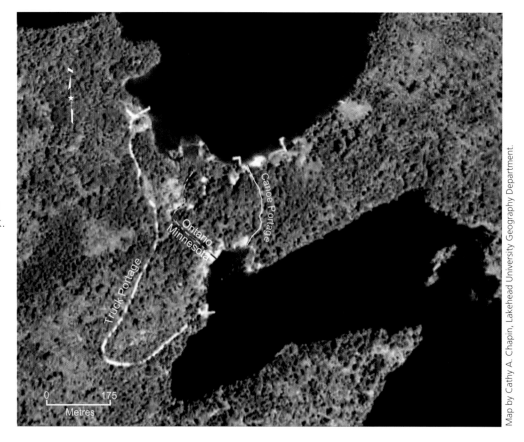

Map by Cathy A. Chapin, Lakehead University Geography Department.

Quetico-Superior region in the higher land a little farther east.

It is not surprising that Native people camped at the Basswood Lake end of the portage since the area below the rapids would have been a prime site for netting fish. Prairie Portage is a resource-rich location with an abundance of fish, wild rice, and a variety of berries continued to be used by Native people through the voyageur period. The artifacts found at Prairie Portage indicate that people have camped near both ends of the portages on both sides of the river, and the abundance of pottery shards and domestic tools such as scrapers indicate that the campsites, especially on the Basswood Lake side, were more than just temporary. Native families apparently lived there for extended periods.

Prairie Portage was a place where generations of kids played, stone tools were sharpened, fishing nets repaired, and meals prepared. Fish was often on the menu since they were plentiful below the

The rising sun illuminates the base of the rapids at Prairie Portage on only a few days close to the summer solstice.

rapids. Meat obtained by hunting varied greatly over time. The Palaeo-Indians probably ate caribou, while during the warm period around seven thousand years ago, white-tailed deer were more likely to be consumed. Meals of moose with wild rice were undoubtedly a staple in more recent times.

In addition to Prairie Portage, numerous archaeological sites have been found on Basswood Lake on both sides of the border from Prairie Portage to the Basswood River and from Jackfish Bay to North Bay. These sites, which encompass everything from the Palaeo-Indian period to the Native people who were on Basswood when the first European explorers arrived, indicate a long and intimate relationship between Native peoples and Basswood Lake. The lake is amazingly diverse. There are shallow, dark-water,

135

productive bays on the southern half of the lake where warm-water fish species such as bluegills and crappies live. Some of these bays have wild rice and are surrounded by basswood, red maple, and black ash trees. The northern half of the lake is very different. It has deep bays surrounded by red and white pines and clear, deep water favoured by lake trout.

In 1785, Alexander Mackenzie wrote about Native people on Basswood Lake in his journal: "The population was very numerous; this was also a favourite part, where they made their canoes, &c. the lake abounding in fish, the country round it being plentifully supplied with various kinds of game, and the rocky ridges, that form the boundaries of the water, covered with a variety of berries."[1] Mackenzie also noted that they depended primarily on fish and wild rice that "grows spontaneously in these parts."[2] Wild rice still grows in profusion in the southern half of Basswood with large stands in Hoist Bay, Back Bay, and Wind Bay. In addition, Manomin Lake (*manomin* is Ojibwa for wild rice) and Rice Bay on Basswood Lake have names indicating high rice production in the past. Only meagre amounts of rice, however, are found in these two locations today.

Clifford Ahlgren, an ecologist who worked extensively on Basswood, has noted that the Ojibwa periodically burned U.S. Point on Basswood, a long, rocky peninsula where fire could be confined in order to maintain good blueberry production. The increased berry production caused by fires may be the reason an Ely-Winton Historical Society map of Basswood Lake calls this area the "Ojibway blueberry hills." This periodic burning may have caused the Ojibwa to name the lake *Bashe Menon Sagaigon* (also written as *Baasi-minan-sag*), which means "dried blueberry lake."

ARRIVAL OF EUROPEANS: PRAIRIE PORTAGE AS A CULTURAL CROSSROADS

In the 1700s and 1800s, Prairie Portage, being both a heavily used portage and a habitation area, was a cultural crossroads where Native peoples and Europeans unavoidably interacted. During this period, it was an important location where people new to this environment — explorers, voyageurs, traders, and settlers — could be taught by people who had lived and prospered there for thousands of years. The European newcomers were literally and figuratively following in the footsteps of Native people and learning survival skills proven to work in this environment from them.

The Native people also learned from the Europeans and obtained copper kettles, guns, fishhooks, iron axes, and other items that they quickly incorporated into their everyday life. They also were victims of diseases such as smallpox, influenza, tuberculosis, measles, and chicken pox that devastated their populations. In the long run, the Native peoples received the worst of the exchange. An entry in Alexander Mackenzie's 1798 journal noted that: "This great extent of country was formerly very prosperous, but now the aggregate of its inhabitants does not exceed three hundred warriors; and among the few whom I saw, it appeared to me the widows were more numerous than the men."[3]

During the voyageur period, the portage between Sucker Lake and Basswood Lake (the present-day Prairie Portage) was known as Gros Portage des Bois Blanc. In a 1797 journal, the Canadian explorer and surveyor David Thompson refers to the portage by the English name of Great White Wood Carrying Place. Many of the journals from this period mention Native peoples living at the Basswood end of the portage. John Macdonell, a clerk for the North West Company, notes that his brigade bought a canoe from Ojibwa living at Prairie Portage to replace a damaged one.[4]

It can be very confusing reading about Prairie Portage in many of the earliest journals written by explorers and voyageurs until it becomes clear that they are referring to the portage between Swamp Lake and Ottertrack. This portage is now known as Monument Portage because of the prominent border markers located there, but was known as Prairie Portage during the voyageur period. The earlier name is probably a reference to the wet, grassy nature of the east end of the portage.

There is no "prairie" at today's Prairie Portage, but the name comes from the large open fields where horses were kept when logging was in its "hay" day in the late 1800s and early 1900s. According to Jeep

LaTourell, whose family runs the truck portage and who is a veritable font of knowledge on Basswood Lake, a large area was cleared for pasture on the Minnesota side of the border. The fields, now mainly converted back to forest, ran from the current mechanical truck portage westerly along the shore of Inlet Bay. Hay for the horses came across the Four Mile Portage from Fall Lake and was brought by barge to Prairie Portage.

A dam, located at the Sucker Lake end of the portage, was built in 1902 to raise the water levels behind the dam, thus facilitating logging and the movement of logs. The dam elevated the water on Sucker Lake enough to make it possible to travel by boat from Moose Lake to Prairie Portage without portaging. Moose, Newfound, Sucker, and Birch lakes

Courtesy of the John B. Ridley Research Library, Quetico Park Information Pavilion.

This 1912 photograph shows the wooden dam built by the St. Croix Lumber Company at Prairie Portage.

then became, in effect, one lake connected by narrows. The level of Sucker Lake was raised enough to cause some of the water to overflow and form Sucker Creek on the Canadian side. Some accounts indicate that the water flowed down the portage. If that was the case, the portage used now only dates back to the construction of the dam in the early 1900s and the old portage, or portions of the old portage, is now Sucker Creek. This overflow created the unusual situation of having a creek and a river flowing parallel to each other while both drain the same body of water.

The dam was rebuilt in 1939 and again in 1955 after it was breached in 1954. In 1968, the dam gave way again and the water levels on Moose, Newfound, and Sucker lakes dropped between 1.5 and 2.5 metres. To minimize the maintenance costs and decrease the chance of future dam failure, the wooden dam was replaced with a concrete structure in 1975, and once again it was possible to travel to Moose Lake without portaging. Today's easy access by motorboat from Moose Lake has changed the dynamics of Basswood Lake and greatly increased the usage of Prairie Portage by both canoeists and fishermen in motorboats.

THE RECENT PAST

Robert Readman, the chief fire ranger in Quetico prior to the creation of the Quetico Forest Reserve in 1909 and later one of the original park rangers, stated that commercial fishing was occurring on Basswood Lake in 1906 and there are reports of commercial fishing occurring as early as 1892. Commercial fishing also occurred from Basswood Lake east along the border to Saganaga Lake, and a two-hundred-metre-long, narrow-gauge railway at Prairie Portage was used to haul fish from those lakes to Basswood. From there, the fish were transported to Hoist Bay and then taken over the Four Mile Portage to Winton, Minnesota. The narrow-gauge railway was also used to move a variety of other material, including logging equipment and supplies, from one end of the portage to the other. Undoubtedly, it was used for a variety of other purposes as well, such as moving supplies for the 1917 boundary survey.

The Chosa family has played a significant role in the history of Basswood Lake. Their roots go back to the fur-trade era. Leo Chosa was a man of mixed French-aboriginal ancestry who trapped in the Hunter Island area prior to 1909. He eventually settled on Basswood Lake and married Annie Dufault, whose Ojibwa grandmother was born on the lake. In Oberholtzer's 1909 journal, he mentioned stopping at a rading post run by Leo Chosa on an island on Basswood Lake. The following summer, Leo Chosa wrote a letter protesting the expulsion of people of the Lac La Croix and Kawa Bay Reserves from their hunting grounds on Hunter Island during the winter. He was deeply involved in commercial fishing and opened a refrigerated fish-processing plant in Winton, Minnesota, in 1914. In 1927, Leo Chosa opened a small store and minnow

In 1917, a survey crew used the narrow gauge railway at Prairie Portage, which appears to have wooden rails, to haul supplies.

business on the United States side of Prairie Portage and ran this business until his death in 1955. His daughter, Leonore Driscoll, took over running the store until it closed in 1964. Among the many members of the Chosa family, Henry Chosa operated towboats on the lake, and Tommy Chosa, Leo's nephew, was a highly regarded guide on Basswood Lake for many years.

When the Four Mile Portage was the primary tourist entry access to Basswood Lake, Cabin 16, also known as Ottawa Island, was strategically located where people heading into Canada could clear Canada Customs and obtain Quetico Park permits. Ranger stations on Bayley Bay and King's Point were situated to handle people who entered Basswood somewhere other than over the Four Mile Portage. The construction of the dam at Prairie Portage substantially increased the number of people using the Moose Lake chain and changed the flow of people

into Basswood Lake, and Prairie Portage became a primary entry into the lake and Quetico Park. In 1948, the Charles L. Sommers Boy Scout Canoe base made special arrangements to have a Canada Customs officer stationed at the base during the summer. This continued until the customs agent began working out of a tent at Prairie Portage in 1952. The following summer a Canada Customs station was built at Prairie Portage, and operated until 1999. Now, tourists entering Canada at this location must first obtain a CanPass, a remote border-crossing permit.

PRAIRIE PORTAGE BECOMES A QUETICO PARK ENTRY STATION

In 1954, Quetico Park followed the lead of Canada Customs and a park ranger sold park permits out of a tent while the site for a ranger station was being cleared. The station was built the following summer and remained in that capacity through 2008. As of 2009, the former Customs building houses the Friends of Quetico store as well as space for selling park permits and fishing licences, and the former ranger station is now a staff residence.

Its location on the southern edge of Quetico, with easy access from Ely, Minnesota, makes Prairie Portage by far the most heavily used entry into the park. Still a very busy and dynamic place, it is not nearly as active as in the decades prior to the quota system when there were many days with three or four hundred people entering the park by way of Prairie Portage. In 1978, a visitor quota was applied limiting the number of groups entering Quetico; only fifteen canoe groups may enter the park through Prairie Portage each day and the group size must not exceed nine members.

The only way that Mike and Priscella O'Brien, park rangers during many of the busiest years at Prairie Portage, could keep up with the paperwork was to obtain information about canoeists entering the next day from outfitters and spend the evening filling out fishing licences. Open for business from 7:00 a.m. until 6:00 p.m., they commonly sold over sixty permits a day, and there were lineups at the outhouses as well as at Canada Customs and the ranger station. With the traffic going in both directions over the portage, there were sometimes over one hundred canoes at the site. Space was often at a premium at both ends of the portage.

Since motors are allowed on most of the Minnesota side of Basswood Lake, there is also a flow of motorboats over the truck portage on the American side. Since the passage of the Boundary Waters Canoe Area Wilderness Act in the United States in

Canoeists arriving at and departing from the Basswood end of Prairie Portage in August 2001.

1978, there have been sporadic conflicts over the use of motorboats on Basswood Lake and lawsuits over the use of vehicles on the truck portage on the Minnesota side of the river. Having the motorboat and canoe portages on opposite sides of the river has ensured that little contact occurs between the two groups, and has helped create parallel universes of motorized and non-motorized users of Basswood Lake. These portages mirror the divide that separates the two groups that have an important element in common — the love of spending time on Basswood Lake and in the Quetico-Superior area.

HUMAN ACTIVITY INCREASES BOTANICAL DIVERSITY

The ground-hugging common plantain on the trail to the Canadian ranger station has survived being trampled by numerous park visitors.

Prairie Portage is a striking botanical crossroads where plants from the boreal forest, the deciduous forest, and the prairies have all taken root. The long human habitation and the variety of uses of both sides of the river — permanent and seasonal Native encampments, logging camps and horse pastures, trading posts, ranger stations and Canada Customs, truck and canoe portages — have greatly added to the plant diversity. Species inadvertently and purposely introduced by Europeans and other immigrants thrive in the disturbed and heavily used portions of the site. Dandelions and a multitude of other introduced species are growing on the lawns and the lawns themselves seem like an unconscious attempt to return the prairie to Prairie Portage. Some of the prairie species that thrive in the disturbed, open areas probably originated as seeds in the hay when horses where kept on the American side of the portage.

Common plantain, called "white man's foot" by the Iroquois since it seemed to follow wherever Europeans walked, grows along the various paths at Prairie Portage and along many other portages throughout the Quetico-Superior region. It is regarded as being "trample-proof" since its leaves are tough, leathery, and lie flat on the ground. It also can recover quickly from damage as it stores energy for growth and repair in its root system. Henry Wadsworth Longfellow's poem "The White Man's Foot" refers to this characteristic of common plantain:

> Wheresoe'er they tread, beneath them
> Springs a flower unknown among us
> Springs a White-Man's Foot in blossom[5]

Walter Hurn, a ranger at King's Point on Basswood Lake in the 1920s, constructed a remarkable garden modelled after those in the English countryside where he grew up. The garden contained a colourful mosaic of flowers in addition to a variety of garden vegetables. Sigurd Olson wrote: "You would never believe that a garden patch up there in the wilds would mean very much but it did — more, in fact, than most of us ever cared to admit. Coming out of the bush where all vegetation runs riot to suddenly find clean gravel walks, vegetables in straight rows and a profusion of flowers when for a long time we had known only muskeg, rocks, and timber did something to us."[6]

As King's Point hasn't been occupied since the 1950s, most of the garden plants have been displaced by native plants. A few domestic plants, however, have survived, including some stunted rugosa roses. In 1985, when we were the rangers at Prairie Portage, we moved two rugosa rose plants that were struggling to survive from King's Point to Prairie Portage. It is hoped that these roses will thrive for many more years in their new home and continue to keep the spirit of Walter Hurn alive on Basswood Lake.

Two plants to be avoided are also present at Prairie Portage. Poison ivy grows in profusion along the trail between the portage and the residence for park staff. Spotted water hemlock, which has been called the most poisonous plant in Quetico, can usually be found near the mouth of Sucker Creek. This plant closely resembles water parsnip, which does have an edible root. The two plants can be confused with fatal results. Shan Walshe wrote that the French name for the plant "is carotte de Moreau, in memory of a voyageur who mistook it for water parsnip and consequently was poisoned."[7]

Arrowhead, a plant with small, edible tubers that was sought out and eaten by Native people, also grows in the mouth of Sucker Creek. Blueberries, raspberries, and saskatoons (also known as juneberries) are all edible berries found throughout the Quetico-Superior region and are found in scattered locations at Prairie Portage. Thimbleberry, a shrub with a bland but edible berry, also grows along the trails. It is common in British Columbia and is found in only a few scattered locations in Northwestern Ontario.

Shan Walshe spent many years searching for and cataloguing the plants in Quetico. One of his most surprising discoveries was the presence of Jerusalem artichoke at the site of the abandoned

Hudson's Bay Post on Inlet Bay, just three kilometres northwest of Prairie Portage. In spite of its name, Jerusalem artichoke is a sunflower, not an artichoke. It is native to North America and has no connection to the Middle East. Other than that, the name is accurate. The plant grows to over two metres tall and has large, edible tubers. Shan found the plant in 1974 when the old fur-trade site, now completely grown in, was still open enough that sun-loving plants, like Jerusalem artichoke, could survive. For thousands of years, Jerusalem artichoke was a major source of food for Native peoples who lived on the prairies or where prairie plants would grow. Although primarily a prairie species, it does well in our climate and we've grown them for food for over twenty years in our gardens in both Atikokan and Thunder Bay. Shan's find indicates that they may have been used by Natives on Basswood or were grown for food at the Hudson's Bay post on Inlet Bay. Jerusalem artichoke apparently is a "plant artifact," a remnant of past human actions on this site.

Tree species that grow in relatively few places in Quetico Park are growing at Prairie Portage. In 1986, we noticed a basswood seedling struggling on the banks of Sucker Creek, just a few metres from the wooden bridge that used to lead to the ranger station and now low leads to the staff residence. In spite of our urgings, the seedling didn't survive. However, there are mature basswood trees growing along the shores of Basswood Lake. Some can be found in the shallow, productive bays on the Minnesota side of the lake and a few also grow along the Basswood River.

Until a few years ago, a huge red ash grew near the shore in front of the ranger station and there are still many others between the ranger station and the portage. Both northern red oak and bur oak are found along the pleasant trail that follows the river on the Canadian side from the dam down to the lake and along the shore east of the dam. Some of these oaks are very gnarled and twisted and give the impression of great age in spite of their relatively modest size. Grey squirrels have moved north with the warmer weather of the last few decades and they are now well established in both Thunder Bay and Duluth. If these squirrels discover the small stand of oaks along the river, they may become part of the future at Prairie Portage.

THE SAGA CONTINUES

To portage a canoe at Prairie Portage means to participate in a twelve-thousand-year-old tradition. The special magic of Prairie Portage lies in its long record of human use. Nowhere else in the Quetico-Superior area is the presence of the human past as apparent as it is at Prairie Portage. It is essential that we learn how to manage the current use of this busy, significant site in such a way that the rich history that came before is preserved.

In addition to its memorable history, Prairie Portage also has a noteworthy recent past. During the years we were rangers there in the 1980s, many people who had considerable impact on the Quetico-Superior area, including Johnny Sansted, legendary guide and trapper; Bob Cary, editor and writer; Al McKenzie, Canada Customs agent; Tommy Chosa, guide; Shan Walshe, Quetico Park naturalist; and Joe Seliga, canoe-maker, often visited or passed through Prairie Portage. This diverse group of exceptional people, who helped make Prairie Portage come alive for me, has taken what Bob Cary called the "last portage." They are now part of Prairie Portage's heritage.

PART THREE

GLIMPSES INTO THE ECOLOGY OF QUETICO PARK

Quetico Park is a captivating blend of deciduous and boreal forest with a sprinkling of species from the prairies. As a result, organisms as diverse as Calypso orchids and caribou lichen, silver maple and stunted black spruce, prairie goldenrod and wild ginger, all grow in a land where whisky jacks overlap with blue jays, moose co-exist with white-tailed deer and bog lemmings live near woodland jumping mice.

Hidden within the rich, mixed forests and the lakes that surround them are miniature worlds where mystery abounds. The subnivean world of the pukak; the deep, dark recesses of large lakes; the underground network of plant roots and fungi; the lives of carnivorous plants in acid bogs; and winter inside a beaver lodge are some of the small, obscure environments that are examined in the essays that follow.

David Abram, who possesses an unusual combination of talents in ecology, sleight-of-hand magic, and anthropology, states that we have lost our appreciation for what "we share with the soaring hawk, the spider, and the stone silently sprouting lichens on its coarse surface."[1] Ecologists, however, are increasingly finding evidence of the physical ties that exist between species previously thought to be totally independent and self-sufficient. The symbiotic relationships between moose and bacteria, ravens and wolves, and orchids and fungi are investigated further in this section.

Two chapters focus on research that has been carried out in Quetico Park. Moose research involved the use of innovative techniques to learn more about moose behaviour during the rut. The research also provided scientific data on the duration of the rut that was influential in having the opening of moose-hunting season in Ontario moved back a few weeks to avoid the main time period when bull moose are most vulnerable. A ten-year study of red and white pine regrowth after forest fires of varying intensities and at different times of the year provides hope for the future of these magnificent pines in the Quetico

Beautiful ground lichens are part of the lilliputian worlds that are found in inhospitable habitats throughout Quetico Park. These fruticose lichens, British soldiers, and a form of caribou lichen, were found at the base of an overturned tree near Jasper Lake.

Park forests of tomorrow. The extensive research in this study resulted in some surprising conclusions, while other findings reinforced already established beliefs.

Twenty thousand years ago, the earth experienced a major global warming that signalled the beginning of the end of the last ice age. The Quetico-Superior region has undergone significant climate and ecological changes since then. The changes occurring now, however, are apparently man-made. Quetico Park simply has a different "feel" to it now than it had in 1976 when I started working at Beaverhouse Lake. The mid and late 1970s were years of very cold winters and deep snow. Lakes are freezing later and breaking up earlier now than they did just thirty or forty years ago. There are exceptions — the late ice-out in 2008 is a recent example — but the trend over the last few decades has been for warmer and drier weather. The vegetation and wildlife that first attracted me to this area decades ago are now under relentless pressure from a warming environment.

In 1911, John Muir, one of the founders of the Sierra Club, wrote: "When we try to pick out anything by itself, we find it hitched to everything else in the universe."[2] Plants and animals don't live in isolation and the "hitching together" of moose and wolves, bumblebees and flowers, and beavers and poplar trees are fairly obvious. Ecologists, however, are also finding fascinating interactions in unexpected places. Trees are now known to be connected, via a soil fungus, to other trees, shrubs, and mushrooms. Plants have even been found to communicate with other plants. Some plants infested with insects apparently send out chemical signals that alert other plants of the approaching danger. This gives plants some time to produce toxins in their leaves to discourage and even kill the herbivorous insects. For other dangers, however, plants have no defence. Imagine their alarm when loggers start their chainsaws or when gardeners start weeding the garden or pulling up carrots.

Interesting, unexpected findings are being made by biologists every year. It is exciting to hear about these new discoveries, but some things may be best not to know. The call of a loon across a northern lake is a haunting, evocative sound. I'm not sure I want to know what they are saying.

CHAPTER NINE

SYMBIOSIS: REMARKABLE PARTNERS

Each of us is a walking ecosystem. Although we each appear to be an isolated, independent organism, we are actually a fluctuating mixture of self and non-self. We have trillions of bacteria living on our skin, mites in our eyebrows and eyelashes, and fungi on our tongue and in our hair. In addition to those on our skin, over a kilogram of bacteria reside in our intestines. Some of these microbes, such as the bacteria in our large intestine that produce vitamin K essential for blood clotting, are crucial to our survival.

Most organisms, however, simply discover that we have interesting neighbourhoods — intestines, armpits, and crotch — that are pleasant places to live. We can think of our bodies as a "habitat" for these organisms, just as a forest is home to red squirrels and moose. Although there are a few organisms like lice, intestinal worms, and amoeba that cause disease or discomfort, the vast majority lives in harmony with us and cause us no harm.

The German botanist A.B. Frank is credited with coining the term "symbiosis" in 1885 to describe the close, prolonged association between two or more different organisms of different species. Although disease is usually the first thing that comes to mind when we think of the interaction between microbes and ourselves or other animals or plants, that is only a small part of symbiosis. Just a few years after Frank introduced biologists to symbiosis, the German biologist Anton De Bary had the "vision to see that the intimate associations of microbes and plants were just as likely to lead to mutual dependence and innovation as they were to mutual destruction."[1] Ecologists then began to look in earnest at the variety of ways organisms work together for their mutual benefit.

The animals and plants that inhabit Quetico Park appear, at first glance, to be totally isolated, independent entities. In reality, however, they too have other organisms living on them, in them, or in such intimate association that they constantly interact. Symbiosis plays a major role in the ecology of the Quetico landscape. Researchers continues to turn up new evidence of the vital role that symbiotic relationships play in virtually every aspect of relationships between living things. These relationships can occur in any combination of organisms — plant and animal, two animals, plant and fungus, fungus and animal, bacteria and fungus, or bacteria and animal. It's even beginning to seem as if all living organisms function more effectively with symbiotic partners.

SYMBIOTIC RELATIONSHIPS

There are three types of symbiosis: mutualism, commensalism, and parastism. Relationships between organisms are called mutualism if both organisms benefit from the association, commensalism if only one organism benefits and the other is unaffected, or parasitism if one organism lives on or in another to the detriment of the host. Since parasitism can result in diseases that directly affect humans, it is more intensely studied and better understood than either mutualism or commensalism.

Degrees of symbiosis can range from occasional, casual interactions to total interdependence. In most symbiotic relationships the organisms strongly interact and influence each other, but each organism keeps its own identity. This is the case with the mutually beneficial relationship between a honeybee and the flower it is pollinating, the commensal relationship between you and the bacteria on your skin, and the parasitic relationship between a cold virus and a person with a cold.

Occasionally the symbiotic relationship between two organisms is so complex and involved that the result appears to be an entirely new and different organism. Lichens, those tenacious life forms found on rock ledges, tree trunks, old cement sidewalks, and other seemingly inhospitable places, are usually made up of an algae and a fungus. In the case of lichens, the extent of this symbiotic interaction is so intricate that the borders separating one organism from another become very blurred and the two species look and act like a single organism.

COMMENSALISM AND PARASITISM

Any canoe trip through the Quetico-Superior area will expose a person to parasites. Wood ticks will gladly attempt to suck human blood, as will bloodsuckers. Bloodsuckers and large wood ticks are merely annoying, but other parasites can seriously affect human health. The small deer tick can carry a bacteria that causes Lyme disease, an ailment that can result in severe nervous system, heart, and joint problems. Giardia is a protozoan (a single-cell organism) that affects humans, but it is also a parasite that infects cats, dogs, cows, beavers, deer, and other mammals. Typically found in lakes, streams, or ponds that have been contaminated by beaver, muskrat, dog, or human feces, giardia is also known as "beaver fever." Giardia infections can occur through ingestion of dormant cysts in contaminated water and, since giardia can be present in beaver feces, drinking water from a beaver pond, creek, or river used by beavers or near a beaver lodge is not a good idea.

The effects of plant parasites can easily be seen on most canoe trips in Quetico Park. Although most plant parasites are either microscopic or tiny insects not readily seen, their effects can be readily apparent. The dead tops on white pine often signal the presence of white pine blister rust and birch blight causes birch trees to prematurely drop their leaves. A close examination of plants along a portage trail or at a campsite will probably reveal some with swollen, abnormal growths known as galls. These galls, tumour-like structures that surround and isolate the parasite inside, can be caused by anything from a virus to insect larvae.

Indian Pipe is a white, ghostly looking plant that is also known as corpse plant, ice plant, and ghost flower. This unusual plant does not contain any chlorophyll and acquires its nutrients from fungi that interact with its roots as well as the roots of conifers. Since Indian Pipe doesn't photosynthesize, neither the fungus nor the tree gets anything in return. In this complex interrelationship between Indian Pipe, symbiotic fungi, and trees, the Indian Pipe apparently acts as a parasite. Although Indian Pipe seems to act like a plant parasite, some botanists believe it also gets some of its energy from dead and decaying organic matter in the soil and is better described as a saprophyte.

Lichens growing on tree bark, turkey vultures eating the carcasses of animals killed by wolves, and

Indian Pipe, lacking chlorophyll, obtains its energy from its association with the roots of other plants.

barred owls utilizing abandoned crow nests, are examples of commensalism since they appear to benefit only one species without harming the other. A miniature example of commensalism in plants is the small spines on twinflower seed capsules that are dispersed by small mammals. The seed capsules attach to the fur of mice and voles and the seeds of

The rounded seed pod of a twinflower has spines that attach to the fur of small mammals.

the tiny but ubiquitous twinflower are transported away from the parent plant much like we transport burrs that attach to our clothing.

In some instances, commensalism can be hard to distinguish from mutualism since relationships between different species are often not well enough understood to be certain that only one species is benefiting from the relationship. Many naturalists, trappers, and ecologists have commented on the special relationship that exists between wolves and ravens. Wolves not only kill their prey, but they also open the body cavities so that ravens, turkey vultures, and other scavengers are able to feed on

what is left behind. Other animals, not usually considered scavengers, such as mink, pine marten, and whisky jacks will also take advantage of these carcasses, especially in the winter when food is scarce. Many biologists feel that this is commensalism since ravens and other scavengers clearly profit by eating wolf kills, while wolves don't seem to benefit from the relationship with the scavengers.

Other observers, however, believe ravens provide wolves with clues that prey are in the vicinity and signal their location by circling over them and calling loudly. If this is the case, then wolves are also profiting from the relationship with ravens and their interaction should be regarded as mutualism. Berndt Heinrich's observations led him to note that ravens and wolves work together so closely that maybe ravens "had evolved with wolves in a mutualism that is millions of years old, so that they have innate behaviors that link them to wolves, making them uncomfortable without their presence."[2]

MUTUALISM

In many cases of mutualism a plant is aided in reproduction by an animal seeking food. The hummingbird and honeybee obtain nectar or pollen while they inadvertently spread the pollen from one flower to another. Red squirrels feed on the seeds in pine cones and the nuts of the beaked hazel. They also scatter them far from the parent plant by

Red squirrels consume large numbers of beaked hazel nuts, but they also inadvertently distribute them by caching them for later use and forgetting to retrieve them.

placing them in caches and sometimes forgetting about them. These relationships that spread pollen and seeds far from the parent plant greatly impact the ecology of the Quetico-Superior landscape, but other examples of mutualism are at least as significant even though they are far more subtle.

In numerous cases of mutualism, the organisms are vastly different in size with the smaller one living inside, or attached to, the larger. In Quetico, there are many examples of symbiotic bacteria living inside animals. The vegetation eaten by a moose is high in the wood fibre known as cellulose. Moose, like other mammals, don't have enzymes that digest this tough, fibrous material. Some bacteria, however, can digest cellulose. Bacteria with this

capability inhabit the digestive system of domestic cows, moose, and Quetico-Superior animals such as the white-tailed deer, snowshoe hare, and beaver. The presence of the bacteria allows these animals to obtain adequate nutrition from twigs, buds, branches, and other plant parts high in cellulose. The relationship between these animals and bacteria is mutualism since both the grazing animal and the bacteria benefit. Neither moose nor snowshoe hare nor beaver could survive on foods available in the wild without these bacteria. In return, the bacteria get a warm, safe place to live and, as a bonus, they get chewed food delivered directly to them. The relationship for many of the bacteria abruptly ends, however, when they are deposited in a pile of feces on the forest floor.

The two species of alder that live in the park are able to grow in places where other plants have great difficulty. Alder are able to thrive where water levels fluctuate between very wet and very dry and nutrient levels are low. Their survival is possible because they form mutualistic symbiotic relationships with a fungus and a nitrogen-fixing bacteria that live in bulbous growths on their roots. The bacteria absorb nitrogen from the atmosphere and convert it to nitrates, a form that can be used by the alder. In return, the alder provides sugar (food) to the bacteria through photosynthesis. Because of this relationship, alders are able to grow in many locations in Quetico where most plants can't survive. The alder/nitrogen-fixing bacteria combination also increases the nitrate levels in the soil, thus improving soil conditions for future plant growth.

This type of symbiotic relationship that is so important to the productivity of our forests, also plays a vital role in our production of food. Farmers and gardeners use the association between nitrogen-fixing bacteria and domesticated plants to enrich the soil in gardens and agricultural areas. Alfalfa and the various edible legumes, such as the numerous varieties of peas and beans, have nitrogen-fixing bacteria associated with their roots. Their symbiotic relationship with nitrogen-fixing bacteria increases the levels of nitrates, an important ingredient in fertilizers, in the soil. Wild members of the bean family in Quetico, such as white clover and American vetch, also harbour nitrogen-fixing bacteria in their roots and add to the nitrate levels in the soils where they grow.

SYMBIOTIC FUNGUS

Although symbiotic relationships can occur between any combination of organisms, the relationships between plants and fungi are especially important in the Quetico-Superior ecology. Plants, including everything from Calypso orchids to giant white pines, appear to be separate and independent organisms above the ground. Their independence, however, vanishes underground where fungal connections to other plants or even to other fungi, form a network of interconnected life. It is known that many plants in the Quetico-Superior, including trees like white pine, black spruce, and birch, grow faster when their roots grow in association with a fungus.

The symbiotic relationship between plant roots and a soil fungus is known as mycorrhiza. Mycorrhiza, which means "fungus root," was first identified over one hundred years ago. It was originally believed that these underground relationships are a relatively rare occurrence, but it is now thought that over 95 percent of all plant species form these symbiotic relationships. With mycorrhizal connections, the thread-like underground fungus becomes an extension of the plant's roots and the clear distinction between the two becomes blurred. Most soil fungi are decomposers that obtain nutrients from decaying material in the soil. By attaching themselves to a plant's roots, they act as underground extensions of the plant and assist the plant in absorbing nutrients from the soil. The fungus also benefits from the association by having direct access to the energy produced by the photosynthetic plant. Fungi have been found to utilize up to half of the plant's photosynthetic production in exchange for aiding the plant to obtain nutrients. In political jargon it is a "win-win situation," but biologists refer to it as mutualism.

Fungi are extremely efficient at obtaining nutrients, such as phosphates, from the soil because they produce enzymes that break down complex organic matter into smaller substances that are easier to absorb. Tree roots are unable to do this, and in areas that are usually low in nutrients, such as

Quetico Park and the rest of the Quetico-Superior, their symbiotic relationships with fungi are crucial for their survival. The interactions with soil fungi must be especially important for trees growing in the small pockets of soil in bedrock and on cliffs.

SYMBIOTIC MUSHROOMS

The fungi that live in the ground, including those involved in mycorrhizae, are thin threads and a hand lens or a microscope is needed to see them clearly. A mushroom is the visible, reproductive body — the "fruiting structure" of a fungus — that appears on the surface. Except for the brief time that the fungus is producing spores in the above-ground mushroom, the organism is simply a mass of fine threads (known as *hyphae*) in the soil. Many mushrooms are saprophytes — an organism that derives its nourishment from dead organic matter — and their hyphae are used to extract nutrients from dead and decaying plant material. Black morels and the common supermarket mushrooms are examples of saprophytes.

Many of the non-saprophytic mushrooms that grow near the base of trees have their underground portions in direct contact with tree roots. Birch trees, including the familiar white birch, have a number of these symbiotic partnerships. Two common non-saprophytic species, one poisonous and the other edible and delicious, are found in Quetico Park. The red-and-white fly agaric mushroom, also known by its scientific name, *Amanita muscaria*, and the edible chanterelle mushroom, *Cantharellus cibarius*, form underground networks with birch and pine trees that benefit both the trees and the mushrooms. As in most other mycorrizal associations, they each benefit from their underground connections. Mushrooms obtain valuable sugar energy from the tree, while the tree obtains nutrients from the

This *Amanita muscaria* mushroom grew near Beaverhouse Lake in Quetico Park.

mushroom whose hyphae excel at extracting nutrients from the soil. Trees with mushroom connections also appear to be less susceptible to soil pathogens and more resistant to frost damage.

AN UNSEEN, UNDERGROUND WEB

Surprisingly, sometimes *more* than two species are symbiotically linked underground. It has been shown that some of the food produced by one plant may pass through a mycorrhizal fungus in the soil and end up being utilized by another plant. These plants, quite often from different species, have an underground connection through a fungus.

Consequently, any white birch at a sunny spot at the edge of a clearing in Quetico may have some of the food (energy) that it produces by photosynthesis transferred, via underground fungal threads, to a Jack pine growing in a more shaded area. Since these exchanges are seldom just in one direction, the white birch might, in return, receive some nutrients the Jack pine obtains from the soil. These relationships may involve many species since the Jack pine's roots could also be in association with other soil fungi that are connected to other plants.

The idea that an unseen fungal network links many plants underground is simply astonishing. The extent and importance of this network, however, is only beginning to be understood. These fungal networks can apparently span many generations of trees and persist as individual trees die and are replaced by others. Some ideas, such as the interconnections between living things, are expressed in religions and in cultural beliefs long before scientists discover them. The interconnectedness of living things found in Buddhism and Hinduism is central to many other religions and cultures, as well. Richard K. Nelson, an anthropologist who lived with the Koyukon in Alaska, was told by an elder that "… the country knows. It feels what is happening to it. I guess everything is connected together somehow, under the ground."[3]

SYMBIOTIC BEINGS ON A SYMBIOTIC PLANET

Biologists have traditionally emphasized the ecological and evolutionary importance of competition for resources. One of the basic tenets of evolution is that resources are limited and there is competition between individuals for these scarce resources. The statement "survival of the fittest" often summarizes this competition among species.

Recently, there has been an increased interest in symbiosis and the role of collaboration between different species. Fitness can be increased by co-operation as well as by competition. Plants obviously compete for nutrients, water, and access to sunlight. However, it is becoming more apparent that a plant can also obtain nutrients and water by cooperating with a fungus.

The American physician and biologist Lewis Thomas, wrote: "A century ago there was a consensus that evolution was a record of open warfare amongst competing species, that the fittest were the strongest aggressors. Now it begins to look different. The greatest successes in evolution, the mutants who have made it, have done so by fitting in with, and sustaining the rest of life."[4] As we have seen, our forests are loaded with plants and animals that compete most effectively by assisting each other. This co-operation between species, known as symbiosis, is proving to be the rule rather than the exception.

Lynn Margulis, a pioneer in research on symbiosis, has proposed that symbiosis plays a central role in evolution. She has turned the old cliché "nature red in tooth and claw" on its head by stating: "Life did not take over the globe by combat, but by networking."[5] Her catchphrase that we are "symbiotic beings on a symbiotic planet" is increasingly supported by biological studies. It is now apparent that the health, range, and diversity of life in the Quetico-Superior area have been greatly increased because of symbiosis.

CHAPTER TEN

LICHENS:
ENDURING, DELIGHTFUL, ORGANIC CRUD

Lichens were among the first signs of life in the Quetico-Superior area after the glacier's retreat. The movement and weight of glacial ice crushed and pulverized the earth's surface and left behind a mixture of bedrock and various sizes of broken rock. Due to their symbiotic nature, lichens were better equipped to grow on these barren substrates than were plants. Recent studies on succession following the retreat of alpine glaciers in Alaska have shown that lichens appear within one year of the retreat of the ice and they probably were growing just as quickly after the retreat of the continental glacier at the end of the last ice age. Because lichens produce weak acids that speed up the weathering process, they helped set the stage for the rich and diverse ecosystems that followed.

Lichens formed a thin veneer of life that, in addition to initiating biological activity, also intercepted and trapped dust and silt created by the glacier. This increased the pace of soil development and helped create a richer environment for the spores of mosses and the seeds of plants that could then become established among the clumps of lichens and the pockets of soil. Although lichens are known as "nature's pioneers" because of their ability to become established on newly exposed surfaces such as the bedrock and boulders left behind by glacial activity, these tough, pioneer organisms continue to thrive in Quetico Park. They manage to cling tenaciously to rock faces released from glacial ice over twelve thousand years ago while continuously colonizing freshly eroded sections.

Lichens are often overlooked because they are so common that they become part of the background. It's not hard to find lichens; simply look where other forms of life find the conditions too harsh to survive. In addition to sheer cliff walls and the surfaces of large boulders, they also live on the trunks of mature trees, the branches of living and dead trees, and in the shaded acidic soils under pines. They can also be found on antlers shed by moose and deer and on decaying bones. Lichens even grow on the shells of living tortoises and on the exoskeletons of insects.

Lichens grow on a variety of surfaces, including bone. This cow moose skull, which has probably lain on the ground for only a year or two, already supports a light coating of lichens. This photo was taken near the Pickerel River.

SYNERGETIC SYMBIOSIS

Beatrix Potter, who is best remembered for her children's books about Peter Rabbit, was an early advocate of the idea, first proposed by Swiss botanist Simon Schwendener, that lichens are symbiotic associations of two different organisms. When doing intricate drawings of lichens, she concluded that Schwendener's "dual hypothesis" was correct. Her lichen illustrations, drawn prior to her becoming a writer and illustrator of children's books, are still held in high regard for their detailed and accurate portrayal of the delicate beauty of these extraordinary organisms. The scientific establishment in the late 1800s, however, did not take radical ideas, especially those coming from a woman artist, very seriously. The dual nature of lichens was an idea that eventually gathered momentum and spread slowly through the scientific community. In 1929, noted authors and biologists H.G. Wells and Julian Huxley stated, "A lichen is no more a single organism than a dairy farm is a single organism."[1] After decades of study and the extensive use of microscopes, genetic analysis, and laboratory experiments, the symbiotic nature of lichens is now well established.

Lichens are able to grow in inhospitable places because they are composed of two organisms working together: a fungus and a photosynthetic partner. The photosynthetic partner, also known as a photobiont, produces the sugar (food); the fungus provides a protective cover and absorbs the water and minerals that both partners need. The photosynthetic part of the lichen is usually an algae, but in some cases it is a type of photosynthetic bacteria known as cyanobacteria. The algae or cyanobacteria have the critical role of producing food for the lichen. The fungus gives the lichen its overall shape and structure and produces pigments that shield its partner from ultraviolet light. These pigments are responsible for the wide variety of colours found in lichens. The fungus also has fine but tough threads that securely attach the lichen to the surface it's growing on and also absorb water, minerals, and other nutrients. Acids secreted by the fungus are strong enough to slowly break down rock into minerals that are utilized by the lichen.

The interrelationship between the fungus and the photosynthetic partner is both intriguing and complex. Since one lichen partner makes food by photosynthesis and the other partner offers protection and is good at extracting nutrients, together they make a potent combination. Their symbiotic partnership allows lichens to survive where neither partner could live on its own. Lichens are a perfect example of the dictum that "the whole is greater than the sum of its parts."

The photosynthetic partner and the fungus blend into each other to the extent that magnification is needed to resolve where one ends and the other begins. They become so reliant on each other that they cease functioning as wholly separate organisms. The apparently new organism is even given a new scientific name and a common name even though it is an amalgam of two different organisms. An example of this is the red-capped ground lichen known as British soldiers. It has the scientific name *Cladonia cristatella* but is composed of two separate entities — an algae and a fungus — each of which also has its own scientific name.

Although much is known about many of the common lichen species, many of the lichens are unknown and unnamed. Recent studies in forests in the Pacific Northwest and the northeastern United States found many new species in the canopies of old-growth trees. It is exciting that new species probably also exist in the canopies of the old-growth red and white pines — which have hardly been examined — in our region. Recently, biologists found that some lichens are made up of more than two species. They discovered lichens composed of a fungus and both an alga and a cyanobacterium. A symbiotic relationship among three different species opens up a whole new world of interactions that lichenologists are eagerly exploring. Joe Walewski, in his enjoyable and informative book *Lichens of the North Woods*, notes that "the more we learn about lichens, the more we realize how much we don't know."[2]

Most biologists believe that both the fungus and its photosynthetic partner benefit from their relationship and that the relationship is an example of mutualism. Some biologists, however, propose that only the fungus benefits; that the photosynthetic partner is a captive of the fungus and that the relationship is a mild form of parasitism. In support of the idea that the fungus is the dominant partner, lichenologist Trevor Goward of British Columbia has described lichens as "fungi that have discovered agriculture."[3]

Whatever the nature of the relationship, it is apparent that the symbiotic nature of lichens gives them an advantage over other types of organisms, especially in very harsh environments. Lichens are found in the heat of the Sahara desert and in the extreme cold of Antarctica where very few plants, fungus, or bacteria survive on their own. Lichens can survive long periods of drought and they simply shut down in the extreme cold of winter and the extreme heat of summer. Consequently, they are found in some of the hottest and driest places on this planet and also in some of the coldest.

Lichens are able to photosynthesise at temperatures as low as -20°C. The ability to photosynthesize at temperatures well below freezing gives lichens a huge advantage over plants in cold climates. It allows lichens in areas like the Quetico-Superior region to begin producing food in late winter when there is still ice on the lakes and deep snow in the woods and, at the other end of the growing season, to continue photosynthesizing after lakes have frozen.

LICHEN GROWTH FORMS: CRUSTOSE, FOLIOSE, AND FRUTICOSE

Lichens are found in three main growth forms: crustose, foliose, and fruticose. Crustose lichens are basically two-dimensional and form a crust on the surface on which they are living. Crustose lichens are commonly found on rock but also grow on bark and rotten wood. They look like old, thick dabs of paint and have been described by geologists as "rock-obscuring organic crud." Geologists use a rock hammer to knock off a surface piece of rock so that they can see what the rock, rather than the lichen on the rock surface, looks like. Crustose lichens, the slowest growing form of lichen with some species growing less than a millimetre a year, can be extremely old. One example, a colony of yellow map lichens in northern Sweden, was found to be over 4,550 years old. The rate of lichen growth has been determined on old gravestones by comparing crustose lichens on photographs taken over one hundred years apart. The slow growth of crustose lichens has also been used for dating artifacts, including the stone statues on Easter Island.

Most of the cliffs, bedrock, and boulders in the Quetico-Superior landscape are covered with crustose lichens that come in a variety of colours. Shades of grey seem to dominate, but brown, black, white, orange, red, yellow, and even blue lichens also occur. Lichens with a blue tint grow on sloping bedrock along the shoreline at King's Point on Basswood Lake.

Foliose lichens are leaf-shaped and are usually yellow-green, brown, or grey. They are the most rapidly growing type of lichen, but even their

Luxurious crustose lichens of several colours grow on a Beaverhouse Lake cliff.

relatively rapid growth rate rarely exceeds two-and-a-half centimetres a year. A common example of a foliose lichen found in in Quetico Park is *tripe des roche* or rock tripe. This very large, scaly lichen is commonly seen on lakeside boulders. During extended periods of hot and dry conditions this foliose lichen looks like large, black, lifeless scales on the rock. It survives these dry periods and quickly revives with the first rain, turns grey, and becomes softer to the touch. This unappealing lichen can be boiled and eaten as an emergency source of food. Survivors of airplane crashes and others who have run out of food have survived by eating rock tripe. The Franklin Expedition in the 1820s[4] subsisted for eleven days in the Canadian Arctic eating this lichen after running out of food on an Arctic trek.

Fruticose lichens, the third growth form, either stand upright and are described as "shrub-like" or are hanging filaments described as "beard-like." They grow on thin, nutrient-poor soils and decomposing wood. Fruticose lichens can be found growing with moss in damp areas and frequently grow along the gravelly edges of Quetico Park and BWCAW portage trails. There are a wide variety of small, shrub-like fruticose lichens that grow on the ground. In some locations, such as along the fringes of the old logging road east of French Lake, growths of fruticose lichens resemble a miniature forest. The shapes — goblets, funnels, wands, horns, and cups — are diverse and fascinating. Most are drab, but

A variety of fruticose ground lichens, including British Soldiers with their red hats, dominate the growth at the base of a small, dead spruce tree. Luxurious growths of small lichens are commonly found in difficult habitats such as this gravelly edge of a Quetico Park portage trail.

made a tasty snack when walking in the bush, I tried this lichen and found it had a pleasant but bland taste that changed to bitter if chewed for very long. Many lichens have a bitter taste, possibly because the fungal partner often produces toxic chemicals to keep insects and animals from consuming them, a good reason to avoid eating any lichen or fungus, including mushrooms, unless it is known for sure that it is edible.

LICHEN HABITATS

Lichens grow on a wider range of surfaces than plants do, and they even grow on plants. They grow on the bark of trees and are especially plentiful on the bark of old-growth pines. They don't usually damage these trees; they merely use them as substrate. Lichens also grow on trees and shrubs that are dead or dying and the branches of these trees are often covered with a variety of lichens.

red-capped British soldiers and red-fruited pixie cups add colour to the miniature landscapes.

Reindeer lichens, also known as caribou lichen, caribou moss, and reindeer moss, are fruticose lichens frequently encountered in the Quetico-Superior region. A variety of different lichens are lumped together under these terms and caribou evidently eat all of them. Although eaten year round, these lichen are the primary source of food for caribou in the winter and are occasionally eaten by moose.

Old man's beard is an example of the "beard-like" form of fruticose lichens. Having been told that it

Some lichens have specific nutritional needs and can only be found in specialized natural habitats in the Quetico-Superior area. An example is the nitrogen-loving lichens found on cliff faces and boulders that regularly get splattered with bird droppings. Commonly seen below raven nests, they utilize the nutrients in the droppings found below nests and perches. An excess of bird droppings, however, can kill vegetation growing on the ground below the nests. This is most obvious below eagles' nests and in great blue heron rookeries.

Lichens grow in abundance on this seven-centimetre (three-inch) tip of a branch on a dying spruce tree on an island in Cache Bay.

Cliffs are vertical mosaics with almost as many species of lichens as the number of plant species you'd find on a similar-sized plot of ground. The diversity of lichens on a cliff depends on the pitch, rock type, and orientation of the cliff. Those lichens that require more water can be found on north-facing cliffs or areas that regularly get runoff from above. Species that can survive with very little moisture are

165

usually found on unshaded, south-facing cliffs. Only those places where rock has recently broken off, or areas of exceptional dryness, are totally devoid of lichens. Areas that have a combination of adequate light and some moisture trickling down from above are usually the richest in lichen diversity and growth.

The type of rock is also an important factor in what species of lichen grow. The cliffs on Quetico Park's Emerald Lake are high in lime and have a very different variety of lichens from those found on the siltstone cliffs on Knife Lake or the granite cliffs on Quetico Lake. The Emerald Lake cliffs have striking orange lichens that brighten up the lake even on the dullest of days. The orange lichens on granite cliffs in the northern part of Quetico are equally compelling, but are usually of a different species.

Lichens can also grow on a wide variety of man-made surfaces. They are found on asphalt shingles, brick buildings, cement bridges, sidewalks, and even on stained glass. A study in France showed that sixteen species of lichens grew on one large, old stained-glass church window. The growth of lichens on stained glass is a problem with many of the old churches in Europe. Lichens also grow on natural surfaces, such as stone, that have been altered by man. Cemeteries feature a remarkably diverse community of lichens growing on gravestones. The varieties of lichens is determined by the type of rock and the orientation of the gravestones.

Most of the man-made structures in Quetico-Superior support the growth of lichens. The few

Orange and grey crustose lichens enliven a gravestone in Thunder Bay, Ontario.

old abandoned Ministry of Natural Resources and United States Forest Service buildings have abundant growths of lichens. Even the buildings still in use and regularly maintained, such as the Quetico Park ranger stations, have places where lichens manage to flourish. Lichens also usually find places on signs, docks and wooden bridges — like the one over Sucker Creek at Prairie Portage — where they can grow.

LICHENS AS ANIMAL FOOD AND SHELTER

Many creatures in the Quetico-Superior area, from chickadees to moose, utilize lichens for food or shelter. Both the barren-ground caribou that lived here

166

at the end of the ice age and woodland caribou that occupied the area as recently as seventy years ago relied on reindeer lichens for a major part of their winter diet. Caribou use their large hooves to dig through the snow to get to the lichens and leave large circular depressions, known as "craters, " when they are feeding in the winter. The word *caribou* comes from a Mi'Kmaq word that means "one who digs." Moose and white-tailed deer also consume lichens, but not nearly to the extent that caribou consume them. The exception can be in the winter when the snow is deep and food hard to find. Deer are at a disadvantage because they have small hooves and, unlike caribou, are not adept at digging through snow to get at the reindeer lichens underneath.

Some fruticose lichens, such as Old man's beard, hang down from tree branches. This hair-like lichen can be over thirty centimetres long and, since it hangs down from branches, is accessible even when snow is deep. Deeper snow can even make some available that the deer can't reach when there is little or no snow. Often, there is a browse line visible, with Old Man's Beard found only above the height deer can reach. Although important as a survival food, it is evidently not heavily utilized when other foods are available.

Northern flying squirrels, which inhabit the Quetico-Superior region, are known to eat significant amounts of lichens and also to use lichens to line their nests. Red-backed voles also consume lichens, especially during the winter when food is scarce.

Birds don't eat lichens very often but many species — including common mergansers, ruby-throated hummingbirds, and boreal chickadees — use lichens as nesting material. Although many lichens are edible, a few are poisonous. The wolf lichen (*Letharia vulpine*) contains a toxic, bright yellow pigment and it was used to poison wolves and foxes in Scandinavia. This species also occurs on the west coast of North America but is not found in Quetico Park.

PICTOGRAPHS, LICHENOGRAPHS, AND LICHENS

Lichens grow on the same cliffs where pictographs are located and have grown over the paintings on many sites. The location of pictograph sites was undoubtedly influenced by the presence or absence of lichen growth. Cliff locations with overhangs that reduced the amount of surface moisture, and therefore the amount of lichen growth, were ideal locations for placing paintings. Orientation is another factor, and the vast majority of pictographs have enough of a southern exposure so that the sun helps in keeping the surface relatively dry. If conditions remained the same, pictographs placed in these locations hundreds of years ago should still have relatively little lichen growth and should still be visible today. However, cliffs also change with time and ideal locations in the past may now have thick lichen growth that totally obscures the paintings underneath. The crustose lichens found on cliffs grow so slowly that their progress in covering a pictograph has been used to try, with relatively little success, to date pictographs.

In some places in North America, lichens were scraped away to leave an image surrounded by undisturbed lichens. These images, known as lichen-oglyphs or lichenographs, obviously have a limited life span unless they are periodically renewed. They have been found on Lake Superior and Lake of the Woods, but, to my knowledge, nowhere in the Quetico-Superior landscape.

There is a reference to an inscription in lichens in *A Tippy Canoe and Canada Too*, a charming book for young adults from the 1940s by Sam Campbell.[5] The book describes a quest to find Sanctuary Lake, a Quetico Park lake of unsurpassed beauty. The canoeists were seeking a mysterious lake where Joe, a legendary Indian guide, had written his name in lichens on a small cliff. Sam Campbell's books have inspired decades of dedicated readers and a few canoeists seek out specific locations mentioned in his writings. When Marie and I were rangers at Cache Bay we met two separate groups on quests to find Sanctuary Lake with its lichen inscription.

LICHENS AS POLLUTION INDICATORS

Although lichens are extremely hardy, they don't stand up very well to air pollution. Due to their susceptibility to damage and even death from air pollution, lichens are reliable air-quality indicators. Since they don't have root systems, they get almost all of their nutrients from the air or from the surface they are growing on. Consequently, some lichens are sensitive to sulfur dioxide from coal, some to acid rain, and others to other gases or heavy metals found in polluted air.

Lichens obtain most of their moisture from rain and consequently also take up many of the pollutants that are dissolved in the rainwater. For this reason, lichens were found to be the most radioactive organisms tested after the Chernobyl nuclear disaster. Lichen diversity has been found to drop dramatically when air pollution increases and the disappearance of lichens from European cities has been documented for the last one hundred years. Many species that were common in urban areas around the world are now difficult to locate. *Hypogymnia physodes*, a species that is found on the bark of conifer trees in the Quetico-Superior area, is a sensitive barometer of air pollution, and, when sulphur levels are high, it dies off.

Students at Two Harbors High School north of Duluth, Minnesota, are conducting an interesting, long-term study of lichens. The project was started by Dennis Herschbach in the 1970s with the goal of introducing his biology students to scientific research and lichens. They are finding lower quantities and less diversity of lichens downwind from Highway 61 and in the denser populated areas around Two Harbors. Their results mirror other, more extensive studies conducted by universities and government agencies.

HIDING IN PLAIN SITE

Lichens are remarkable. Because they are a combination of two different organisms, they can photosynthesize like a plant while decomposing like a fungus. They utilize their dual natures to survive in places where conditions are harsh and nutrients hard to find. They are superb examples of how organisms that co-operate and work together can out-compete individual organisms.

Lichens grow almost everywhere and tend to be overlooked because they simply become part of the background. On the cliffs and boulders of the Quetico-Superior landscape, they form a living veneer that often obscures the rock beneath. On your next trip, take a small hand magnifier, like those that geologists use, and closely examine objects at your campsite — the log you sit on around the campfire, the rock from which you dive into the lake, and the place where you set up your tent. All will have lichens growing on them; indeed, it can be difficult to find a surface that doesn't contain any. A magnified view helps to bring these diverse and colourful organisms, which usually blend into the background, into the foreground where they belong. It is easy to become as captivated by lichens as Henry David Thoreau, who described his fascination with lichens as being so strong it "prevents my seeing aught else in a walk."[6]

CHAPTER ELEVEN

THE ORCHID AND THE FUNGUS:
SYMBIOTIC PARTNERS

While portaging my canoe across a flat, rocky portion of the Silver Falls portage between Cache Bay and Saganagons Lake, I looked down and noticed an unusual, multicoloured flower growing just centimetres from the edge of the trail. Although not far from the descent to Saganagons Lake, I welcomed an excuse to put the canoe down, rest for a moment, and examine the flower that had caught my attention. To my amazement it was a Calypso orchid, an elusive plant I had been searching for for many years. Having always looked in swamps and wet areas where I thought orchids should grow, I was astonished to find one growing in a dry, relatively barren area where hundreds of people must have nearly stepped on it. The combination of small size and relative rarity makes the Calypso orchid a difficult plant to find in Quetico. Distinguished by its vivid colouring and intriguing shape, it is also known as the fairy slipper orchid. The plant is only several centimetres tall, but the small flower is simply stunning.

My fascination with orchids and symbiotic relationships began when I saw that Calypso orchid unexpectedly growing along the Silver Falls portage. I couldn't help but wonder why this orchid was growing in such an unlikely place and why there was just one. Since orchids are primarily tropical plants, there had to be something special occurring to allow this plant, and orchids in general, to grow in cold northern forests.

ORCHIDS AND SYMBIOSIS

Susan Orleans, who has written a book about people obsessed with orchids, has called orchids "the sexiest flowers on earth,"[1] and there are many other references that link orchids and sex. The name orchid derives from the Latin *orchis*, which means testicle and refers to the shape of the plant's tubers. Scholars in the Middle Ages even suggested that orchids grew from the sperm of wild animals that had fallen to the ground. *The British Herbal Guide* of 1653, however, indicated that there was a female sexuality to orchids. It recommended that orchids be handled

Surprisingly, a Calypso orchid grows alongside the Silver Falls portage between Saganaga and Saganagons lakes.

with care because "they are hot and moist in operation, under the dominion of Venus, and provoke lust exceedingly."[2] Why, then, are flowers that are "hot and moist in operation" found in the cold and often dry Quetico?

There are over thirty thousand species of orchids in the world and the vast majority of them are found in the tropics. Orchids first evolved in the warm and moist areas of the world and are the most at home there. As they spread out of the tropics, they evolved special traits and made adaptations that allow them to grow in colder climates. Their seeds, so tiny that they are sometimes referred to as "dust seeds," lack the food resources that are found in most seeds. The combination of the tiny seeds and the associated problems that arise from their small size, have caused botanists to refer to orchids as being "born prematurely." In order to germinate and survive, orchids require a symbiotic relationship with a fungus to provide the nutrients necessary for germination and growth.

Due to the destruction of natural habitats and the rampant collection of orchids for sale to private orchid growers, many of the world's wild orchids are threatened with extinction. One approach to slow the rate of extinction is to grow some of the threatened orchids "in captivity." In order to do this, botanists need to deermine which soil fungi are required to form symbiotic relationships with the endangered orchids. This can be a slow process because the type of soil fungus that forms a symbiotic relationship with an orchid may be different for each species of orchid. Grace Pendergast, a British orchid expert, and a team of researchers at the Kew Royal Botanical Gardens in England have been searching for the specific fungus, from thousands of candidates, that interacts with each threatened orchid species. British biologist Tom Wakeford has described their technique. They put:

[A] few of the pinprick-size seeds of a particular species in the middle of a small dish of sterilized nutrient jelly. On the edge of the dish they place a small colony of a species of fungus. The seeds soon prepare to germinate, but are unable to grow with no food source. However, from the edge of the dish a web of fungal threads, each smaller than a fiber-optic strand, weaves its way toward the embryonic plant. Pendergast and her colleagues then cross their fingers. Will the two organisms be compatible? If they are, then when the thread reaches the embryo there is the biological equivalent of a flash of lightning, and both organisms start growing faster.[3]

The germination of orchid seeds and, for many orchid species, the subsequent growth of the plant are both dependent on a symbiotic relationship between the orchid and a fungus. Orchids are able to survive, and even thrive, in conditions and environments far removed from most of their tropical relatives only if a suitable fungal partner is in the soil. The orchids found in Quetico and the rest of the Quetico-Superior region are successful because there are compatible fungi in the soil. Without this, orchids couldn't grow here.

Of the orchids growing in Quetico, the symbiotic relationship of the moccasin flower, *Cypripedium acaule,* has been the most thoroughly studied. Its seed, which is smaller than the period at the end of this sentence, requires a specific soil fungus from the genus *Rhizoctonia* in order to successfully germinate and begin its development into a mature plant. Moccasin flowers (also known as the pink lady's slipper) are thought to be an extreme case of a symbiotic relationship with a fungus. They are not just aided by their association with a fungus; they require it for their very existence. If the fungus *Rhizoctonia* isn't present, the seeds don't germinate and the moccasin flower doesn't grow — no fungus, no plant. There are few examples of plants, other than orchids, that are this reliant on another species.

The moccasin flower is notoriously hard to transplant and even harder to grow from seed, apparently because of its dependence on a fungus that isn't present in many soils. A few years ago, an acquaintance in Thunder Bay told me he had successfully transplanted one in his backyard after a number of tries. Seemingly, his transplant worked because

Photo by Marie Nelson, Thunder Bay, Ontario.

A sensuous moccasin flower was found near the edge of a beach on a campsite on Beaverhouse Lake.

he took a lot of soil containing the fungus with the plant and in this way created an environment very similar to that from which the moccasin flower had been taken. Transplanted orchids require a location that is suitable not only for the orchid, but for the fungus, as well. Since moccasin flowers can take ten years from germination to reach the flowering stage, they are extremely vulnerable to being picked. Consequently, plants in parks and wilderness areas should not be picked or disturbed. Even outside of protected areas, it is better to simply leave them in the wild. The best way to protect orchids, or any plant for that matter, is to preserve the integrity of the land on which they grow.

QUETICO-SUPERIOR ORCHIDS

I am not sure if we should be surprised that there are so few orchids in Quetico — Shan Walshe listed just twenty-three species for the park — or if we should be amazed that there are so *many* species of orchids in the relatively cold environment along the Minnesota-Ontario border. Although northern orchids are limited in number, they grow in a wide variety of habitats and their beautiful, exotic flowers can be found in shaded coniferous forests, on rocky ledges, and in wet, swampy areas. However, despite the park's supporting a variety of orchids, most of them grow in specialized habitats and are fairly hard to find. The moccasin flower is the only orchid that is frequently seen in Quetico and many others, such as the Calypso orchid, usually require diligent searching.

The moccasin flower, one of the park's largest and most beautiful orchids, is usually in flower by the middle of June and is found throughout the area. This radiant pink flower is known by a variety of names, including pink lady's slipper and stemless lady's slipper. The moccasin flower and other closely related lady's slippers grow in northern climates around the world, and in all countries the names are remarkably similar. In Germany it is called *Frauenschuh* (woman's shoe), in France it is known as *Sabot de Venus* (Venus's shoe), and in Russia it is *Mariin Bashnachock* (Mary's slipper). This hardy plant can be found in a variety of habitats, although it seems to prefer the acid soils of coniferous forests where most plants have difficulty growing. The adaptable moccasin flower and the fungus *Rhizoctonia* are also at home on sandy soil under Jack pine, in wet black spruce forests, on the edge of acidic bogs, on dry, rocky soil, and even on exposed rocky ridges

There are two other lady's slipper orchids in the Quetico-Superior region. The yellow lady's slipper, *Cypripedium calceolus,* has been found in only two locations in Quetico Park and is also rare in the BWCAW. The showy lady's slipper, *Cypripedium reginae*, is the state flower of Minnesota. The Quetico-Superior area is near the northern edge of its range, and as a result it is rare in the BWCAW. There have been no reported sightings in Quetico Park.

The Calypso orchid, *Calypso bulbosa*, belongs to a sub-family of orchids composed of over ten thousand species, most of which are tropical plants that grow in trees. Yet, due to co-operation with a soil fungus,

The Calypso orchid can grow in Quetico because of its association with an underground fungus.

Arethusa is an orchid that is occasionally found along the edges of bogs in Quetico.

it has adapted to a much shorter growing season and long, cold winters. This orchid has a circumpolar distribution and can be found in Siberia, Sweden, Finland, and Russia, in addition to the United States and Canada. In spite of its wide distribution, nowhere is it regarded as a common plant and in some states and countries it is rare or endangered.

There are numerous bog orchids in the Quetico-Superior, including three large, beautiful pink orchids — the Rose Pogonia orchid, *Pogonia ophioglossoides*; the grass-pink orchid, *Calopogon pulchellus;* and swamp-pink orchid, *Arethusa bulbosa.* They sometimes grow on mats of vegetation along the shoreline of lakes and boggy creeks. Thus,

Photo by Marie Nelson, Thunder Bay, Ontario.

This hooded ladies' tresses orchid, rare in Quetico Park, was found growing in silty sand on the shore of Beaverhouse Lake.

that are strikingly different from those of other plants. The leaves are said to resemble rattlesnake skin and at one time were thought to be a treatment for snakebite. There are two species of ladies' tresses orchids, hooded ladies' tresses, *Spiranthes romanzoffiana,* and slender ladies' tresses, *Spiranthes gracilis,* in Quetico and both have small flowers that spiral around the stem and resemble braided hair.

Two of the orchids found in the Quetico-Superior landscape lack chlorophyll and are unable to make their own food by photosynthesis. Spotted coralroot, *Corallorhiza maculata,* and early coralroot, *Corallorhiza trifida,* are called coralroots because they have short, stubby, underground stems (rhizomes) that resemble coral. Since these plants are unable to supply food for themselves, mycorrhizal fungi associated with their rhizomes and roots have to supply all their nutritional needs by obtaining food from nearby plants or from dead organic matter.

these flowers can sometimes be seen without getting out of the canoe.

Some orchids with unusual characteristics can also be found. Two species, dwarf rattlesnake plantain, *Goodyera repens,* and greater rattlesnake plantain, *Goodyera tesselata,* have unusual mottled leaves

A BIT OF THE TROPICS IN THE QUETICO-SUPERIOR

Orchids are not only sexy and beautiful, they are also a clear and dramatic case of plants that are totally dependent on fungi for their very survival. The symbiosis between orchids and soil fungi makes it possible for plants that are more at home in the hot, moist conditions in the tropics to grow in the Quetico-Superior.

Although orchids require fungi for seed germination, the "infection" by the fungi is apparently greater for northern orchids than for tropical ones. These plants with tiny seeds and intricate, showy blooms need all the help they can get to successfully live so far north. It is the symbiotic interaction between a plant and a fungus that makes it possible for canoeists to see the Calypso orchid, a migrant from the tropics, growing in Quetico beneath boreal trees such as black spruce and Jack pine. As the human impact on the landscape continues to increase, plants that require undisturbed habitats and have other specific needs will become more dependent on wilderness areas such as Quetico Park and the BWCAW for their continued existence.

CHAPTER TWELVE

ANTLER LOGIC:
MOOSE RESEARCH IN QUETICO PARK

Concern over the dwindling moose population was the original impetus that led to the protection of Quetico in 1909. These animals were heavily hunted in the early 1900s to feed the men in the logging and mining camps thriving in northwestern Ontario at that time. As both enterprises were labour-intensive and the men required large quantities of food, game animals in the vicinity of the camps were killed to supply meat for the workers. Moose, known as "pine beef," were harvested so intensely that the Ontario government was pressured to create a reserve to ensure their survival. Since the government was also eager to protect the large stands of pine in the area, it established the Quetico Forest Reserve in 1909 — the first official designation of Quetico as a special place.

Quetico's original status as a forest reserve and later as a provincial park gave moose the protected status that allowed them to not only survive but to flourish. By the 1970s, the moose population in Quetico Park had increased to the degree that they became the subject of a major scientific study.

MOOSE RESEARCH IN QUETICO PARK

Although the moose population in northwestern Ontario had remained relatively stable for several decades, several years of near record successful hunts in the early 1970s had moose biologists concerned about the long-term viability of the animal in the area. In those years of high harvest, moose-hunting season for hunters using rifles opened near the beginning of October, a time when the moose rut is still near its peak. It was becoming apparent that there was a significant increase in mortality of bulls when moose-hunting season and the rut overlapped. Moose biologists felt that more research was needed to obtain a better understanding of the timing of the moose rut so that the hunting season could be adjusted to miss the main part of the rut when bulls were the most vulnerable.

Hunting isn't allowed in provincial parks and aerial surveys indicated very high moose densities in the northeastern corner of Quetico Park. Since this area was logged just prior to the logging ban in

1972, logging roads gave researchers easy access to the potential research area and the cutovers provided good visibility. The combination of these factors suggested that Quetico could provide an ideal location to study the behaviour of moose during the rut without the influence of hunting disturbance.

Plans for a study of moose in Quetico Park originated with discussions in 1974 involving Tim Timmermann, the regional moose biologist for the Ministry of Natural Resources who was an expert on moose management and the driving force behind Ontario's use of selective hunting and quotas to maintain the moose population; Dr. Tony Bubenik, a wildlife researcher for the MNR who was born in Czechoslovakia and who would, over the course of his career, write nearly three hundred scientific papers; and Shan Walshe, the Quetico Park naturalist who excelled at calling moose and was enthusiastic about working with two moose experts. It was fortunate that this dynamic trio, all excellent fieldworkers who relished the joys and difficulties of working in a wilderness park, were available to conduct this important field study.

The first two seasons of the study, 1975 and 1976, were dedicated primarily to Tony Bubenik's investigations into the behavioural response(s) of bull moose to a dummy antlered moose head. When conducting research in Alaska, he came up with the innovative — and seemingly bizarre — technique of wearing a styrofoam moose head complete with interchangeable moose antlers of varying sizes. He used the moose head to study the responses of bull moose during the rut to different-sized antlers and different head motions. Apparently, he was the first person in North America, if not the world, to use this research technique. He may have obtained the idea of using a dummy moose head from Native Americans who disguised themselves with antlers and hides to closely approach their prey when hunting. These Quetico Park investigations were an important continuation of his Alaskan studies, later continued in Algonquin Park, into the role of antlers in the determination of social rank.

Bubenik used a life-size, styrofoam head that was covered with dark fabric and had variably

Tony Bubenik wears an antlered moose head in the study area near McKenzie Lake.

Courtesy of Tim Timmermann, Thunder Bay, Ontario.

This large, mature bull moose was called into the research area.

sized foam antlers that could be interchanged. He wrote, "The antlered head of a bull moose is the only center of visual attention for both sexes. Because of their importance as a visual stimulant, a bipedal man with an antlered head is as readily accepted as any quadrupedal one, despite the presence of human scent. Ergo, I was able to study communication among moose by wearing an antlered dummy moose head."[1]

Bubenik's research, with assistance from Timmermann and Walshe, involved calling in a moose and observing and photographing its responses to the size of the antlers and to the various movements of Bubenik's moose head. He found that when he wore antlers larger than those of the bull that was called out, the other bull would simply assess the size of his antlers and quietly walk away. When he wore antlers noticeably smaller than those of the other bull, the other bull would ritually paw the ground, move its head, and attempt to make it clear that he was the dominant bull. These assessments of comparative antler size are made by bulls so they don't waste valuable energy in combat that they could more profitably use in locating interested females. It was only when Bubenik put on antlers very similar in size to the other bull's antlers that the other bull would actively thrash the ground, become agitated, and be ready for physical conflict. He then knew it was time to take off the antlered head and look for a safe haven.

From 1977 through 1980, the research concentrated primarily on collecting data about the timing of the moose rut. This study was conducted by Ontario Ministry of Natural Resources wildlife biologists Tim Timmermann, Rick Gollat, John McNicol, and Mike Buss. They monitored moose activity along old logging roads in the study area in the northeast corner of the park, particularly concentrating on the areas to the north and west of McKenzie Lake and along part of the portage from Lindsay Lake to Cache Lake.

During September and early October they recorded fresh moose tracks, thrashing activity, rut pits, and other evidence of moose encounters. Eight towers, some of them from Bubenik's previous investigations, were used to observe moose responding to calls. The towers were also used at night, especially in 1980, when infrared night vision scopes were employed to observe the response to calls by moose after dark.

Their findings indicated there was very little rut activity until the antlers were rubbed free of velvet, which usually occurs at the very end of August or beginning of September. As the rut progressed, a general pattern of increasing moose mobility was observed. Thrashing, the hitting and rubbing of a bull's antlers on small trees or shrubs during the rut, began in early September and increased in frequency until it peaked during the last two weeks of September. Thrashing helps change antler's colour from the light bone hue just after the shedding of the velvet to a chocolate-brown colour as wood resins, bark, and sap help taint and stain the newly exposed, hardened, velvet-free antler surfaces. Alder and willow were the main species that were thrashed, especially those found along the logging roads, trails, and the edges of beaver ponds.

Both bulls and cows produce pheromones, highly volatile chemicals that trigger behavioural responses. During the rut, bulls advertise their sexual state by dispersing these chemicals in their urine. Bulls dig shallow pits with their hooves and then urinate in the pit. They then roll in the mixture of mud, urine, and sex pheromones. This activity, which apparently is done to make the bull more enticing to females, only occurs during the rut. The

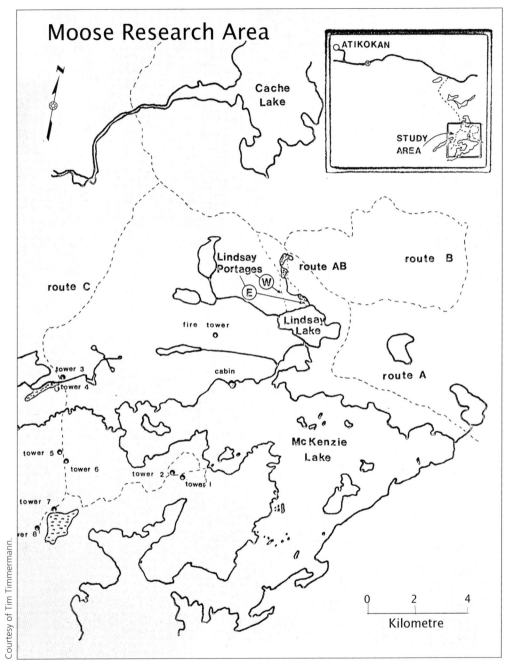

MAP 15: MOOSE RESEARCH AREA NEAR MCKENZIE LAKE
This map depicts the study area that was used for the determination of the duration of the moose rut, the movements of moose during the rut, the response of bull moose to calls, and other relevant information about moose behaviour during this important time of the year.

rut pits discovered during the study were of two types: either large dish-shaped pits that the bulls urinated and rolled in, or much smaller pits with no evidence of wallowing. One grassy meadow near McKenzie Lake had active rut pits during all four years of the study. The areas with the most intense rut activity were generally open alder-ringed areas that the bulls could use for thrashing.

The most obvious indicator that the rut was past its peak was the increasing caution shown by the bulls when responding to a call. At the peak of the rut, the bulls called in were very aggressive. After the first week of October they were less apt to respond, and, if they did, they were generally more timid and less apt to come into the open. Although there was considerable variation in the timing of the rut from year to year, the peak of the rut occurred during the last two weeks of September and the first week of October. All the indicators — fresh tracks, thrashing, rut pits, and response to calling — substantiated these findings.

In the years prior to this study, the moose-hunting seasons opened in the first week of October. As a result of the report submitted at the completion of the study, the researchers recommended that the opening of moose season be delayed "to the end of October or beginning of November to completely eliminate the rut-induced effects, which result in increased vulnerability to the bulls."[2] This important recommendation was taken into account and the opening of moose season in Ontario was moved

back so that only the very end of the rut was included in the rifle moose-hunting season. Archery season, which requires getting closer to the animal, is open during the peak of the rut.

ANTLERS

Antlers are deciduous — they fall off every year. Like leaves, they grow during the spring and summer and are shed when their function is completed. Moose, deer, elk, and caribou have antlers that are regrown and discarded every year. Horns, on the other hand, are permanent. Horns, such as those found on mountain goats, bison, and domestic cattle, are never shed and continue to grow throughout an animal's life.

Antlers originate from bone bases, known as pedicles, which are located on the forehead. The hardened antlers are similar to bone, but they are relatively soft and flexible as they are growing. Antlers, like trees, become larger by increasing in diameter and lengthening from their tips. The cells at the tips of antlers are among the fastest-growing of any known cells, which is remarkable, considering the hard, dense final product.

Growing antlers are covered with a soft, fuzzy material known as velvet, which gives the antlers a brown and furry appearance. The velvet contains small arteries and capillaries that bring blood to the antlers growing underneath. These blood vessels carry the minerals that are deposited to form the antler and they leave their imprint on the growing antler. These meandering grooves, clearly visible on the surface of a hardened antler, show where the blood vessels in the velvet used to be. Velvet-covered antlers are easily damaged, especially during the first few months of growth, because they are relatively soft. Just before the velvet is stripped off at the end of the summer, the antlers become hard and bone-like. If the antlers are damaged when they are velvet-covered and growing, they can be deformed into bizarre shapes. If, for example, a bull falls and damages the antler on just one side, the undamaged side will continue to grow normally while the damaged side will develop an unusual shape.

Since velvet-covered antlers are sensitive, a bull is aware of their size and apparently can detect when they come in contact with anything. The sensitivity

One side of this set of moose antlers, from an animal shot north of Quetico Park, was damaged while growing and still in velvet.

of the velvet allows the bull to judge the size of his constantly growing antlers that he can't see. Even after the velvet is off the antlers in the fall, the bull retains a sense of their final width and uses this information when moving through the woods.

Near the very end of August, the levels of testosterone increase in bulls and the flow of blood to the antlers is shut off. The growth of the antler then stops and the velvet dries up and starts to peel off. Bulls rub the velvet off on small trees and shrubs. Vince Crichton, a moose biologist from Manitoba, has documented bulls eating this velvet, apparently in order to retain the valuable nutrients it contains. When the velvet is gone, the antlers become the hard, bony "finished product" that play such an important role in determining the reproductive success of a bull moose.

A yearling's first set of antlers are small "spikes" that may have small forks at their tips. Each succeeding year, the overall size increases until maximum antler size is reached, usually between the ages of seven and ten. As bulls age beyond this, their antlers usually get smaller. In addition to age, the bull's genes and his nutrition are also important factors. Not much is known about the importance of genetics in antler growth, other than that it is an important factor. Good nutrition is essential for a bull to grow a large, healthy rack. Since antlers are composed primarily of calcium, phosphorus, and protein, moose must have access to foods high in these nutrients. Many biologists believe one reason these animals spend so much time in shallow water eating aquatic vegetation in the summer is that these plants are high in minerals.

In his later years, Tony Bubenik worked on his antler research with his son, George. Recently, George, a retired University of Guelph biologist, and his son Peter, a mathematician at Cleveland State University, published a paper on their research on moose antlers. They tested the theory, first proposed over twenty years ago by Tony, that palmated moose antlers may function as amplifiers of sound. They found that large moose antlers improved sound reception by nearly 20 percent. Their research verifies Tony's suggestion that "the palms of moose antlers may amplify incoming sounds and so aid in moose communication."[3] When asked if he was surprised that their research verified his grandfather's earlier speculation, Peter replied, "I expected it to be true, my grandfather knew his stuff."[4]

The size of antlers on a large bull moose is impressive, but in the past there were animals with antlers that make moose antlers look puny in comparison. The Irish Elk lived in the British Isles and across northern Europe until it became extinct at the end of the last ice age. Based on their skeletons, these early animals are thought to have been only slightly larger than a large bull moose in the Quetico-Superior area. However, Irish Elk had incredible antlers that, on the largest specimens, measured over four metres from tip to tip. It isn't known why they were so huge, but, like moose,

This discarded moose antler was found near Cirrus Lake.

deer, and caribou today, they were probably used to intimidate other males and impress females. It was possible for Irish Elk to have such large antlers as they lived in open, grassy areas and did not have to manoeuvre them through forested areas.

It seems surprising that the male Irish Elk, like today's bull moose, caribou, bull elk, and buck deer grew antlers during the summer only to discard them every winter. Tony Bubenik, however, provided an interesting theory:

The advantage in discarding the old and growing new antlers each year is that it provides the capability of annually changing antler size and shape to correspond to changes in body condition. In this way when a

186

breeding male is strong, he produces impressive antlers that advertise his prowess; when he grows weaker (through injury, disease, or old age), he produces smaller antlers that indicate he is out of the competition and thus will not provoke antagonism from a superior rival.[5]

For decades, Tony Bubenik's research revolved around the role antlers play in determining the status of males and their success in passing their genes on to the next generation. He summarized his research results when he wrote, "I was able to provide evidence that the antlers of large deer are organs of paramount social importance: they did not evolve as weapons for fighting and incapacitating. Antlers are primarily indicators of age and fitness, that is, of status and rank, visually assessed by females when selecting a mate."[6]

Cows ultimately make the determination (much like females in human societies) as to which male or males they will mate with. For cow moose, size — the size of the antlers — does matter.

A young bull moose eyes an indifferent cow moose. This interaction took place along the road near French Lake on Quetico's northern border.

ANTLERED PICTOGRAPHS

Some of the most memorable rock paintings in the Quetico-Superior area are of moose and other antlered animals. The bull moose on Lac La Croix and Hegman Lake are especially striking. The Lac La Croix bull moose was used as the symbol for Quetico's 75th anniversary. An overzealous government official, evidently fearing that someone would be offended, castrated the depiction of the pictograph used as the official symbol.

The bull moose on the cliffs in a narrow section near the east end of Crooked Lake, an area that is also referred to as the Basswood River, is known as the "eccentric moose" or "pipe-smoking" moose. This moose is depicted as having small antlers — or no antlers at all — but has an impressive, elongated bell (the flap of skin hanging from the neck). To me the moose looks more like it is swallowing a canoe than smoking a pipe, but either way it is eccentric. Not all of the moose depicted in pictographs are male; there are cow moose at Lac La Croix and an evocative cow and calf on Darky Lake.

A magnificent caribou with antlers almost as long as the body can be found on a cliff near Montgomery Lake with another caribou (this animal, however, has also been identified as a moose) not far from it. There are no rock paintings that, in my opinion, definitely portray deer, although there are a few pictographs where the species depicted is definitely debatable. One of these, an antlered head on Quetico Lake, has been identified as a caribou, a moose, and an elk in different references.

MOOSE ENCOUNTER

Swamp Bay of Saganaga Lake, where moose are frequently seen, is just a short paddle from the ranger station at Cache Bay. I heard moose calling in late September when Marie and I were the Cache Bay rangers in 1984, and, knowing about Tony Bubenik's use of antlers, I was inspired to try calling moose to see how they would react to my homemade moose antlers. I made a moose-rack replica out of cardboard and reinforced it with thin strips of wood. The result of my efforts only vaguely resembled moose antlers, but I decided to give them a try.

I left the ranger station before dawn and paddled into Swamp Bay in my one-man canoe with my antlers and my trusty Olympus camera. Cow calls could be heard in the distance well before sunrise, and later I heard the sound of a bull grunting near the shoreline. I imitated a bull call with the hope that one would be enticed to come into the open along the shore and was surprised and elated with the quick response. The bull appeared just after sunrise. I was about thirty metres away, holding up my antlers with one hand and trying to focus the camera with the other. A good look at the bull made me aware that my homemade antlers were noticeably larger than those it sported. Bubenik had found that when a moose was confronted by a bull with larger antlers, it simply walked away from a confrontation. Unfortunately for me and my hopes of getting close-up photos of an aggressive moose from the safety of my canoe, Bubenik was right. The young bull looked at my antlers and walked back into the woods. It either realized that it was no match for the large antlered creature in front of it, or simply thought I was a human in a canoe holding up cardboard antlers. I may have had a better chance of getting good photos if I hadn't used the antlers.

MOOSE IN QUETICO'S FUTURE

One of Quetico Park's success stories is that the moose population, which had sunk so low that the Quetico Forest Reserve was formed in 1909 to protect them, rebounded to one of the highest moose populations in Canada by the 1970s. It is ironic that the last logged area in a wilderness park became the site of a significant scientific study. Logging was terminated in Quetico in 1972 and there was a short period of time when the bridges over the French and Cache rivers were still intact, giving easy road access to the study area near McKenzie Lake, and there was still easy viewing in cutovers. Fortunately, Ontario moose biologists seized this opportunity and conducted meaningful research that not only increased our understanding of the moose rut and the behavioural significance of moose antlers, but also helped convince government officials to move the opening

of moose season to a later time so it would miss the peak of the rut.

Moose and other antlered animals have played an important role in Quetico's past and will continue to play an important role in the future. The population of antlered animals has been in flux in the Quetico-Superior region since the glacier's retreat. Barren-ground caribou, woodland caribou, moose, white-tailed deer, and possibly elk, have all been, or currently are, in the area. The higher temperatures over the last few decades have improved conditions for deer and white-tailed populations have increased throughout the Quetico-Superior region. Deer are moving into areas, such as the moose research area around McKenzie Lake, where they were seldom seen twenty-five years ago.

Researchers in northwestern Minnesota have recently concluded that warmer temperatures over the last few decades are the primary reason for the declining numbers of moose in northwestern Minnesota. With most predictions calling for a continued increase in temperatures, the future doesn't seem very promising for moose in the Quetico-Superior landscape. In the early 1900s, hunting pressure caused a significant decrease in moose populations and now higher temperatures appear to be putting new stresses on moose. It is unfortunate that moose, the animal whose declining numbers played a major role in the original establishment of Quetico, are again decreasing in numbers because of human activities, as the 100th anniversary approaches.

CHAPTER THIRTEEN

SNOWSHOES, BLACKFLIES, AND CARNIVOROUS PLANTS

A few times each summer I put on a pair of snow-shoes and go for a walk. I slide my sandalled feet into the snowshoe harness, make sure I have insect repellent, and head out onto a bog. I use ski poles for balance, walk carefully so as not to crush any pitcher plants and keep an eye out for pools of water where I might sink. Wearing snowshoes allows me to stay on top of the squishy surface of a floating bog. Without them, the floating bog mat sinks fairly quickly under each step. Since snowshoes spread a person's weight over a large area, it is possible to stay on top, provided you do not stand in one place for long. It can be difficult getting onto a floating bog in the summer, but, once on top of the mat, it's surprisingly easy to move about wearing snowshoes.

SUMMER SNOWSHOEING ON FLOATING BOGS

The idea for using snowshoes in the summer on Quetico Park bogs came to me when I saw a photo of a bog researcher in the northeastern United States wearing them. I've also been told that Cree guides use snowshoes to retrieve geese during the hunting season in the James Bay area of northern Ontario. People whose work depends on moving around in boggy places have shown that snowshoes function well in these areas, even in the summer.

The bog researcher and the Cree guides wore trad-itional wooden snowshoes that evidently work fine if kept well varnished. I only used wooden snowshoes once in the summer, and the sagging webbing con-vinced me that plastic or metal snowshoes would be more practical. I have found that inexpensive plastic snowshoes with rubber bindings or the lightweight aluminium-frame snowshoes work very well. Sandals or cheap, canvas shoes and a long, stout stick or ski poles for balance are the only other items needed. The wide baskets on old ski poles are helpful since they don't poke through the floating mat, but they do have a tendency to get caught in the vegetation.

On hot days, a T-shirt and shorts are comfort-able attire. Many bog plants are in bloom in early

It is wise to walk carefully, whether on snowshoes or on foot, on a floating bog. They are fragile environments in Quetico Park and elsewhere, and care must be taken when visiting them.

summer when the bugs are at their peak and these bogs have a much wider variety of swarming, biting insects than I have ever encountered anywhere else in Quetico. Insect repellent and sunscreen — items seldom required in January — are treasured items when snowshoeing in the summer. Temperature is only one of the differences between summer and winter snowshoeing. If you fall in the winter it is merely an inconvenience; in the summer you not only get wet, but you may have great difficulty getting back up again.

One must use caution when taking cameras, binoculars, or other items that water could damage when snowshoeing in the summer. There are several kinds of wetlands in Quetico Park and the Atikokan area, and I learned by trial and error that use of snowshoes in either swamps or marshes can create numerous problems and promote swearing because of the open water and the unpredictable nature of their surfaces. Bogs, especially floating bogs, on the other hand, can be terrific places for such an activity.

Bogs are characterized by a wet, spongy, acidic substrate composed chiefly of sphagnum moss on which a limited variety of shrubs, herbs, and some stunted trees grow. Those bogs that consist of a floating mat of sphagnum moss with pitcher plants, sundews, buckbean, bog cranberry, leatherleaf, and a few orchids such as Arethusa and Rose Pogonia growing on it are known — not surprisingly — as floating bogs. Most are found along quiet bays of lakes or on the edge of slow-moving rivers or creeks, although some are found in shallow depressions surrounded by forest. But beware — the floating mat often has more than ten metres of water beneath it.

Snowshoeing in bogs can be a wonderful experience, but it has to be done with caution. The advantage of snowshoes is that they spread your weight over a large area — this is also their greatest disadvantage. Since they greatly enlarge your footprint, they also increase your chance of stepping on sundews, pitcher plants, and other vulnerable plants. If you decide to snowshoe on bogs, minimize the time spent on the bog, walk carefully, and refrain from going in large groups. Boardwalks that extend out into floating bogs are the best way to get a good look at bog plants without damaging the vegetation. The Kingfisher Lake Outdoor Education Centre, located just north of Thunder Bay, Ontario, has a boardwalk that extends onto a floating bog and has proven to be an ideal way for hundreds of students to learn about bogs and see pitcher plants, sundew, and other bog plants without injuring the plants in the process. A similar boardwalk is found at the visitor centre in Orr, Minnesota, southwest of the BWCAW.

Bogs have a tenuous existence and the forest around them is slowly encroaching. Many floating bogs have filled in over time and the water beneath the floating mat has been replaced by wet soil. When this occurs, there is enough substrate for shrubs and trees, primarily black spruce and tamarack, to survive, creating what are commonly known as black spruce bogs. Here, the soil beneath the spongy vegetation allows a wider variety of plants to take root and, consequently, a wider variety of herbs, shrubs, and trees are found than on floating bogs.

THE APPEAL OF BOGS

The seldom-visited ecosystems known as bogs have a particular attraction for me because of their fascinating and unique variety of plants. Sphagnum moss, the primary component of floating bogs, can absorb up to twenty times its own weight of water, and, in addition to its amazing ability to absorb water, it also has antibacterial properties. Not surprisingly, early cultures in both North America and Europe with access to this moss used it for diapers. Because of its antibacterial properties, it was also used as an absorbent dressing in the First World War.

Another feature of this unusual plant is its ability to increase the acidity of the surrounding water as it grows. The acidic environment created by sphagnum significantly decreases the amount of bacteria and other decomposers in acid bogs. The resulting slow decomposition leads to an accumulation of partially decomposed organic material known as peat. However, the acidic conditions make life difficult, or even impossible, for many plants. Relatively few species — such as leather-leaf, bog laurel, Labrador tea, pitcher plants, bog rosemary, cotton grasses, sundews, and cranberries — can survive and even thrive, in this waterlogged and acidic environment.

The low level of decomposers means that bogs are low in nitrogen, phosphorous, and other recycled nutrients, and since bogs are stagnant pools, they lack the circulation necessary to supply nutrients from other sources. In addition, their only source of fresh water is rain, which is almost totally lacking in nutrients. Because of this scarcity, the plants grow very slowly; in fact, it seems surprising that anything can grow at all. Quetico Park biologist Lisa Solomon has found that some of the black spruce in bogs are well over a hundred years old and yet these stunted trees are only a few centimetres in diameter.

Some orchids are able to extract scarce bog nutrients with the assistance of fungus associated with their root systems. Rose pogonia, Arethusa, and grass pink are beautiful, showy orchids that can be found in many, but definitely not all, floating bogs in Quetico Park. Nitrogen is essential for plant growth, but plants in bogs have difficulty getting enough nitrogen for growth and reproduction. Some, such as leather-leaf and Labrador tea, even retain some of their leaves over the winter so they don't need to use scarce nutrients to grow all new ones in the spring. A few others take another unusual route — they compensate for the shortage of nitrogen and other nutrients by obtaining it from insects. Some drown the insects, some trap them on sticky leaves, while others suck their victims into tiny underwater bags.

ADAPTATIONS TO LIFE IN A BOG

Plants are constantly under siege by a wide variety of insects. Their leaves, stems, and roots are devoured by both adult insects and their larvae. It is somehow reassuring that a few plants can turn the tables on bugs and become the eater rather than the eaten. Plants in acid bogs have difficulty obtaining sufficient nutrients and they have devised ways to kill insects in order to obtain food. These insect-eating plants, also known as insectivorous or carnivorous plants, are found almost exclusively in acid bogs in Quetico.

Sundews and pitcher plants are two types of plants whose insect-killing activities can be directly observed in bogs. Interestingly, they use very

Leaves of round-leaved sundews are covered with drops of sticky fluid that both attract and help capture prey.

different methods to capture their food. Sundews trap insects on sticky drops of fluid on their leaves. Pitcher plants, on the other hand, drown and digest their prey in a pool of liquid found in their large basal leaves. Sundews are living fly-paper and pitcher plants are drowning pools.

Although sundews are small plants, they catch the eye because of the reddish hairs that cover the leaves. There are two species of sundews in Quetico, and they differ primarily in the shape of their leaves. The round-leaved sundew, *Drosera rotundifolia*, is fairly common throughout the area while the spatula-leaved sundew, *Drosera intermedia*, is relatively rare. Both species are very small and the round-leaved sundew has leaves that are usually less than a centimetre in diameter. Both species have hairs tipped with glistening drops of sticky fluid that attract insects by their colour and smell. When insects land on the leaves to

A sundew leaf folds around insect prey. The prey will be digested and the leaf will open again and possibly capture another victim. This sundew photo was taken from a boardwalk at Kingfisher Lake, north of Thunder Bay, Ontario.

investigate, they are often glued to one or more hairs. The more they struggle to free themselves, the more gooey hairs they contact and the leaf begins to slowly fold around them. The bending of the leaf has been described as being similar to closing the fingers of the hand over the palm. The tiny leaves usually trap mosquito-sized insects, but creatures as large as damselflies and dragonflies can occasionally be seen struggling to free themselves. Glands associated with the hairs release enzymes and acids that digest the insect and the plant then absorbs the nitrogen and other nutrients from the insects. Ironically, the most common prey of sundew — mosquitoes, gnats, and midges — are the same insects that pollinate the plants.

The pitcher plant, *Sarracenia purpurea*, is named after the odd, pitcher-shaped leaf that rests on the waterlogged mat of a bog. The pitcher is a modified leaf with the upper surface of the leaf forming the inside of the pitcher. It is covered with striking reddish-purple veins and is usually about half-full of a liquid that looks like water. It is very apparent that the shape and colour of pitcher plants vary greatly, even within a small bog. There is considerable debate about whether this is due to ecological differences within the bog, variations in food uptake, or is simply caused by genetic differences.[1] A large, solitary flower hovers over the pitcher on a long stalk. Pitcher plants can be seen from a distance due to these unusual, waxy red flowers that are visible well above the plant.

The nectar on the lip of the pitcher attracts insects such as bees, flies, wasps, mosquitoes, ants, and beetles. While feeding on the nectar, some insects find that the slippery sides make the pitcher a lethal waterslide. The top of the inside of the pitcher is lined with downward-pointing hairs and they make it very hard for an insect to crawl out once it is in the

The digestive liquid that contains enzymes is found inside a modified leaf of this Quetico Park pitcher plant.

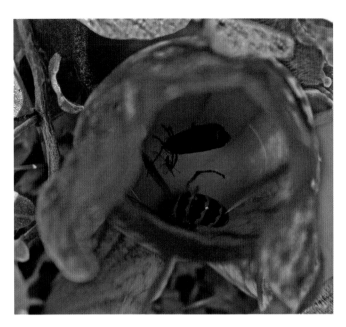

A wasp and another insect, larger than most victims found floating in the modified leaf, constitute a feast for a pitcher plant in this floating bog just north of Quetico.

been found in pitcher plants. When you look into a pitcher plant, it is common to see dead and decaying prey floating in the water. This past summer, about one-fourth of the pitcher plants that I looked into had dead insects floating in them. I was, however, really surprised to find that a few also had insect larvae wriggling in the pitcher's liquid. Some plants had four or five small worm-like larvae and one had what appeared to be a small beetle swimming on the surface of the liquid in the pitcher. The beetle may have been trapped and simply looking for a way out before the acid had enough time to eat through its durable exoskeleton. There is a chance, however remote, that it may have found a way to survive in the acidic pool.

Bog ecologists have found that the acid pool in a pitcher plant is a micro-ecosystem where as many as seventeen different species of insect can thrive in the acidic conditions and enzymes that digest other insect species. Stephen Heard, a Canadian ecologist from the University of New Brunswick, found that the larvae of three insect species — a fly, a midge, and a mosquito — "feast on the carcasses of other insects until the days become short and it is time to prepare for winter. Then they fast, so that when the plant is buried in snow and the pitcher pool freezes solid, no particles will remain in their digestive systems to sprout ice crystals and burst their guts. In spring the water thaws out and they start eating again. By early July they reach adulthood and fly off in search of a mate and a new pitcher plant to hold a new generation."[2] Amazingly, they manage to overwinter in a frozen

liquid. The liquid in the pitcher is very acidic and contains enzymes produced by the plant that slowly digest prey. The prey varies from smaller insects to large beetles and wasps. By acting as a predator, the pitcher plant obtains the nutrients it needs from bog insects rather than through its root system.

Pitcher plants are insectivorous plants since they primarily consume insects that have drowned in the pitcher, but they are more accurately called carnivorous plants since they can also kill and consume other non-insect species. The partially digested remains of mites, spiders, and the occasional small frog have pool of acid and carry on in the spring as adults. Some of the insects that overwinter in the pitcher plant may also pollinate the flowers of the pitcher plant and help secure a future home for their offspring.

Bladderworts are carnivorous plants that take a much different approach to capturing their prey. There are six species of bladderworts in Quetico Park. They all consume much smaller prey than pitcher plants or sundews and capture their prey underwater. In addition to their normal leaves above the water, they also have underwater leaves that are modified to capture tiny creatures. These leaves form tiny bladders, just barely visible to the naked eye, with an inwardly opening lid. The bladders are gas-filled and have a partial vacuum. When a tiny organism, such as an insect larvae or even a micro-organism, touches hairs around the bladder opening, the lid opens and the prey is sucked into the bladder. The organism is then digested inside the bladder. When digestion is completed, the water is pumped out and the trap is reset for the next victim.

PLANT EATS FROG

Donning a pair of snowshoes in the summer provides access to the unique environment created by acidic conditions in northern bogs where life can be difficult, or even impossible, for most organisms. Bog plants are fascinating, but there isn't much diversity in this challenging environment. Trees that survive in an acid bog are stunted and it is intriguing to look down at the cones growing near the tops of mature trees over one hundred years old. These small plants, stunted trees, and relative lack of diversity make a floating bog resemble tundra. The swarms of bugs and the cool air rising from the vegetation adds to the feeling of being on tundra. On a floating bog, however, a pool of acidic water — rather than permafrost — underlies the soggy mat of plants.

The release of acids by sphagnum is the primary reason for the acidic conditions in bogs. Paradoxically, pitcher plants create a small, concentrated acid pool within the larger, more diluted acid pool that lies beneath and pervades the bog. The small acid vat not only allows the pitcher plant to digest insects, but the plant sometimes digests frogs, as well. In an acid bog, instead of the usual food-chain sequence of a frog eating insects that have fed on plants — the plant occasionally eats the frog. Contemplating this while snowshoeing in shorts and a T-shirt on a hot July day, it somehow seems right.

CHAPTER FOURTEEN

A RAVEN'S KNOWLEDGE

All northerners, regardless of where they live, have one bird species in common — the raven. Not only is this large black bird found all across northern North America, it is also found in Greenland, Iceland, and across northern Europe and Russia. The raven is at home in Uppsala, Sweden, as well as Upsala, Ontario. Although predominantly a northern bird, ravens are one of the most widely distributed birds in the world. In North America, they have extended their range beyond the tundra, boreal forest and mixed forest, and, consequently, live in the high desert country near Ely, Nevada, as well as in the pine forests of Ely, Minnesota.

In the Quetico-Superior, the raven's range overlaps with that of its close relative, the common crow. The primary difference is that the raven, *Corvus corax*, is much larger than the crow, *Corvus brachyrhynchos*. The raven also has a larger, thicker beak and has a wedge-shaped tail rather than the squared end of the crow's tail. Ravens are found throughout the Quetico-Superior area, but crows are more common in the BWCAW than in Quetico.

Crows, however, seem to be increasing throughout the Quetico-Superior region, possibly due to the gradual warming over the last few decades. These birds usually migrate south during the coldest winter months, but over the last few decades crows have been leaving later, coming back earlier, or not leaving at all. Ravens do not migrate south for the winter, but stay in the north and rely on their intelligence, adaptability, and omnivorous feeding habits to get through our long, cold months. Ravens mate well before migrating birds even consider heading north and are usually on their nests incubating their eggs by late March. Their colour serves them well in the cold since their inky-black feathers allow them to absorb more heat from the sun, a feature that comes in handy when spending hours on the nest at a time when cold, snow, and freezing rain are not only possible, but very probable. Ravens don't merely survive the winter — they thrive and even prosper.

Drawing by Mary Lambirth, Blackduck, Minnesota.

Ravens live year-round in the Quetico-Superior and are completely at home even in the coldest weather.

RAVEN ECOLOGY

I love watching ravens fly. They delight in performing an assortment of unusual aerial acrobatics — even flying upside down on occasion. Since ravens don't rely on speed or manoeuverability to obtain food, it seems unusual that they would be such skilful flyers. Birds fly primarily for practical purposes: searching for food, avoiding predators, or simply moving from place to place. Ravens, however, often appear to cavort in the air with joyous abandon simply because it is fun. Their most exuberant flights occur during their mating season in late winter. Then they can be seen chasing each other and performing aerial acrobatics. These flights involve a mixture of upward zooms, steep dives, and innovative and intricate manoeuvres that are performed while flying in tandem, as well as when flying separately. They move together, wing tip to wing tip, as if their routine is choreographed and they are hearing music played just for them. While it is certainly understandable that mating flights would be passionate and lively, they also do barrel rolls, swoops, and flips at other times of year. Ravens even seem to enjoy flying on those -30°C and -40°C winter days when no other birds can be seen in the frigid skies.

Biologists have noted that ravens make a wider variety of sounds than any animal other than humans. Their most striking and unusual sound is a single bell-like note they make while flying in late winter that seems to be associated with their mating season. This odd, ringing sound would be surprising coming from a peacock, but is especially strange coming from a hulking, black bird.

The call that I have heard the most often is a deep call that sounds like "kraa" and is sometimes repeated many times. It is similar to the "caw" call of the crow, but is much deeper and less strident. They also make a "clunk" or "thunk" sound that is unlike any other bird sound I have ever heard. In contrast to these distinctive, unmelodic one-note sounds, they can also make very soft, musical sounds that make the raven the world's largest songbird. Raven vocalization is primarily an indication of their social nature. A biologist studying raven calls in Alaska described thirty different raven calls, indicating that ravens have a large vocabulary that allows them to discuss a wide variety of topics. They are capable of communicating with the other ravens about the location of the nearest food, the presence or absence of predators, or simply to pass on the latest juicy bit of raven gossip.

Ravens are both predators and scavengers. As predators, they eat eggs and kill frogs, snakes, mice, voles, and young and wounded birds. They also consume a variety of insects and other invertebrates. Thunder Bay naturalist Scot Kyle has labelled ravens the "bikers of the bird world" because they "dress in black, are big, and they are mean."[1] I'm not sure about the "mean" reference, but they do occasionally act as predators on surprisingly large animals. About ten years ago, farmers near Dryden, Ontario, and in The Pas, Manitoba, reported that ravens were killing their sheep and cows. The birds were apparently landing on the heads of these farm animals and driving their beaks into the eyes of their prey. Ravens killing small birds and mice is not surprising, but killing domesticated animals as large as cows with a few hard, well-placed blows is an impressive feat.

At the other end of the food spectrum, they also eat plant foods, and have been observed consuming large amounts of blueberries. The extremely diverse diet of a Quetico raven can include large and small mammals (in any state of freshness or decay), snakes, turtles, frogs, toads, minnows, crayfish, tadpoles, eggs, nestlings, worms, insects, seeds, and berries. Ravens are omnivores and opportunists of the highest magnitude. When it comes to food preference, ravens, like humans, are specialists in non-specialization. Ravens, however, obtain the vast majority of their food by acting as scavengers. With less food available in the winter, they rely heavily on animal carcasses provided by accidents, malnutrition, wild predators, or human hunters. They take advantage of animals killed by vehicles by flying along highway corridors and feeding on the road kills.

In wilderness areas, ravens are dependent on moose and deer carcasses provided by wolves. A large number of ravens usually indicates the presence of a concentration of food—usually a dead animal. Driving to Atikokan a few years ago, I noticed five or six ravens circling over the French River just north of the highway. I snowshoed down to the river and found a deer carcass surrounded by raven tracks. Wolf tracks — those near the carcass were nearly obliterated by raven activity — could be clearly seen on the ice, and patches of hair and blood made it clear that the deer was killed on the ice and dragged to shore. The scavenging of wolf kills is the primary reason that ravens are able to to remain in Quetico Park and the BWCAW during the winter.

Ravens generally build their nests in trees. In the Quetico-Superior area, they commonly nest in old white pines since the branches give them protection from the elements. Unlike bald eagles, ravens often nest well back from the lake, which means that their nests often go unnoticed. Since the young are usually flying by mid-May, the nests are no longer in use when canoeists enter the Quetico-Superior in large numbers.

When a good site is available, they nest on the sunny sides of cliffs. They seek out locations where they can build a nest under an overhang. A nesting site on the cliffs on the north shore of Quetico Lake has a large overhang that completely protects the nest. I first saw this wonderful Quetico Lake

ABOVE

A raven's nest sits under an overhang on a Quetico Lake cliff. This nest, south-facing and with protection from snow and rain, has been utilized by ravens for decades.

RIGHT

This raven's nest is found in the framework of a transmission tower in Thunder Bay, Ontario.

cliff nest in 1976 and it is still in use over thirty years later.

As ravens nest much earlier than most birds, they are on the nest when the weather is still cold. As a result, the nests are usually situated facing south to obtain as much solar heat as possible. Since the eggs are being incubated when both snow and freezing rain can occur, nests with an overhang to protect both the incubating adult raven and its chicks is a huge advantage. In addition to using trees and cliff ledges, ravens also use man-made structures for nest platforms. There are reports of ravens nesting on highway overpasses, high-rise buildings, billboards, and church steeples. Ravens are even nesting in a large, metal transmission pylon in a residential area in Thunder Bay, Ontario, and in another transmission tower near Shebandowan Lake along the highway between Thunder Bay and Atikokan.

WOLVES AND RAVENS

Ravens have a multi-faceted, symbiotic interactions with wolves. They obviously benefit from this relationship because the wolves not only kill the animal, they also open the carcass so the ravens can get at the meat and organs. Wolves also apparently benefit from their association with ravens by obtaining signals of the locations of prey from ravens. There have been numerous reports of this signalling by ravens who circle over moose, primarily old, malnourished, or injured animals — and call loudly.

While conducting research in the Superior National Forest, Fred Harrington found that ravens respond to wolf howls in the fall and winter — even when humans were doing the howling. He noted that when he howled, "ravens abruptly changed their flying course, approached me and appeared to search (zig-zag flight, hovering), suggesting they were attempting to find me."[2] Being very dependent on carrion in the winter, ravens know that howling wolves often indicate a fresh kill.

During twenty-seven years of field research on Isle Royale in Lake Superior, Rolf Peterson found that ravens were present at every wolf kill site, often within sixty seconds of a moose's death. A raven can eat and stash up to two kilograms of food a day. If there are ten ravens at a kill site, they will consume as much in one day as one wolf. A solitary wolf or a pair of wolves has to spend much time trying to keep ravens and other scavengers away from the kill. Researchers on Isle Royale have speculated that a major reason that wolves hunt in packs is so that they lose less food to ravens.

David Mech, a wolf researcher who worked on Isle Royale and in northern Minnesota, wrote about the numerous times he had observed wolves and ravens engaging in what appeared to be "play." Ravens pull the tails of wolves and even occasionally land on their backs. The wolves chase the ravens but don't seem intent on catching them. Mech noted

Ravens feast on a deer carcass in northern Minnesota as a wolf watches.

Photo by Jim Brandenburg/Minden Pictures.

that it "appears that the wolf and raven have reached an adjustment in their relationship such that each creature is rewarded in some way by the presence of the other and that each is fully aware of the other's capabilities. Both species are extremely social, so they must possess the psychological mechanisms necessary for forming social attachments. Perhaps in some way individuals of each species have included members of the other in their social groups and have formed bonds with them."[3]

RAVEN MYTHOLOGY

The raven plays a major role in the legends of many Native American cultures. Many Ojibwa and Cree tales from Minnesota, Ontario, and Manitoba feature ravens. In these tales ravens are often "tricksters," creatures that are capable of heroism and courage, but also of trickery and even deceit. In Pacific Northwest mythology, the raven plays a central role and is known as both a creator and a folk hero. Richard K. Nelson, in his magnificent book *Make Prayers to the Raven*, notes that the raven plays a central role in the mythology of the Koyukon in northwestern Alaska. For the Koyukon, the raven is a complex character that is simultaneously an "omnipotent clown, benevolent mischief-maker, buffoon, and deity."[4]

In early European cultures, ravens also played significant roles. My Norse ancestors, like many Native American cultures, not only believed they could learn from these intelligent and adaptable birds, but also wove them into their mythology and spirituality. In Norse legends two ravens, Hugin (thought) and Munin (memory), flew off at dawn and observed what was happening in the far-flung Norse realm. They returned in the evening, perched on the shoulders of the Norse god Odin, and whispered to him what they had learned during their day's travels. Information received from ravens, because they could observe and understand things that were beyond the comprehension of mere humans, was considered to be extremely valuable. In Ireland, the phrase "raven's knowledge" means to know all and to see all.

Although ravens are no longer common in England, they were so abundant in London in the late 1600s that the King was petitioned to get rid of them. Since many Englishmen held ravens in high esteem, there was opposition to this extermination plan. According to the book *Ravens in Winter*, the raven extermination was not completed because a family of ravens lived in the Tower of London and a "soothsayer advised the King that if he removed all the ravens from the Tower a great disaster would befall England and his Royal Palace would crumble into dust. The King, not wanting to tempt fate, decided to keep six ravens and appoint a Keeper."[5] The ravens are still there today, but their wings are clipped to ensure that they don't leave the Tower. The Tower ravens don't successfully breed, but whenever one dies, another raven is brought in to replace it. Another centuries-old English tale states that a raven's head buried at the base of the Tower of London protects London from invasion. Ravens are also featured in voyageur lore. According to some accounts, a raven feather was used to initiate voyageurs into the "black feather brigade" when he made his first crossing of the Arctic Divide.

Design by Lisa Sorenson, Atikokan, Ontario.

This design is used by the Dragons of the Black Feather dragon boat team in Atikokan, Ontario. Ravens are part of the mythology, including that of contemporary Canadians, of people around the world.

Individuals, as well as cultures, sometimes feel a special bond with ravens. Sigurd Olson was cross-country skiing near Ely, Minnesota, when he "saw a raven circling overhead, and knew it was watching our progress over the trail as a flock of them had watched over me when I was travelling on the rotting ice of New Found Lake to the east. They had warned me that day, for ravens know when the ice is bad and the hunting is good. This time we were safe, for there was no ice to cross, and the bird soared and soared high in the blue without even coming close."[6]

RAVEN INTELLIGENCE

Ravens and crows are known for their intelligence and many biologists consider them to be the most intelligent birds of all. They exhibit their intellect in numerous ways, such as by opening clamshells by dropping them on rocks or pavement. According to an article in the journal *Behavioral Ecology*, crows in California pick up walnuts in their beaks and fly high enough to break them open when dropped on pavement.[7] It has also been reported that carrion crows, a close relative of ravens, have been observed waiting for the lights to change on a university campus in Japan. When the lights are red, the crows hop in front of the cars and place walnuts, which they acquired from nearby trees, on the road. When the lights turn green, the birds fly way and vehicles drive over the nuts, cracking them open. When the lights turn red again, the crows join the pedestrians in the crosswalk and pick up their meal.

Ravens have been subjected to numerous examinations and tests of their intelligence. They quickly solved the problem of how to efficiently move doughnuts from one location to another. When confronted with multiple doughnuts, a raven will pass its beak through the hole of one doughnut and grab the edge of another — a perfect solution to the two-doughnut one-beak problem. Some raven researchers have concluded that some of their problem-solving abilities approach or even surpass those of the great apes.

The late Konrad Lorenz, a renowned animal behaviourist, had a pet raven. He once fed this raven after it had brought him a piece of laundry that it had obtained from a clothesline. The raven, thinking it had been rewarded for bringing laundry, made repeated raids on neighbour's clotheslines. The raven kept bringing wet socks and undergarments until it realized it was not going to be rewarded again. Another indicator of ravens' intelligence is their ability to adapt and thrive in towns and cities as well as in wilderness areas. In addition to utilizing buildings and other man-made structures for nests, ravens have also made other adjustments to living in close association with humans.

In towns and cities ravens routinely inspect garbage cans, raid dog food dishes in backyards, and habituate garbage dumps, just as they search for animals that have died of natural causes or been preyed upon in the wilderness. In Atikokan and Thunder

Bay, they can be seen routinely inspecting the back of a hunter's or trapper's half-ton truck, looking for morsels of meat and picking up choice scraps of food from garbage bins behind restaurants. Always the opportunist, ravens will take advantage of humans whenever possible. One raven was seen flying across the road at the French Lake campground with a whole sandwich in its beak.

NOBLE TRICKSTERS

Dr. Lawrence Kilham, author of *The American Crow and Common Raven*, was attempting to shoot a raven for a scientific collection when:

> a raven came circling overhead. That was it. I lifted my single-barrel, 20-gauge shotgun and fired. One small feather drifted down as the raven continued circling, seemingly undisturbed. I lowered my gun, searched my pocket for another shell, and was reloading when I looked up. The raven was back sooner than I expected. Just as I looked up he took a shot at me. A large purplish splotch (the raven had been eating crowberries) landed on the front of my hat. I took it off and gazed in astonishment. One can say that it was all fortuitous, but that is not the way it seemed to me. The experience left me with the feeling that ravens, in addition to being sharp mentally, may have a sense of humour."[8]

Either that or the raven was simply shooting back with the best weapon it had.

Ravens have many attributes that we usually associate with humans: they have a sense of humour, use tools, are unusually intelligent, interact to an unusual extent with other species, and enjoy playing. Like us, ravens have also successfully made the transition between wilderness and human-dominated landscapes, and thrive in environments as diverse as the Arctic and Death Valley.

In the mythology of many cultures, ravens are regarded as tricksters with a dual nature. They can be noble and compassionate, but they can also be lazy, selfish, and deceitful. Based on these attributes, we may have more in common with these intriguing creatures than we want to admit. I can't help but think that if ravens have their own mythology, their observations of complex and contradictory human behaviour would lead them to believe that humans should play the role of the "trickster" in raven folklore.

CHAPTER FIFTEEN

FIERY INTERLUDES IN AN ENDLESS DANCE

My generation grew up with visions of the horrifying destructiveness of forest fires. A Walt Disney movie from the 1940s depicted a raging forest fire where "crazed, screaming animals flew, galloped, ran and crawled from hideous tongues of flame, stopping only long enough to warn their friends. Some were burned. Many wept. They lost their families and their beautiful, happy homes."[1] Although this fire occurred only in the imagination of the animators of the film *Bambi*, their vision of the destructiveness of fire left a lasting impression in the mind of the public.

Bambi was released in 1942, and two years later the Smokey Bear campaign to reduce forest fires began. In 1950, fire fighters in New Mexico rescued a bear cub with burned paws. He was treated and became the living symbol of Smokey Bear. Growing up in the era of Bambi and Smokey Bear, I watched as Bambi narrowly escaped a raging forest fire and just took it for granted that Smokey was right when he said that forest fires are bad.

My first encounter with the effects of forest fires came while paddling through recently burned areas on Camel and Metacryst lakes in Quetico Park in the mid-1970s. It was a shock to see a blackened, seemingly lifeless forest after the healthy, green forests we had encountered on our trip prior to reaching the burned area. My harsh, negative first impression of fire was reinforced when I conducted archaeological surveys after the large fires in Quetico in 1995. It takes a long time to be convinced of the benefits of fire when you look at skeletal trees in a seemingly lifeless, burned-over area. For me, it wasn't an issue of "can't see the forest for the trees" but rather "couldn't see the future forest for the blackened trees."

In 1995, large fires burned in Quetico Park and I was able to take photos of the fire aftermath on Pickerel Lake. For the next three years I was able to go back and take photos of the same locations. It was fascinating to watch the yearly changes in the vegetation over that short time span and document the resurgence of life after the fire. After reading about the effects of forest fires, talking to fire ecologists, and — most importantly — observing the dramatic revival of a forest in the years

This landscape was barren one month after a very hot, intense fire burned the north shore of Pickerel Lake in 1995.

Three years later at the same location on Pickerel Lake, the vegetation, with a predominance of fireweed, has transformed the land, and there are many more changes yet to come.

following a fire, my opinion of forest fires changed dramatically. I became convinced that preventing fires in wilderness parks over a long period of time is not necessarily beneficial and can even cause ecological damage. Most forests, including those in the Quetico-Superior, have evolved with fire. Decades of active fire suppression have greatly changed their composition.

A day after a fire, smoke continues to rise from the smouldering remains of a small fire north of French Lake in 1977.

Researchers who work with the living aftermath of forest fires — healthy, living trees — are the most persuasive advocates for the positive long-term effects of forest fires. Their research has led them to the conclusion that forest fires have many beneficial effects for both the plants and the animals that depend on them. Because forest fires generally burn in a "patchy" fashion, they leave a mosaic of intensely burned, lightly burned, and unburned forests. This results in a more diverse new forest with a greater mixture of plants and animals than what is found in forests that haven't burned for a long time. Even intensely burned areas rebound in a few years into young stands of pine. Throughout Quetico,

211

even-aged stands of pine resulting from fires can be seen along many waterways. In the aftermath of the 1995 fires, young, healthy stands of pine are growing on the north shore of Pickerel Lake and along large sections of Kawnipi Lake. Older stands of pine, resulting from forest fires in the last fifty years, can be found on Saganagons, Metacryst, and Baird lakes as well as numerous other locations. The mature red and white pines at The Pines on Pickerel Lake are also most likely the result of a fire that burned over two hundred years ago. Miron L. Heinselman and Clifford Ahlgren stand out as individuals who not only conducted fire ecology research in what is now the BWCAW, but who were also effective in educating the public on both the positive aspects and the complexities of forest fires. Heinselman was a forest ecologist with the United States Forest Service from 1948 until 1974 and spent much of that time studying the effects of fire on northern Minnesota forests. Clifford Ahlgren and his wife Isabele worked for the Wilderness Research Foundation on Basswood Lake, now located on Fall Lake, north of Ely, Minnesota, and were research associates with the College of Forestry at the University of Minnesota. For over three decades, Heinselman and the Ahlgrens wrote articles that inspired others to study fire ecology and worked to make the public more aware of the benefits of fire in forests.

Heinselman became a strong advocate for the advantages of fire upon discovering that trees in stands of old-growth had fire scars showing that they had survived numerous fires and that the even-aged stands of trees he investigated were probably the result of forest fires. He concluded that both the origin and the subsequent health of old-growth stands he investigated were fire-dependent. The results of his detailed studies of forests of all ages and types convinced him that the suppression of fire was having a negative effect on the forest ecology of the BWCAW, and he became an outspoken advocate for fire at a time when this was not a popular view.

THE PAST IN FLAMES

Long before the arrival of the first Europeans, Native peoples altered the environment by periodically setting fires in some locations. Clifford Ahlgren described the use of prescribed burns to stimulate the growth of blueberries by the Ojibwa on a long rocky peninsula on Basswood Lake known as U.S. Point. He stated: "In the 1800s and possibly earlier, this ridge was periodically burned over by the Ojibway to keep the forest back and maintain the open conditions in which blueberries thrive."[2]

It isn't known if the use of fire to improve berry habitat on Basswood Lake was an exception or if Native people in the Quetico-Superior commonly used fire this way. In other locations in North America, Native people used fire to improve the habitat for game animals prior to the arrival of Europeans, and that practice may have occurred in the Quetico-Superior, as well. It would seem that determining the frequency of forest fires — whether man-made or natural — from hundreds or even thousands of years ago would be an impossible task. Scientists investigating sediment cores from the bottom of lakes, however, came up with a way to do this. While conducting an analysis of pollen from sediments from lake bottoms, they found that small pieces of charcoal were present in some layers of sediment and that the charcoal in sediment layers from the past hundred years or so matched the years for known fires.

A team led by Albert Swain from the University of Minnesota extended this correlation between charcoal in lake sediments and the dates of forest fires into analysis of sediments from earlier time periods. They analyzed sediment cores from the bottom of Lake of the Clouds, located south of Ottertrack Lake. From this evidence, they calculated that the fire cycle over the past one thousand years in the Quetico-Superior area was about seventy to eighty years. They also found that charcoal was found at about the same frequency all the way back to the retreat of the glaciers. They concluded that "fire has been an important factor in determining the composition of the forest vegetation in the BWCA during the past 10,000 years at least."[3]

Miron Heinselman took a more direct path and looked for evidence of past fires in the trunks of living trees in the Superior National Forest in northern Minnesota. He compiled a chronology of forest-fire years by examining fire scars and counting growth rings to determine the exact year that fires occurred. The ages of major forest stands were determined by taking small cores from living trees and counting the tree rings. He supplemented this field data by examining evidence collected by land surveyors between 1873 and 1907 to verify his fire dates and find information on other fires. In so doing he compiled a record of fire history that extends back to the early 1600s.

When conducting field studies of old-growth pines, Heinselman found that "the oldest stand found dates from a disturbance, probably a fire, in about the year 1595."[4] This group of three red pines are in a stand of fire-scarred pines on Three Mile Island of Sea Gull Lake that was scarred by fire in 1692, and again in 1801. As these trees were well over one hundred years old when LaVerendre travelled the border route in 1731 near the beginning of the fur trade, they have lived through the entire European era in the Quetico-Superior area. Recent fires have been a threat to these ancient pines. The 2006 Cavity Lake Fire burned a portion of Three Mile Island and the 2007 Ham Lake Fire also threatened the island.

Surprisingly, Heinselman found that over one-third of the total area burned between 1610 and 1972 occurred in a span of just thirteen years — from 1863 to 1875. His studies also showed that some areas are far more susceptible to fires than other areas. He determined that the largest, second-largest, and fifth-largest fires during his study period all occurred in the area between the southern shore of Saganaga Lake and the southern boundary of the BWCAW. The tendency for this area to burn continued with both the 2006 Cavity Lake Fire and the 2007 Ham Lake Fire. The other region of high fire frequency was a swath of land south of Lac La Croix. At the other extreme, the land south of Basswood and Crooked lakes had very little fire activity between 1610 and 1972 and relatively little has burned in the years after his study.

Heinselman obtained information on forest fires prior to 1595 by using Swain's data of charcoal in lake sediment cores. By combining data from sediment cores, written records, fire scars, and tree rings, Heinselman was able to extend the record of forest fires in the BWCAW back to the post-glacial period. He found that intervals between fires varied greatly depending upon the types of trees in the stand. Jack-pine forests burned more frequently than forests that were predominantly red or white pine. He concluded that the average interval between fires for a given area in the BWCAW before European settlement was about one hundred years.

An extensive study of the fire history of Quetico Park was carried out in 1975 and 1976. The objectives of the study by G.T. Woods and R.J. Day, researchers from Lakehead University in Thunder Bay, Ontario, and the Ontario Ministry of Natural Resources were to determine the extent and frequency of past fires, study the ecology of the forests now present in Quetico Park, and investigate the role of fire in the origin and perpetuation of Quetico's forests. Like Heinselman, they also found that the average span

between fires varied from forest type to forest type. In addition, they determined that in areas dominated by Jack pine and black spruce, fires occurred much more frequently than in forests dominated by red and white pine. Woods and Day determined that, before fire suppression began in 1920, the average interval between fires for a given area was seventy-eight years. It is remarkable, and reassuring, that three separate studies — Swain's analysis of lake sediments, Heinselman's research in the BWCAW, and the Woods and Day study in Quetico Park — all found fire intervals between seventy and one hundred years for the years prior to fire suppression.

Woods and Day found that 75 percent of the study area burned between 1860 and 1919, an additional 17 percent burned from 1920 to 1939, and only 4 percent burned after 1940. As a consequence of the extremely small area burned since 1940, they found very few young forests and a dramatic increase in the length of the fire cycle to 870 years. Most of the forest communities were between 40 and 120 years old and were the products of the 1860 to 1940 fires. Their study concluded that without the reintroduction of fire, Quetico's forests would to develop into "overmature, decadent stands composed mostly of uneven-aged shade tolerant hardwoods and conifers … If Quetico Park is to be maintained as a true wilderness area and natural forests are to exist within its boundaries, wildfire must be reintroduced."[5]

Quetico Park and BWCAW forests are changing from the predominantly pine forests of the 1700s to those composed predominantly of balsam fir and poplar. This is primarily due to the significant decrease in the number of acres burned each year after active fire suppression began in the early 1900s. The development and use of airplanes and other modern technology around 1940 resulted in a further dramatic decrease in the amount of forest that burned each year.

The realization that fire suppression was greatly altering forests in the Quetico-Superior area and the desire to create a more natural forest mosaic by returning fire to the landscape eventually led to the creation of fire-management plans in both the BWCAW and Quetico Park. Fire-management plans have the difficult task of balancing the ecological health of the forests, the safety of canoeists, and the economic interests of those outside the boundaries of the wilderness areas. Personnel in both Quetico Park and the BWCAW have found that most people will accept forest fires in wilderness areas as long as they feel assured that human safety is the first priority and that fires allowed to burn will be carefully monitored and aggressively fought if they threaten to burn outside of the wilderness area.

The increase in the amount of land burned since the fire-management plans went into effect has brought the average interval between fires (fire cycle) closer to what it was prior to the beginning of active fire suppression. In 2007, Quetico Park reported that the fire cycle was 298 years, a dramatic drop from the 870 years that was found for the active suppression period between 1940 and the release of the Woods and Day report in 1976. The decrease in the fire cycle is primarily the result of the large 1995 Quetico Park fire, but more relaxed fire management policies have also contributed to the decline.

Although the fire cycle is declining, there is still a long way to go before the fire frequency in Quetico reaches the seventy-eight-year cycle that prevailed prior to active suppression in the 1920s. Since active fire suppression began, there haven't been many large fires in the Quetico-Superior. Much of the area burned in the Quetico-Superior in this period was due to large fires during the exceptionally dry years of 1936, 1995, 2006, and 2007. Although fires occurred on both sides of the border in 1936, Quetico was the hardest hit when over sixty-five thousand hectares (one hundred sixty thousand acres) burned in six fires during that year.

In 1995, large-scale wildfire on the scale of the fires documented by Heinselman and Woods and Day from pre-suppression times returned. More than twenty-five thousand hectares (sixty-two thousand acres) of forest burned in Quetico Park, most of it in a large fire (known as Fire 141) in the southeast part of the park. At its peak, almost half the park was closed to travel that year and a portion of the Dawson Trail Campground had to be evacuated. Portions of the spring and summer of both 2006 and 2007 were also dry and large fires occurred both years in the BWCAW. The 2006 Cavity Lake Fire was a July fire that was suppressed from the beginning but still burned over twelve thousand hectares (thirty thousand acres). The 2007 Ham Lake Fire was an early spring fire that started outside of the BWCAW and burned many cabins as well as over thirty thousand hectares (seventy-five thousand acres) on both sides of the border.

Although the health of the forests in Quetico Park and the BWCAW is best served by the reintroduction of fire, it is a difficult task to successfully accomplish this without areas outside of the wilderness also burning. The fire-management plans in Quetico Park and the Superior National Forest are, above all, management plans that cautiously attempt to return fire to wilderness areas. The key word is "cautiously," as they still actively suppress fires that begin when conditions for the fire spreading is high, and monitor fires that are allowed to burn.

QUETICO PARK FIRE ECOLOGY RESEARCH

Fire ecology has been a hot topic for research in both Quetico Park and the BWCAW over the last few decades. Studies of prescribed burns, influences of fire on biodiversity, relationship between blowdowns and fire, comparison of the effects of logging and fire on eastern white pine, and evaluations of regrowth after spring, summer, and fall fires are a few of the topics that have been researched. Due to my interest in old-growth pines, I will concentrate here on the research in

In 1996, the charred bark at the base of a white pine near Mack Lake is evidence of the fire that burned the previous summer.

Quetico Park on regrowth of white and red pine after different types of forest fires.

The two main types of forest fires — surface fires and crown fires — have very different effects on wildlife and vegetation. Regrowth after both types of fires has been studied in Quetico Park in recent years. Surface fires burn the dead leaves, dry needles, grass, downed branches, shrubs, and small plants but don't rise into the tops of trees. They commonly leave scars at the base of mature trees, especially red pine and white pine, as evidence of their passing. Surface fires are not as common in Quetico-Superior forests as they are in western Canada and the United States. Unattended campfires begin as surface fires, but small conifers such as balsam fir, white spruce, or white cedar can act as fire ladders to lift the flames into the crowns of Jack pine, red pine, or white pine.

Crown fires burn into the tops of trees. They are most common in resinous conifers where they burn the highly flammable living and dead needles, twigs, and branches. These fires are often supported by surface fires that move beneath or just behind the crown fire. Winds are required to keep crown fires moving, and a recent large destructive fire in the Quetico-Superior area, the Ham Lake Fire, was driven by strong winds that caused it to move rapidly and resist suppression efforts. Although surface fires are more common, crown fires tend to be larger and burn bigger areas in the Quetico-Superior.

Tim Lynham of the Canadian Forest Service began his studies of regrowth of red and white pine following Fire 141 in 1995. This fire, the second largest in Quetico Park in over a hundred years, burned with varying speed and intensity depending on the weather and type of vegetation it encountered. It left a mosaic of charred, burned, lightly burned, and unburned forest. Lynham noted that, by working in this area, he and his co-workers "had the rare opportunity to study the impact of a large, high-intensity wildfire in stands of 150 to 300-year-old red and white pine while also investigating re-growth in pine stands burned by low-intensity ground fires."[6]

His team was able to study the aftermath of intense crown fires where 90 percent of the organic layer was consumed, leaving a barren landscape of bare rock and mineral soil. Since 1995 was not a particularly good cone-producing year for either white or red pines, adjacent unburned stands didn't contribute many seeds to the burned areas. Consequently, regrowth the following year was primarily birch and aspen seedlings mixed with smaller plants such as fireweed, fringed bindweed, and big-leaf aster. If the research had been for only one year, the conclusion would have been that the old-growth pine stands in the intensely burned areas were going to be replaced by a primarily deciduous forest.

Subsequent years of research, however, showed how events shifted the balance toward pines.

Fortunately for pine regrowth, 1996 was a good cone crop year for red and white pines and the number of seedlings increased dramatically. The following year, a drought began in Quetico Park that lasted until 1999. Although the drought killed some of the red and white pine seedlings, the protection offered by fireweed and bigleaf aster enabled many of the seedlings to survive. The stressed pines produced another good cone crop in 1998. A blowdown in 1999 knocked over tall pines, resulting in increased sunlight reaching the seedlings and a further increase in red and white pine seedlings occurred in 2000 due to another large cone crop.

The large pine cone crops in 1996, 1998, and 2000 raise the question as to whether the stress from the fire and/or drought might have triggered closely spaced years of good cone production. Lynham's research seems to support the idea that stressed trees put their energy into cone production to increase the chances of survival of the next generation of pines.

Lynham and his crew also studied the regrowth in a red and white pine stand that was burned in a low-intensity ground fire. Similar to their findings in the high-intensity burn areas, there were only a small number of seedlings in the first year after the fire due to the low seed production by red and white pine in 1995. In contrast to the high-intensity fire sites, they found that mortality of pine seedlings was much higher on the low-intensity fire sites. They determined that this was primarily due to the minimal amount of ground cover left after a low-intensity ground fire.

Lynham's team found that red and white pine can germinate in low-light levels, but require higher levels of sunlight to survive and grow into mature trees. This means that seedlings can start on burned sites even when other plants, such as aspen, birch, and fireweed, dominate the regrowth at first. Although there may be enough sunlight to allow the germination of seedlings, they will flourish only if they receive sufficient sunlight to prosper as young trees. This can occur as the fireweed and other pioneer species diminish after a few years and the aspen and birch become thinned. As more competing species succumb to old age and dead trees topple, the pines get more sunlight and start to dominate the site.

Since fires alter the soil chemistry by lowering the pH and increasing some nutrients, soils were sampled in burn areas and compared to the samples from outside the burn. Poplar and birch usually grow rapidly and help keep the nutrients on site after a fire. They provide shelter for young pines and, because they have shorter life spans than red and white pine, they provide nutrients for the maturing pines when they die. Lynham's lengthy study, which ended in 2006, allowed him and his crew to investigate the complex interplay of varying cone production, drought, species interaction, and blowdown on intensely burned crown fire sites as well as low-intensity ground fire sites. The amount of regrowth of red and white pines they documented in both low- and high-intensity burn sites gives hope for the future of these magnificent pines in Quetico Park forests.

A crew under the guidance of Quetico Park biologist Lisa Solomon is monitoring regrowth in recently burned areas throughout the park. One of the areas is the region burned in the 2005 McNiece Lake fire. It is reassuring that one of the largest old-growth stands of red and white pine in Ontario is being monitored and even more assuring that they are finding significant regrowth of both red and white pine in burned areas.

RESURGENCE OF LIFE AFTER A FIRE

Numerous shrubs, herbs, and other vegetation play a major role in re-establishing a forest after a fire. Fireweed (*Epilobium angustifolium*) is probably the plant most associated with regrowth after a forest fire. It produces a large number of seeds covered with fine hairs that, like dandelion seeds, can be transported long distances by the wind. The flowers grow on a long stem and bloom from the bottom up. The bottom flowers are producing seeds in June while those at the top are still in bud and won't produce seeds until September. This unusually long seed production, which covers most of the fire season, is a primary reason for the presence of fireweed after most fires.

In many recently burned locations, two species not commonly seen in Quetico Park forests

Some species of liverworts grow in large numbers the year following a forest fire. These were growing the year after the 1995 fire on Pickerel Lake.

— geranium and liverwort — can be found carpeting the ground to the virtual exclusion of other species. The seeds of Bicknell's geranium (*Geranium bicknellii*) can lie dormant in the soil for over one hundred years. Although fire kills the seeds of most plants, the heating of the soil during a forest fire stimulates the germination of this germanium's seeds. After a fire, it gets a head start on most plants since its heat-resistant seeds are in the ground in a dormant state — a seed bank — until a fire passes through. Liverworts are primitive plants that look like mosses and are named for their flat, leaf-like structures that resemble the lobes of a liver. Some species of liverworts, especially *Marchantia polymorpha*, thrive in post-fire conditions since they grow on exposed mineral soil and their lightweight spores are dispersed into burned areas by the wind. In addition to appearing quickly after forest fires, they can occasionally be found growing in the charcoal of campfire rings of seldom used campsites. They usually persist for only a few years and are succeeded by ground lichens, herbs, and shrubs.

While conducting surveys of regrowth in a recently burned area near Brent Lake, Quetico Park biologist Lisa Solomon noticed dozens of ruby-throated hummingbirds feeding on the fireweed nectar. She noted that, although hummingbirds aren't normally associated with burned areas, it makes sense that the prolific growth of wildflowers in many burned areas provides excellent habitat for them. Researchers have also observed that insect populations that feed on fire-damaged vegetation increase dramatically after a fire. Wood-boring beetles — some species can detect a burn using infrared receptors on their legs — are among the first insects to colonize a burned area. Many species of woodpeckers, particularly black-backed woodpeckers (*Picoides arcticus*) and three-toed woodpeckers (*Picoides tridactylus*), feed on the beetles and their numbers also increase rapidly after a fire. For these birds, not only does their food source increase, but they also gain nesting sites in large, standing burned trees.

Tracks of deer and moose are frequently seen in recently burned areas, sometimes within months of the fire. Other animals don't usually appear in significant numbers until many years have gone by. Lynx fitted with radio collars in the BWCAW in 2007 were found to head directly toward the large area burned on the east side of Quetico Park in 1995. In the twelve years since the fire occurred, the vegetation had recovered to the point where it contained high snowshoe hare populations that attracted the lynx.

AS ESSENTIAL AS SUNLIGHT AND ADEQUATE MOISTURE

Thirty-five years ago, Miron Heinselman set the tone for future work in the Quetico-Superior area when he wrote: "Fire largely determined the composition and structure of the presettlement vegetation in the Boundary Waters Canoe Area as well as the vegetation mosaic on the landscape and the habitat patterns for wildlife. It also influenced nutrient cycles, and energy pathways, and helped maintain the diversity, productivity, and long term stability of the ecosystem. Thus the whole ecosystem is fire-dependent."[7]

Heinselman's fire history studies in the 1960s and 1970s provided the base of knowledge on which others, in both Quetico Park and the BWCAW, have built. Research focused on fire ecology has greatly increased our understanding of the role of fire in area forests. Investigations into the history of Quetico-Superior fires have clearly shown how fire has consistently been an integral part of Quetico-Superior forests since soon after the glaciers retreated. While fire can be a powerful, destructive force, we are now more appreciative of its constructive, regenerative powers. In contrast to the teachings of *Bambi* and Smokey Bear, fire is as essential to the long-term health of wilderness forests as sunlight and adequate moisture.

In *The Wild Trees*, Richard Preston notes that: "Time has a different quality in a forest, a different kind of flow. Time moves in circles, and events are linked, even if it's not obvious that they are linked. Events in a forest occur with precision in the flow of tree time, like the motions of an endless dance."[8] We are increasingly aware that fire is an intimate partner in this long, intricate ecological dance.

CHAPTER SIXTEEN

TAILS BENEATH THE SNOW:
LIFE IN THE PUKAK

The winter woods can be silent and seemingly devoid of life. The deep and persistent cold of a Quetico-Superior winter forces most birds to migrate, some mammals to hibernate, and plants to make "antifreeze" to keep their cells from freezing while they store their resources underground. The impression is that the forest's inhabitants are asleep and that life will awaken in the spring.

There is, however, an "underside" of winter. A world of complex tunnels, icy columns, and bustling life exists under the snow. This environment — where a mouse is a large mammal, the largest predator is the size and shape of a banana, a tree trunk is a critical obstacle, the wind never blows, and the sun doesn't shine — is a haven for the small. The Inuit word for this miniature world is *pukak*.

I first became aware of the pukak and life under the snow in the 1970s when reading *Wild Harmony: Animals of the North* by William O. Pruitt. He vividly describes how a red-backed vole, an animal I had never heard of, spends the winter in the pukak, a place I never knew existed. He emphasized the significance

of scale — small animals living in habitats of which large animals like ourselves are unaware — and the importance of the pukak as the winter home for small creatures that have a major impact on the ecology of Quetico Park simply because of their numbers. Surprisingly, the total weight of mammals living under the snow in the pukak in mid-winter often exceeds the weight of the mammals living above the snow.

GEOTHERMAL HEAT AND A BLANKET OF SNOW

For large mammals, including humans, deep snow is a hindrance to travel and survival. When the snow is deep, animals deplete valuable energy resources finding food and avoiding predators. Occasionally, extreme winters can have devastating effects on wildlife. During the winter of 1995–96, exceptionally deep snow caused the populations of white-tailed deer to drop dramatically in both northern Minnesota and northwestern Ontario. That winter,

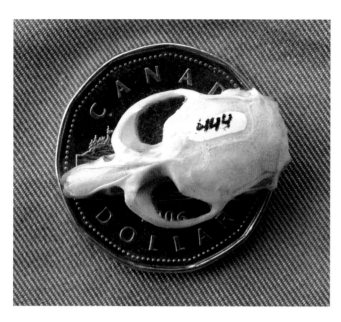

The skull of a red-backed vole has openings for the large eyes that, as in most prey animals, provide good peripheral vision. This specimen from Lakehead University in Thunder Bay, Ontario, was photographed on a Canadian loonie to show its relative size.

even moose, whose long, stilt-like legs make them well adapted to moving through deep drifts, were dragging their bellies in the snow.

In contrast, deep snow is beneficial for most small mammals. For chipmunks, mice, shrews, and voles, a major threat to their surviving the winter is the lack of sufficient snow rather than too much. Snow actually provides a refuge for them. The small size of these mammals makes them very susceptible to the cold. Hypothermia and freezing to death are constant threats and they have to find a way to avoid the cold if they are to survive the long winters in the Quetico-Superior region. Small mammals use leaf mould, pine needles, and other decaying vegetation as insulation when the temperature plummets. They can also utilize rotting stumps and tangles of downed limbs and branches for both insulation and protection and can burrow into the soil. Snow, however, offers the best protection for these small creatures. Living under frozen flakes seems like an unlikely way to avoid the cold, but snow is actually a very good insulator. Acting as a blanket over the earth, the snow keeps the ground level habitat of the pukak at a liveable temperature.

Fluffy, falling snow is comprised of over 90 percent air and even snow on the ground can contain as much as 70 percent air. It is the air trapped between the crystals that makes snow a good insulator. The blanket of snow traps the heat radiating up from deep in the earth and also insulates the ground from the cold air above the snow. When there is no snow, or insufficient snow, the ground heat is lost into the atmosphere.

The amount of snow needed to keep the soil surface temperature near freezing even in the coldest weather — called the heimal threshold — depends on the outside temperature and how packed-down the snow has become. Researchers have found that the snow depth required to reach the heimal threshold varies from twenty to thirty centimetres, depending on the amount of compaction. Quetico Park usually has snow of this depth by late November or early December, but in some winters that depth isn't reached until much later. When the snow reaches this depth, the temperature of the ground layer stabilizes within a few degrees of freezing, regardless of the temperature of the outside air. The warmth that is constantly radiating from deep within the earth slowly decomposes and sublimates the snow crystals at the base of the snow pack. A latticework of ice columns and openings appears and the naturally occurring openings caused by ground vegetation and leaf litter are enlarged.

The network of openings that make up the pukak forms where there are sufficient herbs and other small plants to keep some of the snow from coming in contact with the ground. This causes small openings or cavities that are added to and enlarged by heat coming up from the ground. Pukak layers vary considerably, depending on the habitat and the conditions as the snow accumulates. A mowed lawn will have virtually no pukak, but most areas with undisturbed vegetation will have a pukak layer as long as there is at least twenty centimetres of snow. Where there is little or no vegetation, and there are many such places in Quetico, no pukak layer forms regardless of the depth of snow. Areas with bedrock at the surface, boulder-strewn shorelines, and the ice surface of ponds and lakes are examples of places in Quetico where the pukak doesn't form, regardless of snow depth.

AT HOME IN THE PUKAK

A study of the small mammals of Quetico Park was conducted in the mid-1970s by David Nagorsen from the Royal Ontario Museum in Toronto, Ontario. His team found two species of chipmunks and thirteen species of land mammals smaller than chipmunks. They located and identified three mouse, five shrew, four vole, and just one lemming species. Another researcher, Doug Morris, a biology professor at Lakehead University in Thunder Bay, Ontario, conducts studies on the habitat selection and structure of communities of red-backed voles, meadow voles, and other small mammals found in northwestern Ontario and throughout the

A researcher holds a meadow vole identified by its ear tag on a research plot near Thunder Bay, Ontario.

An inquisitive red-backed vole visits a Quetico Park campsite in September, 2008.

Quetico-Superior region. Much of his research is carried out under controlled conditions on a plot of land about 150 kilometres east of Quetico Park and not far from Thunder Bay.

The most common mammal in Quetico and the BWCAW is one that, in spite of its large numbers, is only occasionally seen at any time of year. The red-backed vole is a plump, mouse-sized animal with a broad chestnut stripe that runs from its forehead to its rump. It is a secretive creature, but can be seen in the early morning and evening, scurrying and scavenging food around campsites in Quetico. Because of its abundance, this vole is important prey for numerous predators and plays a vital role in the ecology of the Quetico-Superior area. Although red-backed voles were just one of fifteen species of small mammals found in the Quetico Park study, they comprised about half of the total animals captured. These voles were found in all of the habitats studied, everywhere from wet meadows to dry, upland slopes. Four species related to the red-backed vole were also found in Quetico Park. The meadow vole, heather vole, rock vole, and southern bog lemming are all more specialized in their requirements and each of these species is found in specific habitats. All are far less common in Quetico than the red-backed vole. Voles and other small mammals are near the bottom of the food chain and are a main source of food for weasels, fox, hawks, owls, and other predators.

Red fox searching for prey in shallow snow in Sleeping Giant Provincial Park.

The populations of these varied predators are, to a large extent, dependent on the populations of these small mammals.

Snow, especially deep snow, helps to protect pukak dwellers from large predators. However, red foxes have been observed jumping into the air and coming down on their front feet to pin voles and mice to the ground. It is believed foxes use their acute hearing to precisely locate these small mammals below the snow and are able to capture them in the pukak even though they can't see them. Smaller predators, like marten and mink, are not small enough to hunt in the pukak, but weasels have extremely slender, sinuous bodies that allow them to follow their prey, primarily voles, mice, and shrews, through the narrow runways under the snow. Weasels are particularly sensitive to the cold because their long, thin bodies have a relatively large surface area from which heat escapes. They, too, find both warmth and food in the pukak.

Long-tailed and short-tailed weasels are common in the Quetico-Superior region and the least weasel, the smallest Canadian true carnivore, has been recorded in Quetico Park. This tiny creature has to elevate its metabolism to stay warm in winter and eats up to half its body weight each day. All weasels have very high metabolic rates and Richard Conniff, a well-known American writer on biological topics, has described weasels as having "the metabolism of a hip-hop dancer on a caffeine bender."[1] Carolyn King, a biologist from England who has studied weasels for over thirty years, reported that she tried to count the heartbeats of a short-tailed weasel but "it proved impossible: the heart was purring like a little sewing machine."[2]

Weasels are renowned for their ability to kill prey much larger than themselves, such as snowshoe hare and ruffed grouse, and are so aggressive that other predators usually avoid them. In one recorded case, however, a hawk flew down and grabbed a weasel in its talons only to be seen falling to its death just seconds later with the weasel's teeth embedded in its throat. Unlike the small mammals they are hunting, weasels frequently enter and leave the pukak, but they are not permanent occupants. Researchers have proposed that pukak dwellers occasionally create tunnels leading from the pukak to the surface of the snow as ventilation shafts to dispel carbon dioxide, which can build up to dangerous levels beneath the snow. Weasels can enter or leave the pukak by using these ventilation tubes or they can simply burrow through the snow.

There are three known species of mice in Quetico Park, and one of them, the deer mouse, is Quetico's second most common small mammal. Two mouse species, the woodland-jumping mouse and meadow-jumping mouse, are primarily seed-eaters and spend the winter in insulated nests below the snow. The deer mouse and both the least chipmunk and the eastern chipmunk, store up food in the fall and spend much of the winter in a state of reduced metabolism and temperature known as torpor. They huddle together for warmth with members of their own species, eat their stored food, and occasionally venture out of their nests to collect seeds and to seek out any other food they can find.

Movement is somewhat constrained in the subnivean world. Some places, primarily places where the pukak doesn't form due to lack of vegetation close to the ground, evidently can't be reached during the winter. Travel is restricted to corridors of ample space through which animals can manoeuvre. Even though corridors can be enlarged and extended, there are barriers, such as downed tree limbs, creeks, and lakes that make some areas inaccessible. The inability to reach spots containing valuable food resources limits the food available in the winter.

Voles, mice, and lemmings are primarily herbivores that feed on the shoots, leaves, bark, berries, and fungi that are accessible to them in the pukak. One drawback to living in the pukak is the finite food supply for these creatures. In addition to the restrictions imposed by the corridors, the plant food available under the snow is limited to what was there at the end of the growing season. Since no new food is being produced to replace what is consumed, the food supply declines throughout the winter.

Shrews are fascinating and poorly understood animals that roam the pukak all winter, preying on insects and the occasional small mammal. Shrews have a novel way of dealing with the decrease in available food in the winter. They simply get smaller.

A shrew found dead on the surface of the snow along the hiking trail east of French Lake that follows the old logging road. This shrew, probably a masked shrew, did not have puncture marks nor any other evidence of what caused its demise.

Their energy needs are decreased by their losing up to 45 percent of their body weight. Their kidneys and other internal organs, as well as their brain, are reduced in size to help them survive the leaner times of winter.

The pygmy shrew, the smallest mammal in our area, and the smallest mammal in North America, gets even smaller in the winter. This shrew is only seven to eight centimetres long and weighs less than a quarter coin. Despite its size, this tiny mammal is a predator. It eats mainly beetles and other insects, but also preys on spiders and earthworms. Shrews generally have the smallest bodies and the fastest metabolism of all the mammals, and the pygmy shrew, being the smallest, has the highest metabolic rate of all. Its heart beats at the astonishing rate of twelve hundred beats a minute. This shrew has to eat almost constantly in order to maintain its metabolism and can starve to death after only a few hours without food.

The pukak is also the winter home of the only poisonous mammal in North America, the short-tailed shrew. This mouse-sized, fairly common, shrew is unusual because its saliva is toxic, allowing it to kill prey larger than itself. Astonishingly, they have been known to kill garter snakes, young rabbits, and snowshoe hares in the summer.

The most common shrew in Quetico, and the third-most common small mammal, is the masked shrew, which is found in almost every habitat in the park. Researchers have found them in habitats as diverse as acid bogs and mature coniferous forests. Like its slightly larger cousin, the arctic shrew, it is thought to mainly eat insects, but has a varied diet that is known to include vegetation and the young of mice, voles, and other shrews. In the pukak it probably feeds primarily on the wide variety of insects spending the winter there. The pukak, otherwise, would be a safe place for insects except for these masked shrews and other insectivores that voraciously eat them. Quetico's fifth shrew, the water shrew, is unusual in that it spends a great deal of time in the water. Little is known about its life in the winter.

Researchers in the boreal forest in Manitoba have shown that plants and fungi under the snow are eaten by a wide variety of insects such as ground beetles, aphids, springtails, and leafhopper nymphs. They, in turn, can be preyed upon by spiders, centipedes, carnivorous beetles, and mites. To complete the pukak food web, these creatures can be eaten by shrews.

LIMITATIONS OF THE PUKAK

The pukak, like all habitats, has its limitations and drawbacks. Carbon dioxide levels can build up and reach dangerous levels, the food supply is limited to what is present when the winter began, and movement is restricted to where the openings in the pukak lead. It is always relatively warm in these tunnels, but the blanket of snow that protects pukak dwellers from the cold also effectively blocks most of the light from entering. When the snow reaches a depth of about thirty centimetres, even the midday sun causes only a faint glow of soft, bluish light to reach the pukak, and only about 1 percent of the light penetrates to the ground when the snow depth reaches double that depth. In the pukak, light penetration is such that organisms can only be vaguely aware of the sun and they are oblivious to the stars, moon, or northern lights.

Because of the dark, animals in the pukak have to rely mainly on their senses of smell, touch, and hearing. This darkness of the pukak is not a major problem for shrews since they have poor vision and rely largely on their sense of smell. Other pukak dwellers also require a keen sense of smell and use it to find a food cache, avoid predators, and detect their own territorial markings or those of other species. Voles, mice, and shrews also utilize their sense of touch to navigate through the complex system of natural openings and tunnels in the pukak. Voles have long, sensitive whiskers around their face and a bracelet of short, stiff hairs around their wrists. They use their whiskers and stiff hairs to determine the width of openings and to probe into crevices. Sensitive hearing allows them to detect faint sounds and to communicate with members of their own species. They can also feel the vibrations of footsteps of a predator approaching on top of the snow.

Populations of the small mammals that occupy the pukak in the winter fluctuate greatly from year to year. They can quickly recover from low populations because they can have many litters in one year and commonly have five or six young in each litter. In addition to having numerous large litters, the females of some vole species are ready to breed when they are just six weeks old. These high birth rates, however, are balanced by high mortality. Most shrews, mice, voles, and lemmings are thought to live only about one or two years on the average. Although predation within the pukak is limited to creatures small enough to travel through the pukak maze, the predatory weasels and shrews that live in or travel through the pukak are effective

and efficient killers. Predation can also come from outside the pukak. In addition to the threat of red fox, wolves, and coyotes, pukak dwellers are also prey for owls that can dive into the snow to snare mice and voles with their talons.

The red squirrel is the one animal whose size places it between those that live above and below the snow. They are active most winter days but spend nights in insulated nests in tree cavities. William Pruitt has noted that during periods of extreme cold, red squirrels move into subterranean tunnels beneath he snow. He stated: "The critical temperature that sends them from the environment of the moose, fox and lynx into the environment of the shrew and red-backed vole seems to lie between -32°C and -34°C."[4]

DANGEROUS TIMES IN THE PUKAK

Over the last decade, Quetico Park has experienced a few winters when there was very little snow until January. In winters when snowfall sufficient for the formation of the pukak is delayed, the period of danger of dying from hypothermia for small mammals is extended. In an article titled "Life in the Snow," Dr. Pruitt wrote, "the period between the onset of sub-freezing temperatures and the development of the snow cover to the heimal threshold undoubtedly gives shrews, voles, and lemmings their severest trials."[4]

An early or late winter temperature of -10°C with little snow cover is much harder on small mammals than -40°C in mid-winter when the snow depth protects them from the cold air. This has been substantiated by long-term population studies of small mammals in Scandinavia indicating that winters without much snow showed a greater decline in small mammal populations than winters with extreme cold.

Another dangerous time is during periods of very warm weather, usually in March or April, when the rapid melting of snow can cause flooding of the pukak. During this transition time, the snow that protected pukak dwellers all winter becomes unstable and changes into a dangerous, cold liquid. Tunnels collapse, mini-avalanches occur, and animals are forced out from under the snow where they become vulnerable to land predators like martens and red foxes, and aerial predators like owls and hawks. Although the pukak can be an unpredictable, unstable environment, it provides a haven for small mammals during times when most would be unable to survive the combination of cold and predators without its protection.

THE MOUSE AND THE MOOSE

Large, bulky creatures, such as humans, are oblivious to the vibrant, thriving communities that live under the snow. An intact web of life — where animals are killed and new life is created — occurs in the vibrant micro-environment under a mantle of snow. In a chapter entitled "Coming of the Snow," Sigurd Olson lyrically described the pukak world beneath his snowshoes as a "jungle of grassy roots and stems, tiny mountains of sphagnum, forests of heather, the whole interwoven with thousands of twisting burrows of meadow mice.... Theirs was a world removed, an intricate winter community, self-sufficient and well organized."[5]

The small mammals in the Quetico-Superior area are able to survive, and even thrive, during our long harsh winters by using snow to their advantage. They evade the extreme mid-winter cold by using snow as a blanket, and the earth as a constant source of low heat. They live in an unexpected, surreal environment and have replaced the bitter wind and extreme cold with confined spaces, dim light and constant coolness. When the snow is deep, the moose and the mouse live in the same woods but in very different worlds.

CHAPTER SEVENTEEN

UNCOMMON SENSE: LIFE UNDER THE ICE

Almost half of the surface of Quetico Park is covered by water. When paddling through this mosaic of lakes, rivers, and wetlands, it is hard to believe that fresh water is a relatively rare commodity in most of the world. Although 70 percent of the earth's surface is covered with water, only 3 percent is fresh water. Canada has more than its share and fresh water is found in abundance in the Quetico-Superior. The varied landscapes and diverse creatures found in and on the water are the primary attractions that draw people to Quetico and keep them coming back.

Quetico is a montage of aqueous habitats — lakes, rivers, ponds, creeks, swamps, marshes, and bogs. People love paddling on them, swimming in them, and seeing the loons, beavers, mergansers, otter, great blue herons, painted turtles, and other creatures that inhabit them. As appealing as these birds and animals are, they are merely part of the background for the thousands of people who come to Quetico primarily to catch the walleye, lake trout, smallmouth bass, and northern pike that inhabit its lakes.

It is the unusual physical properties of water that makes it possible for such an alluring assortment of organisms to exist in Quetico, where the lakes are frozen and cut off from sunlight and oxygen for almost half the year. Fortunately for life in northern lakes and for the bald eagles, the fishermen, and the multitude of other creatures that depend on the fish for food, water's odd characteristics work to their advantage. Three of these remarkable physical properties play especially important roles in the ecology of aquatic ecosystems in the Quetico-Superior area: 1. Solid ice floats on liquid water; 2. water is its most dense at 4°C; and 3. more oxygen dissolves in cold water than in warm water. Without these properties, there wouldn't be the quantity or diversity of life that now exists in Quetico. In fact, if ice didn't float on water, by late winter there wouldn't even be any liquid water left in most lakes to provide a habitat for fish.

Water is the only compound that is found on earth as a solid, a liquid, and a gas. In its liquid phase, such a wide variety of substances dissolve in water that it is known as the universal solvent. This universal solvent and the myriad substances dissolved in it sustain our bodies from within by flowing through our veins as blood. On a much larger scale, this ability to dissolve substances as diverse as oxygen, phosphates, and sodium helps sustain life in oceans and fresh water. The curious physical properties of water also play a central role in how life in Quetico's lakes, rivers, streams, ponds, marshes, and bogs is sustained and distributed.

TURNOVER TIMES

During the summer, the sun warms the water near the surface of lakes and they become layered with the lighter warm water floating above the denser, cooler water below. The temperature of the surface water is dependent on a variety of factors and will vary from lake to lake, but it usually peaks around 20°C in Quetico lakes. The water temperature slowly decreases with depth until the thermocline — an abrupt change in temperature that separates the warmer surface water from the colder deep water — is reached. Below

In the summer, the oxygen and nutrients circulate above the thermocline. The spring and fall turnovers cause the oxygen (concentrated in the upper part of the lake) and nutrients (more concentrated near the bottom) to become distributed vertically throughout the lake.

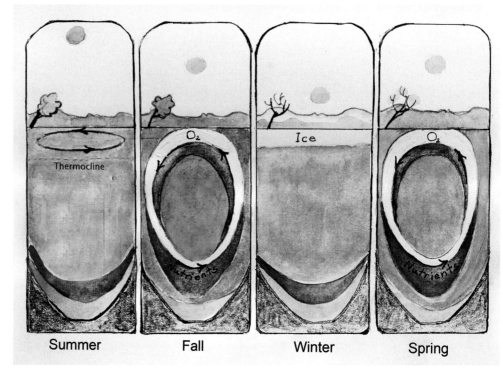

Summer Fall Winter Spring

Diagram by Jennifer Garrett, Atikokan, Ontario.

the thermocline, the temperature quickly drops to a constant 4°C. Like other liquids, water becomes more dense (heavier) as it cools, but it reaches its maximum density at 4°C rather than at 0°C. This unusual correlation between the density and temperature is the reason that water at the bottom of deep lakes in the Quetico-Superior remains at 4°C — the temperature of the densest water — regardless of the season or the surface temperature of the water.

When the temperature of the surface water reaches its peak in mid- or late July, the thermocline, near the surface in early summer when the lake begins to warm, has sunk many metres. The depth of the thermocline, which varies from summer to summer and from lake to lake, will slowly move back up as the water cools in the fall. The sunlight that warms the water also stimulates the growth of microscopic photosynthetic organisms in the water called phytoplankton. Like plants on land, they are the base of the food chain and also produce much of the oxygen essential to other organisms in the lake. Since phytoplankton require sunlight for photosynthesis, most of the plant food and oxygen are produced in the well-lit, upper part of the lake.

In addition to the oxygen obtained from phytoplankton, water also obtains oxygen from contact with the air and, to a much lesser extent, from "seeps" and springs that bring water into the lake. Anything that increases the interaction between air and water raises the amount of oxygen dissolved in the water. Waterfalls, rapids, and wind, especially strong winds that generate large waves, increase the oxygen levels of water. The increased level of oxygen below waterfalls and rapids is one of the reasons that fish are attracted to these areas.

The contact with the air and photosynthetic activity throughout the summer and fall months slowly increases the amount of oxygen dissolved

Suckers spawn in the spring in the fast water below a small rapids in the northern part of Quetico Park.

235

in the surface water. The layering produced by the warming of the water, however, prevents the oxygenated water near the surface from mixing with the water below the thermocline. Most of the activity in Quetico's lakes occurs in the upper portion where, not only is the water warmer, but where the bulk of the food and oxygen are also found. As the oxygen increases in the surface water, nutrients accumulate on the bottom of the lake in the form of organic material, such as leaves, pollen, animal feces, and dead organisms of all kinds. Decomposers, primarily bottom-dwelling bacteria and fungi, slowly break down this organic material into nutrients that dissolve in the water. The layering of the water in the summer and early fall traps these nutrients beneath the thermocline just as the oxygen is isolated in the upper water levels.

The surface water temperature gradually decreases in late summer and fall until the entire lake becomes a uniform 4°C. The autumn winds and lake currents will then mix the entire lake. This mixing of the water throughout the lake in the fall — known as the fall turnover or overturn — allows the highly oxygenated surface water to blend with and replace the oxygen-depleted water from the bottom of the lake. This occurs at an opportune time since organisms, such as lake trout, that are usually found in the deeper parts of the lake require oxygen to be replenished in the depths of the lake. Turnover also allows the nutrient-rich water from the bottom to mix with water from the surface.

The floating "black ice" that forms on lakes just prior to ice-out is clearly present here on French Lake.

Turnover occurs again in the spring when the water warms to a uniform 4°C, as well as in the fall, when the lake water cools to the same uniform 4°C. When the ice melts in the spring, the surface water is 0°C. As the surface water warms, it becomes denser and starts to sink. When the entire lake becomes a uniform 4°C, spring turnover occurs. Just as in the fall turnover, the nutrient-rich water from the bottom mixes with the relatively oxygen-rich water from the surface. The nutrients isolated at the bottom of the lake would not be available for recycling by phytoplankton inhabiting the more biologically active upper layers of the lake if turnover didn't occur. The warm spring sun enhances the growth of the phytoplankton that survived the cold water and dim winter light under the ice.

Most northern lakes have twice yearly turnover, but there are exceptions. Small, but very deep lakes may have only partial turnovers or have a complete turnover only in the fall when winds are strong enough to thoroughly mix the lake. A few small, deep lakes studied in the Quetico-Superior area, such as Miners Lake in Ely, Minnesota, don't turn over completely and have a stagnant bottom layer. At the other extreme, shallow lakes warm to the bottom so summer stratification doesn't occur and their water is mixed by the wind so the oxygen and nutrients become blended without turnover.

In tropical lakes and other areas where the surface water temperatures don't get as low as 4°C, turnover doesn't occur, the depths of the lake are too low in oxygen to support much fish activity, and nutrients get trapped at the bottom of the lake. These lakes are less productive than they would be if the oxygen and nutrients were distributed throughout the lake by turnover as they are in northern lakes.

FLOATING ICE AND OXYGEN-RICH WATER

Anyone who has forgotten to add sufficient antifreeze to a vehicle or who didn't adequately drain the plumbing at the cabin is well aware that ice expands as it freezes. Water is highly unusual in that it expands, rather than contracts, as it changes from a liquid to a solid. If it acted like most compounds, ice would sink as it formed, and during the winter it would be continuously forming at the surface and dropping to the bottom.

The consequences would be enormous. Every cold winter night, as fast as the surface water would freeze, ice would sink to the bottom. This would cause lakes to freeze solid from the bottom up. Rather than "icing over," lakes would "ice under." Quetico Park lakes, with the possible exception of the deepest, largest lakes — such as Agnes, Pickerel, and Basswood lakes — would be solid ice before the winter was over. This would obviously be devastating and many, if not most, aquatic species would not be able to survive these conditions. In addition, the ice at the bottom of lakes would melt very slowly and this would have a cooling effect on our summer temperatures.

Fortunately for the ecology of lakes in the north, ice floats on the top of the water and acts as an insulating layer between the water and the frigid winter air above. Any accumulation of snow on top of the ice adds another, and better, insulating layer that further slows the formation of additional ice. Even with these insulating layers, lakes can still accumulate one metre of ice, strong testimony to the severity and length of our colder winters.

Ice and snow insulate the water from the cold air above the ice, but they also greatly decrease the amount of light entering the water. The combination of low light levels and low water temperatures causes photosynthesis to slow down greatly in the winter. Therefore, the amount of oxygen that is in the water at freeze-up, with only slight additions by seeps and photosynthesis under the ice, has to last until the ice cover melts in the spring. When the ice forms and seals them in for almost half the year, fish and other oxygen-using organisms have to get by on the oxygen present when the ice forms.

Fortunately, lakes at freeze-up have high concentrations of oxygen since the colder the water is, the more oxygen it holds. At freeze-up, the surface water is at 0°C and at this temperature water holds almost 50 percent more oxygen than it does at 20°C. Once again, the unusual chemistry of water works to the advantage of aquatic organisms in the north.

FISH BENEATH THE ICE

As the water temperature drops and lakes begin to ice over, there is a corresponding decrease in the metabolic rates of many fish species. Species that spend most of the time in the warmer parts of the lake in the summer, such as smallmouth bass and largemouth bass, become less active in colder water. This decreased activity — although they still may move considerable distances — lowers their requirements for both food and oxygen, which are both in shorter supply in late winter under the ice than they are in the summer.

The lower water temperatures tend to increase the amount of time required for muscle to contract and this lowers the maximum swimming speed of many fish.[1] Not all species of fish, however, swim slower and become less active in cold water. Researchers have found that some fish spend a substantial amount of time in relatively warm shallow parts of the lake in the summer, such as yellow pickerel (walleye) and northern pike, are able to elevate the levels of enzymes that enable them to maintain a higher metabolic rate in cold water. This allows them to remain active all winter and to continue to actively pursue prey, but probably not at the same intensity as in the summer.

Fish that spend most of the summer in the cold water below the thermocline thrive in cold-water conditions and don't have to make adjustments to remain active throughout the winter. Lake trout, burbot, and a few other species of cold-water fish enter the warmer surface waters in the summer for just short periods to feed. They spend the vast majority of time in the colder water, but can travel everywhere in the lake during turnover in late fall and early spring when the lake has a uniform temperature of 4°C. Due to the unusual chemistry of water, the 4°C lake water that lake trout spend most of their time in is the warmest water in the winter and the coldest water in the summer.

Lake trout are the best known of the fish species whose metabolisms remain high and who continue to be active predators that seek out and catch minnows and small fish all winter. Although the cold does not bother them, they have to contend with decreasing amounts of both available prey and oxygen levels as the winter progresses. It would be interesting to know how lake trout hunt in the depths of the lake where there is little or no light. Even in very clear lakes, light only penetrates to a depth of twenty metres or so, and below that it slowly fades to pitch black. With the sun so low in the sky, light levels are at their lowest in the winter and even during the day lake trout have to capture prey with very few visual clues in the little light that penetrates through the snow and ice. They may use a combination of their sense of smell and their ability to detect movement through vibrations in the water, but a more precise understanding of how they are able to find and capture prey under these conditions is one of the many unknowns of lake ecology.

An interesting, additional fact about lake trout is their scientific name — *Salvelinus namaycush* — which is based on the Ojibwa name (*nahmagoos*) for this fish. To my knowledge, this is the only species whose scientific name contains an Ojibwa word.

Another fascinating cold-water species is the burbot. This odd-looking fish, also known as eelpout, lawyer, or ling, is a freshwater relative of the cod. Burbot has an unusual scientific name, *Lota lota*, a name seemingly inspired by Dr. Seuss. Burbot spawn in the winter under the ice. They gather over a gravel or sand bottom in shallow water and form a writhing, intertwined ball of fish. After releasing their eggs and sperm, the fish thrash about, scattering the eggs, which later fall to the bottom. A large female can lay as many as one million eggs. The embryos develop for four to five weeks in the cold water and hatch when just 3–3.5 millimetres long — one of the smallest of freshwater fish larvae. Burbot have been caught, along with lake trout, in nets at depths of well over one hundred metres in Lake Superior. They are active all winter and are often caught by people ice-fishing. They are also caught in Quetico lakes in the summer by people fishing in deep water for lake trout. Their eel-like shape, elongated fins, and smooth, slimy skin probably account for fishermen commonly throwing them back in spite of their excellent taste. They have a rubbery texture when fried, but are excellent in many dishes, including *mojakka* (Finnish stew). Burbot, boiled and doused in butter is known as "poor man's lobster."

Whitefish and their smaller relative, ciscoes, also remain active under the ice. Ciscoes are also found below the thermocline in the summer, but often enter warmer water to feed. Their wide-ranging travels are responsible for their importance as summer food for lake trout and burbot in deep water and for loons near the surface. The presence of large numbers of ciscoes on Bayley Bay of Basswood Lake, where they can be seen surfacing on still days in the summer, are probably responsible for the concentration of loons that gather there every fall.

OTHER SPECIES BENEATH THE ICE

Since photosynthesis slows dramatically under the ice, very little food is produced and the amount steadily decreases as it is consumed by fish during the winter. It's no wonder that many organisms cope with these conditions by slowing their metabolism so they require less food. Being cold-blooded, the metabolism of frogs slows whenever the temperature decreases. They become lethargic, even in mid-summer, when the temperature drops and they take lethargy to an extreme in the winter.

Some frogs in the Quetico-Superior, including mink frogs and leopard frogs, hibernate under the ice. They scoop out shallow pits in the sand or gravel bottom of ponds or shallow bays of lakes, slow their metabolism and meet their minimal oxygen requirements by simply breathing through their skin. In studying frogs, researchers at Carleton University in Ottawa, Ontario, found that they survive under the ice by entering a "liquid-cooled coma."[2] Researchers snorkelling in Ontario streams in mid-winter have seen leopard frogs wedged between rocks in deep pools. Hibernating underwater and breathing through the skin is a strange way to spend the winter, but other frog species have an even more novel approach. Wood frogs, grey tree frogs, and spring peepers simply seek out a well-insulated place along the forest floor, such as under leaf litter, and survive the winter in a frozen state. Chemicals, such as glucose, act as natural antifreeze and also initiate a series of physiological changes that allow these frogs to survive for months while frozen.

Their metabolism slows down, their hearts stop beating, their breathing stops, and their brains cease to function. In the spring, they slowly thaw from the inside out: the interior organs first and finally the limbs. Bernd Heinrich, a biologist who wrote a fascinating book called *Winter World*, stated that the survival of frozen frogs is "a medical marvel that challenges the limits of our beliefs of what seems possible."[3]

Snapping turtles and painted turtles manage to survive the winter by filling their lungs with oxygen-rich air on the surface and then swimming to the bottom of a lake before freeze-up and burrowing into the mud. Remarkably, this is a dive that lasts for about six months. Researchers have found that a painted turtle's heart beats as little as once every ten or eleven minutes. Since lungs are specialized organs for breathing air, organisms like frogs and turtles have adapted other ways of absorbing oxygen from water. While

Photo by Marie Nelson, Thunder Bay, Ontario.

As its species name indicates, the grey tree frog (*Hyla versicolor*) is able to change its colour. This tree frog, clinging to a branch on the Beaverhouse-to-Quetico-Lake portage, took on the colour of the predominantly green background.

A painted turtle swims near the dock at Prairie Portage.

they lie buried in the mud in a dormant state, they have very low requirements for oxygen. They are able to absorb sufficient oxygen from the water through their skin and through their cloaca, the opening to their reproductive and excretory systems, which is lined with a rich network of blood vessels.

Since snapping turtles often over-winter very close together in an area known as a hibernacula, they are very vulnerable to predation and many can be killed in a short time span. At the site of the long-term study of snapping turtles in Ontario's Algonquin Park, a large number of snapping turtles were killed one winter by otters who ate the viscera out of the hibernating and defenceless turtles.

TOPSY-TURVY WORLD

Conditions faced by organisms under the ice are strangely similar to those faced by organisms at the bottom of the snow, in the pukak. In both places, the temperatures are not far from the freezing point, it is either pitch black or has only dim, filtered light, and the food source is constantly dwindling throughout the winter. In addition, both the sub-ice and the subnivean are topsy-turvy worlds where it is the warmest on the bottom and the coldest on the top. In lakes, however, it is bizarre water chemistry, rather than the earth's heat, that is the primary reason for the relative warmth at the bottom.

The organisms beneath the ice, like those beneath the snow, have met these unusual conditions in diverse and innovative ways. Some hide in crevices between rocks and others bury themselves in the mud, while some undoubtedly use methods that we know nothing about. Winter under the ice is as contrasting in lifestyles as it is uniform in temperature. Organisms in deep hibernation manage to co-exist with active predators. Some aquatic creatures, like lake trout, remain as active in the winter as they are in the summer, while a painted turtle is in hibernation so profound that it takes a single breath that lasts for six months. This odd fact is an example of why the English biologist Richard Dawkins noted: "The essence of life is statistical improbability on a colossal scale."[4]

CHAPTER EIGHTEEN

FLOATERS, STILTERS, AND AGGRESSIVE PLANTS

Finding tracks in the snow and trying to decipher what kind of animal made them, when they were made, and what the animal was doing at the time, reminds me of archaeology. In both tracking and archaeology, one is trying to establish what happened in the past based on a limited amount of physical evidence. The advantage in analyzing animal tracks rather than spear points or clay pipes is that the tracks, as ephemeral as they may be, were made recently rather than hundreds or thousands of years ago. I've usually seen the type of animals whose tracks I find, but I'm never going to come face to face with a Palaeo-Indian or have an eighteenth-century French-Canadian voyageur appear in front of me.

Although both tracks and artifacts can tell a story, it takes someone with the knowledge and practical experience to bring the information to life and make the account very compelling. If the tracks are fairly clear and not too old, most naturalists are very good at identifying the type of animal that made them. The people who have impressed me the most, however, are experienced trappers and intense,

skilled hunters. In order to be successful, they have developed the ability to interpret, rather than just identify, animal tracks. They can often determine when the tracks were made, the sex and age of the animal, the speed at which the animal was travelling, and other facts of value to a trapper or hunter.

FLOATERS AND STILTERS

Each significant snowfall leaves a blank, white canvas that, with time, becomes a map of the comings and goings of numerous creatures. The surface of the snow, however, doesn't give a complete picture of these activities. Mammals chipmunk-size or smaller live in the pukak, the subnivean world beneath the blanket of snow. They seldom venture onto the snow's surface once the snow gets deep enough to provide insulation. However, that same deep snow that benefits pukak dwellers by providing insulation and protection from most predators can also be a major problem to animals living above the snow.

Animals that are too large to enter the pukak have to find ways to travel effectively when snow arrives. There are two main methods of coping with the problem of travelling through deep snow: "floaters" attempt to stay on top, while "stilters" use their

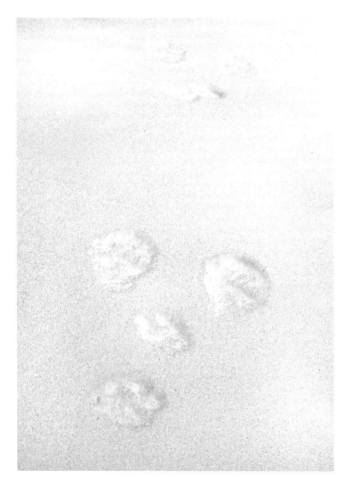

The large feet of snowshoe hares allow them to stay on top of the crusty March snow when other animals, except for lynx, break through.

long legs to keep their torsos above the snow. Some animals primarily use one of these techniques, but most maximize their winter mobility by using a combination of both.

The extremely large feet of lynx and snowshoe hare give them enough flotation to effectively stay on top of the snow. Even in deep, light, fluffy snow, they are able to "float" on top and move effectively when other animals their size are floundering. The winter diet of the snowshoe hare consists of buds, small twigs, and bark of both conifers and deciduous plants. Each snowfall buries some potential food, but it also brings them closer to food that was previously out of reach. With each substantial snowfall, previously inaccessible plants become available foods.

Big-footed lynx are the main predators of snowshoe hare. Other land predators, such as timber wolves and red fox, are hindered by deep snow, but the lynx can pursue and catch snowshoe hare even under those conditions. They seem to be evenly matched in deep snow, but lynx are successful often enough that, in the winter, snowshoe hare commonly make up over 75 percent of their diet.

In the winter, the feet of ruffed grouse also act like snowshoes. In preparation for winter, comb-like rows of bristles grow between their toes in the fall. These bristles transform the ruffed grouse's feet into snowshoes that allow them to manoeuvre on top of the snow while searching for food. During the winter, their food of choice is aspen (poplar) buds, but they will also eat catkins and buds of small shrubs

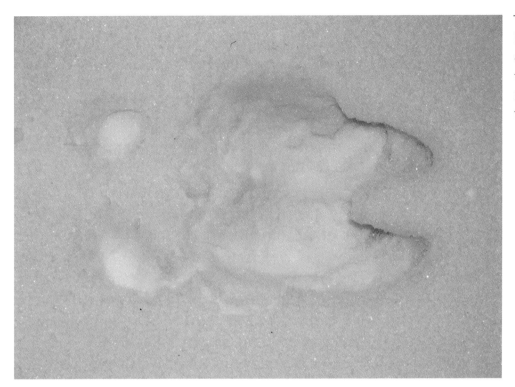

This moose track in shallow snow in Quetico Park clearly show the dewclaws that play a role in helping moose walk more easily through deep snow.

that protrude above the snow. Ruffed grouse often spend cold nights under an insulating blanket of snow and the bristles on their feet are probably helpful in extricating themselves from their snow cave in the morning.

Moose are the ultimate "stilters" and their peculiar high-stepping gait is an adaptation that is ideal when walking in deep snow. It is also beneficial at other times of the year — walking in swampy areas, along lakeshores, or striding over deadfalls and other impediments on the forest floor. Even with their extremely long legs, moose also have adaptations that lessen their sinking into the snow. They have two large dewclaws on the back of each leg a few centimetres above the hooves. These dewclaws, combined with the spreading of their hooves, effectively increase the surface area of the foot in contact with the snow. Both barren-ground and woodland caribou have even larger hooves and dewclaws than moose and this gives them additional floatation in deep snow. They also use their large hooves as shovels to dig through the snow to get to the lichens on the forest floor that are their primary source of winter food.

The relatively short legs and small hooves of white-tailed deer make them vulnerable in deep snow. They are good stilters when the snow is less than forty centimetres deep, but tend to have trouble when the snow gets much deeper. In order to compensate for the difficulties they encounter in deep snow, they apparently select areas with less snowfall for their winter range. White-tailed deer become concentrated in areas with sufficient food and cover and they stay in these "deer yards" and travel the same well-used trails for most of the winter. In spite of these adjustments, snow depth is a major factor in determining where they spend the winter. They expand their range during winters with little snow, but large numbers of deer may die in winters with deep accumulations of snow. Snow depth is one of the important factors that will continue to determine the relative success of moose and deer in Quetico Park and the rest of the Quetico-Superior area.

Predators, such as wolves and red fox, have legs long enough to deal with thirty centimetres or more of snow, but not long enough to deal with deep snow. Consequently, they seem to frequently use the wind-blown areas with less snow, such as open ridges, and often travel on the surface of large lakes. They also have dewclaws that give them more flotation on the snow and also aid them in grasping prey. When snow is deep, a pack of wolves will walk in single file and each wolf steps in the tracks of those ahead. Similar to human snowshoers or a flock of geese, they undoubtedly rotate the difficult task of breaking trail. When a crust develops on the snow in late winter, wolves are usually able to stay on top while moose and deer break through the crust and become easy prey.

TRACKS OF PREDATORS AND PREY

The tracks of a moose, a white-tailed deer, a snowshoe hare, or any herbivore are often found in a fairly straight line. Each animal seems focused on reaching a specific destination, such as a feeding area, or a place to bed down to rest or spend the night. When they find a plentiful food source, however, their tracks indicate that they spend a considerable amount of time moving back and forth while systematically consuming appealing vegetation.

The tracks of timber wolves, red fox, lynx, and other predators, on the other hand, move in a more unpredictable manner as they seek signs of their prey. Their apparently erratic movement is probably the result of responding to smells, sounds, and other stimuli that they detect as they travel. They seem to be very aware of other animal tracks and frequently you can see where they put their noses into a fresh track. Most predators have an acute sense of smell and they are simply getting closer to the information source. When they come across fresh tracks of their prey, they purposefully follow the trail and often save energy by stepping directly in the tracks of their intended victims. When the snow is very deep,

A slide-like trail along the French River indicates an otter's presence in mid-winter.

moose — in spite of their long legs — have to push their way through the snow. They make trails that other animals utilize — in effect, smaller animals use moose as snowplows to help clear a trail for them.

The most distinctive winter tracks are made by otter. Otters have elongated bodies with very short legs and they compensate for their short legs by sliding on their bellies in the snow. They have very dense, short fur oriented toward the back of their body that allows the toboggan-shaped animal to glide efficiently on top of the snow, and they seem to take advantage of every opportunity to do this. This technique doesn't work very well in deep, soft snow, but their tracks are usually encountered along rivers or on lakes where there is more apt to be a crust sufficient to support their weight.

When snowshoeing along the French River in the northeast corner of Quetico Park, I often see otter tracks on the sides of the river. Their tracks clearly show that they swim for stretches in the open water to look for food and come out and travel along the shore or over the ice where the river is frozen. Rough nobs on their rear heel pads, often visible in their tracks, give them better traction on the ice. They also appear to frequently reuse slides that end in open water below rapids. It is amazing that an animal can come out of the water in sub-freezing temperatures and travel over land in a wet fur coat. The otter's extremely short ears, short legs, and heavily furred tail make this behaviour possible by helping to minimize heat loss.

USING SNOWSHOES TO BECOME A "FLOATER"

Humans are good "stilters" until the snow depth reaches a depth of about thirty centimetres, and then our normal walking stride, much different from that of a high-stepping moose, is greatly restricted. By strapping on a pair of snowshoes, we attempt to imitate the large feet of lynx and snowshoe hare and become "floaters." We can choose the size and shape of the feet we wear. Large snowshoes give greater flotation but they also restrict movement in thick vegetation. When choosing the type of snowshoes, a compromise has to be made between flotation and mobility.

A person moves slowly on snowshoes, but when wearing them there aren't many places in Quetico that can't be reached. Cold weather and snow opens up areas that can be difficult to visit at other times of year, such as bogs and swamps. With snowshoes attached, you become an effective all-terrain vehicle that runs on granola bars, beef jerky, and orange juice.

During the winter, there are fewer distractions and the lack of leaves greatly increases visibility. While travelling slowly on snowshoes, unusual shapes, disturbed vegetation, and objects seemingly out of place are frequently noticed. Mushrooms stuck behind branches, freeze-dried by the winter cold, are often seen. A whisky jack or a red squirrel, creatures that would have a hard time surviving our

Anna Nelson uses artificial big feet to enjoy a winter hike in Quetico.

You can even look into the nest and see what materials were used in its construction. Lichens, twigs, pine needles, moose hair, down, leaves, and numerous other items can be found lining the nests. Field guides to bird nests — it is amazing what resources are available — can be used to determine the identity of the most likely builder of the nest.

Evidence of larger animals, in addition to their tracks, is also visible in the winter. Bear claw marks, some of which reach more than two metres off the ground, can be seen on trees that bears have selected to mark their territories. Shrubs and small trees may have broken branches and scraped bark where moose and deer have rubbed velvet off their antlers in the fall. While snowshoeing in the northern part of Quetico Park over the last few winters, I have occasionally noticed where porcupines have stripped the bark off trees to get at the nutritious inner bark.

PASSIVE-AGGRESSIVE WINTER PLANTS

Mid-winter in Quetico is usually quiet with few signs of activity. There are good reasons for the relative inactivity: many of the birds have migrated, some animals are hibernating, and most of the smaller mammals are living under the snow. Plants, the base of the food chain, are in a temperature-induced sleep. They spend the winter in a state of suspended animation, a form of plant hibernation that will end with the warmth of spring.

winters if they didn't store food away during the more productive times of the year, probably cached these mushrooms in the fall. Small bird nests, hidden by leaves in the spring and summer, become conspicuous against the bare winter sky. Many of these nests, above your head at other times of year, are at eye level when walking over deep snow on snowshoes.

Trees and shrubs produce excess energy during the summer that is stored underground in their root systems where it is safe from most animals. It will remain there, securely stored away, until spring, when it will be used to "jumpstart" the plant. Sugars securely stored all winter will then flow as sap to the branches where it is needed to stimulate the opening of buds and growth of leaves and flowers.

The exposed plant above the ground, however, is at risk. Buds, both leaf buds and flower buds, are fully formed in many plants by the fall in preparation for spring. They are packed with nutrition and are potential food for northern herbivores such as ruffed grouse, snowshoe hare, white-tailed deer, and moose. In areas where there is a high concentration of deer or moose, they eat the preferred foods as high as they can reach and winter browsing can have a devastating impact on vegetation. Due to healthy predator populations, unusually high numbers of deer seldom occur in the Quetico-Superior region and consequently, the obvious "browse lines" on plants that are clearly visible in areas of high deer population are seldom seen.

Although they are unable to flee, plants do have a variety of defences. Plants are not passive; they actively attract animals by producing colourful and scented flowers and fruits when it is in their interest to do so. They can also aggressively defend themselves from disease and from being eaten. Many plants, especially those in the desert, have sharp spines or thorns to discourage herbivores. In Quetico, similar but toned-down defences are used; raspberries have small spines on the stem and nettles have irritating hairs on the stem and leaves. Most mixed forest and boreal plants, however, rely on the production of chemical toxins to discourage animals and insects from eating them. They can afford to lose some of their leaves and buds to herbivores, but there is a limit to how much they can lose and still survive.

Plants are particularly vulnerable in the winter. They have a limited number of energy-laden buds and they are incapable of making more until spring so it is essential that they protect them. Since plants are essentially hibernating in the winter, they can only use defences that they prepared during their growing season. Some plants, such as poplar and mountain ash, have a resinous coating on the buds that deters hungry animals. Most northern plants use a more vigorous form of chemical warfare to deter winter browsing. They make unpalatable or toxic chemicals that are often concentrated in the buds. Moose, deer, and other herbivores try to minimize the amount of toxins they ingest and evidently sample plants and then browse heaviest on those that are low in toxins.

Moose means "twig eater" in many Algonquin languages, and this name accurately describes their winter diet. They are browsers in the winter, primarily feeding on the buds of a variety of trees and shrubs. They bite off the end of twigs and the nipped branches are clearly visible where moose have been feeding. Some species, such as red osier dogwood

Moose selectively browse those plants that their senses indicate are both nutritious and low in toxins.

— which Quetico Park naturalist Shan Walshe referred to as "moose candy" — are sought out and heavily browsed. Other species that are apparently lower in nutrients are less tasty or have better chemical defences, are eaten only occasionally.

It is informative, if one encounters moose tracks while snowshoeing, to simply follow them. Although they often travel in a straight line and show no interest in feeding, they routinely zigzag through the woods searching for food. There is usually a wide selection of food above the snow line and moose can usually be very selective in what they eat. Evidence in their tracks will show that they may stop in a patch of moose maple, speckled alder, or willow and heavily browse some plants, lightly sample others, and totally ignore those that are distasteful to them.

Research on varying levels of toxins in plants explains why moose will heavily browse one shrub and leave adjacent ones untouched. Many plant species consistently produce high levels of toxins, while in other species the levels of toxins vary greatly from plant to plant. Studies have indicated that snowshoe hare, moose, and other herbivores sample plants and move on to another if they detect high levels of toxins.

Researchers who have studied the interaction between vegetation and snowshoe hares have found that "hares don't eat new annual growth on plants because that growth contains a high amount of poisonous toxins."[1] Since herbivores usually eat the newer vegetation because it is higher in nutrients, this unusual behaviour by snowshoe hare is apparently an adaptation to newer growth having higher toxin levels. Hares have adopted the policy of avoiding old growth due to the low levels of nutrients and avoiding the newest growth because of the high levels of toxins. This causes them to concentrate on the parts of the plant that are one or two years old. One of the advantages of forest fire in Quetico is that fires increase the number of younger, more nutrient-rich plants that herbivores generally prefer. In the case of snowshoe hare, two or three years after a fire is the beginning of a smorgasbord of plants with growth over one year old that is still high in nutrition.

Herbivores, however, can also develop resistance to the toxins produced by plants. Consequently, plants that are toxic to one species are readily eaten by other species. Spruce grouse, for example, feed heavily on the same spruce needles that are unpalatable or toxic to many other organisms. Monarch butterfly caterpillars, which are occasionally seen in the Quetico-Superior region, not only feed on milkweed plants whose chemicals poison other insects, they also incorporate these toxins into their bodies to discourage birds from eating them. They are able to take the plant's chemical defence and use it to protect themselves.

WINTER'S PROMISE

Plants produce a wide variety of compounds in an attempt to defend themselves from being eaten, as well as for protection from disease. They not only have to adapt to extreme cold, forest fires, parasites, and other hazards of northern life, they also have to protect themselves in the winter, when they are the most vulnerable from being consumed by wildlife. The tough, resilient, and innovative plants and animals encountered while snowshoeing in Quetico are vivid reminders of Henry David Thoreau's statement: "There is a slumbering subterranean fire in nature that never goes out, and which no cold can chill."[2]

When snowshoeing through a winter landscape that seems strangely quiet and seemingly lacking in life, it is always exciting to encounter evidence of that "winter fire" in animal form. Fresh tracks hold the promise of life ahead and I have found that tracks can stir my imagination and allow me to conjure up the animals in my mind and visualize them moving across the land.

Tracks reveal the identity and the activities of animals that we often see and they also provide insights into the lives of those that we only rarely get a glimpse of. Timber wolves, lynx, pine marten, fisher, and other animals seldom seen in the summer leave records of their passing in the snow. I have never seen a cougar or a lynx in Quetico Park but I have come across lynx tracks. I am hoping that cougar tracks, or possibly a cougar, are in my future.

CHAPTER NINETEEN

A COZY WINTER NEST OF BEAVERS

Snowshoeing across a beaver pond just north of Quetico Park on a cold February morning, I was surprised to hear soft murmuring coming from the direction of a beaver lodge. At first I thought the faint sounds must be water moving in the nearby creek or wind in the branches of spruce trees along the edge of the pond. As I moved closer, it became apparent that the muted sounds were coming from inside the dwelling. The unexpected sounds, which ceased as I drew nearer, made me take a closer look at the beaver lodge. Hearing noises from a beaver lodge in mid-winter was totally unanticipated. The snow-covered lodge appeared totally devoid of life, but the sounds I heard made it clear that a beaver family was actively living — not hibernating — inside the snow-covered lodge.

When seen in the summer, beavers are wary of humans, so it was interesting to stand only a few metres from this family and have them aware of my existence, but totally unafraid. Their lodges are protected by a thick, dense mixture of sticks and mud that offers them a wall of security against predators as well as insulation against the winter cold. Beavers are seasonal workers who spend a secure, leisurely winter living off their labours during the open-water season.

I noticed a small, ice-encrusted depression at the top of the lodge where warm air escaping from the lodge had partially melted some of the snow. Warmth from the beavers inside the lodge was gradually escaping into the frigid morning air. In his delightful 1913 book, Enos Mills noted that in a beaver lodge: "Little earthy matter is used in the tip-top of the house where the minute disjointed airholes between the interlaced poles give the room scanty ventilation."[1] Although these tiny openings allow air to slowly pass through, the tightly interwoven sticks and branches prevented me from seeing into the interior of the lodge and, more importantly, do not allow predators easy access to the lodge interior.

On a showshoe hike, I stop to listen for sounds of life in a beaver lodge. If lodges are approached quietly, sounds can sometimes be heard coming from inside, even in the coldest days in mid-winter.

INSIDE A BEAVER LODGE

When paddling up creeks in Quetico Park, I have often marvelled — and sometimes cursed — at the frequency and size of large beaver dams. It is hard to believe that twenty-five-kilogram rodents, using just their teeth and paws as tools, are able to construct dams that can be hundreds of metres long and flood hectares of land. While beaver dams are structures that attract my attention, beaver lodges appear to simply be an ungainly pile of sticks mixed with some mud.

After hearing the noises coming from the inside of a beaver lodge in mid-winter, I decided I needed to find out more about their origin and structure. It appears that these lodges may have evolved from burrows in muddy river or pond banks used by some North American beavers and by their European cousins. The wood and mud lodges may have originated when branches were used to repair weak or damaged burrows. These wood-reinforced burrows slowly evolved into the stick and mud lodges of today.

Peter Marchand, an American naturalist who thoroughly explores the world of his subjects, described how he squeezed his body through an exposed entrance tunnel in a drained pond and crawled into a recently abandoned beaver house. After exploring the inside of the lodge, he noted that:

> Outwardly, a beaver lodge appears to be nothing more than a mud-plastered pile of woody debris — an unkempt heap of odd-sized sticks that occasionally reaches twenty feet in diameter and rises four or more feet out of the water. In this case, the interior turned out to be a marvel of neatness and cleanliness. The earthen floor of the lodge was worn smooth by the countless comings and goings of wet feet on silky clay. The walls and ceilings were trimmed evenly; not a single nub protruded to discomfort a huddling animal.[2]

He found the lodge was composed of a main chamber with bedding of shredded wood and wood chips. An orderly, comfortable space is essential since a beaver family spends most of its winter huddled together in this chamber for warmth and companionship. They also groom themselves and each other and to keep their fur well oiled in this chamber.

In addition to the main chamber, a smaller compartment was found to the side of one of the entrance tunnels. This area, located just above the water level, apparently functions as a place for beavers to dry off before entering the main chamber. Remnants of food in this lower chamber indicated it also functioned as a feeding platform. The lodge is the focal point of a beaver's life. They eat, rest, sleep, mate, and bear their young in a dwelling that also protects them from heat, cold, and predators.

WINTER LIFE IN THE LODGE

The inside of a beaver lodge, insulated with mud and sticks and moderated by the pond water, is a place to escape the heat in the summer and the cold in the winter. A beaver family, usually consisting of an adult pair, the kits born that spring, and the previous season's offspring, over-winter in the close confines of the lodge, which resembles a large eagle's nest that has been turned upside down, deposited in shallow water, and plastered with a coat of mud.

Using temperature probes, researchers have recorded temperatures inside beaver lodges. One study found that winter temperatures ranged from a high of 6°C and a low of -4°C. Although -4°C sounds cold, it is remarkable that chubby rodents can maintain a temperature this high by body heat alone when it is -40°C outside the lodge. Since they have at least twenty centimetres of stick and mud insulation, lodges with from four to ten beavers probably stay very warm on even the coldest January night. Lodges with just two animals, on the other hand, must become very cold, especially if there isn't much snow to supply added insulation.

Beavers have been given the scientific name *Castor canadensis* and the term *Castor* is apparently derived from the Greek word for beaver. Some etymologists, however, believe that the word *Castor* is derived from the Latin word *castoratum*, which means castrated. For most of the year, the male sex organs are tucked up inside the body. To anyone unaware of this, the males would appear to be castrated. The male gonads descend when the female becomes sexually receptive and then the sex of male beavers becomes obvious — even to non-beavers. Females go into heat in January or February — a time when heat is definitely needed in the lodge — and mating usually occurs inside the beaver lodge. For the two adults in the lodge, the long, quiet winter is pleasantly interrupted by this short, but intense, period of physical activity. The female gives birth to three or four young, called kits, in the spring.

In addition to their sexual activity, beavers' long periods of winter lethargy are temporarily broken when they have to leave the lodge to obtain food. They minimize their time in the cold water by constructing a food cache adjacent to their lodge, which has a minimum of two entrance tunnels. Just a short swim from either entrance enables a beaver to reach food that was stockpiled over the summer and fall.

In mid-November at freeze-up, this beaver lodge, with its large food cache on a pothole south of Atikokan, Ontario, is ready for winter.

Beavers obtain food for the winter cache from the trees and shrubs that grow on the land surrounding the pond during the open water season. The food cache is composed of branches and sticks with the bark still on them. Leafy branches that protrude above the water are placed on top of the cache to ensure that snow mounds up and provides an insulating cover to minimize water freezing around their food supply. The wood species in the cache vary according to what is available in the vicinity of the lodge. Trembling aspen (poplar) is the species of choice, but a variety of different species, including willow, birch, and maple, are also included in the cache. Beavers have a monotonous winter diet composed primarily of twigs, which have a very high cellulose content. Their primary source of nutrients, however, is the cambium, a thin layer beneath the bark of the twigs they chew.

Some bacteria can digest cellulose, and beavers have a pouch of bacteria in their cecum, which is located between the small and large intestine. The breakdown of cellulose is a slow process and it isn't completely digested in one trip through the digestive tract. Consequently, beavers eat the soft, gelatinous material that is produced after one journey through their digestive tract. This efficient, but seemingly unsavoury property of eating their feces is known as coprophagy. Beavers share this trait with a few other mammals, including snowshoe hares, who eat food high in cellulose. After the second trip through their system, more cellulose is broken down, excess liquid is absorbed, and the feces resemble compacted sawdust.

ADAPTIONS TO THE COLD

Beavers need a thick fur coat to maintain an adequate winter body temperature. Since they must enter the water to obtain food, they need coats that are waterproof as well as exceptionally warm. Water siphons heat from the body much more rapidly than air does and it is extremely difficult for mammals to maintain an adequate body temperature in cold water without a thick exterior layer of insulating material. Beavers keep their thick fur well-oiled in order to make it water repellent. They obtain oil for waterproofing their fur from glands located near the base of their tails, and spend a great deal of time preening and working the oil into their fur with the aid of a split toenail on their hind foot that acts like a comb. They also have a layer of fat beneath their skin that acts as insulation against the cold, as well as an energy source.

The thick, winter fur coat that keeps beavers warm has also been used by humans for clothing and sleeping robes for thousands of years. In the mid-1500s, beaver fur developed snob appeal and beaver hats became fashionable male headgear in Europe. The demand for beaver pelts nearly drove the European beaver to extinction. The fur trade in North America then became the primary source of beaver pelts and remained that way until silk top hats replaced beaver hats in the late 1800s. The luxurious fur of the beaver was a primary driving force behind the European exploration of Canada and parts of the United States. Two of the main fur-trade routes ran through Quetico — one along the southern boundary from Saganaga Lake to Lac La Croix and the second heading diagonally across the park from French Lake in the northeast to Lac La Croix in the southwest — and they were largely financed by the value of beaver pelts. Interestingly, many of the names of the portages along both of these routes can be traced back to the fur-trade era.

It is hard to believe that a fashion item worn primarily by upper-class Europeans was one of the main economic forces behind the exploration of northern North America. The quest for beaver pelts had a particularly big impact on the advance of Europeans across Canada. The historian Peter C. Newman has written: "Just as the stalking for their ivory tusks lured white hunters into the heart of Africa, so the beaver pelt drew traders from Hudson Bay and the St. Lawrence River toward the snowcapped Rocky Mountains and, eventually, to the shores of the jade green Pacific."[3]

Fur hats and fur coats are no longer fashionable and the beaver population has rebounded. For today's Quetico canoeists, the highest value for a beaver pelt is being able to see it on a living beaver in the wild.

OPEN WATER, LONG DAYS, AND HABITAT CHANGE

Beavers enter the winter very fat and emerge very skinny. Even with all the physiological and behavioural adaptations, their low-nutrition winter diet causes them to slowly lose weight throughout the season. After spending a lazy, but physiologically taxing, winter in their lodge, they are ready to change their lifestyle when the ice is gone. They have to become as "busy as beavers" in the summer so they can remain in their warm, communal nest, live a life of leisure in their lodge, and be "lazy as beavers" all winter long.

Beavers would have a pretty idyllic summer if all they had to do was obtain daily sustenance, raise their young, and take care of their immediate needs. But the fact that they must accomplish twelve months of work in the seven months of open water has given them the reputation of hard workers who seem to labour from sunrise to sunset.

During those seven months they have to build and repair their dams and either make repairs to their lodge or construct a new one. In addition, they not only feed themselves, but they also have to put up food for the entire winter. Beavers are vegetarians who eat a variety of aquatic plants such as the fleshy tubers of cattails and water lilies, and sedges and rushes that grow in the beaver pond or in a shallow bay, creek or river near their beaver lodge. Their summer diet is very different from, and more nutritious than, their monotonous winter diet of tree bark. In addition to obtaining nutrients to sustain themselves during the open-water season, they also have to put up enough food for the entire winter. Beavers prefer the newer bark on smaller branches, so they have to cut down trees in order to reach them. Researchers in Ontario's Algonquin Park found that beavers had the following preferences for food — trembling aspen, white water lily, raspberry, speckled alder, and red maple.

Their love of the inner bark (cambium layer) of trembling aspen and other preferred foods has greatly altered the distribution of trees and shrubs near the shore virtually everywhere in the Quetico-Superior. For paddlers, there isn't a trembling aspen

Beavers clearly left their mark on a poplar tree that was felled near Montgomery Lake not long before this photo was taken.

in sight along many creeks and it may seem that black spruce and tamarack are the predominant trees in Quetico. This is partly due to the preference of those species for wet areas, but the food preferences of beavers are important factors as well. In addition, on hillsides that slope away from a lake and anywhere near a beaver lodge, there usually are no trembling aspen visible for at least fifty metres from shore since beavers usually clearcut any that they can safely reach.

A beaver's bright orange front teeth are shaped like wood chisels and are ideal for cutting down trees and stripping bark from branches. Probably no other animal has teeth that have to withstand such intense and sustained use. The constant wearing down of the teeth is balanced by the fact that the teeth never stop growing. The back surfaces of beaver teeth are softer than the front surfaces. Due to this discrepancy in hardness, the teeth are continuously sharpened as they are used.

Beavers gnaw off the bark and feast on the cambium layer from branches and twigs. The wood that is left after they have removed the outer layers can be used in their building projects. Because the edible outer layers are low in proteins and fats, they must consume vast quantities of bark to obtain the nutrients they need. This leads to the creation of a great deal of construction material. Beavers are very fortunate in being able to use their considerable leftovers as building material because dams and lodges require almost constant maintenance.

Because beavers can live in bays of lakes and on rivers where they do not alter the flow, the classic beaver dam and pond are entirely optional. It is their dam-building activities, however, that flood the landscape and allow beavers to access to areas of water otherwise too dangerous to exploit. It's been said that only humans change their environment more than beavers do.

Beaver dams are comprised of sticks and branches of various sizes, with mud as the adhesive and waterproofing agent, and a few rocks as ballast. Rocks provide weight to help stabilize the dam and they are very apparent in old, decaying dams along dried-up beaver ponds. Although most are of modest size, dams over three metres high and a kilometre long have been reported.

The mud used to make the dam waterproof and to fortify the beaver lodge is obtained from the bottom of the pond. Mud is usually taken from above the dam, thus helping to make the pond deeper. Beavers dive to the bottom to gather it with their front paws and then hold it to their chest as they swim to their destination. If it is necessary to carry mud on land, they walk on their hind legs while clutching the mud tightly to their chest with their front paws.

The ponds created by beaver dams help the beaver in numerous ways. Beavers rarely have predators in the water, but they move slowly on land and can be killed by wolves or bears. The higher water level created by the dam gives them access to trees that would otherwise be far from shore and this minimizes the time they need to spend on land. The higher water level also allows them to transport branches by swimming, a safer and easier method than dragging them on land. On creeks and shallow rivers, a dam is required to elevate the water enough so that the pond doesn't freeze to the bottom in the winter. If this occurred, the beavers' food supply would be encased in ice and frozen tunnel openings would trap them in the lodge. Not only can the pond not freeze to the bottom, but there has to be enough water under the ice so that beavers can swim to the food cache.

The ponds created by beavers are also ideal for aquatic animals such as frogs, turtles, and minnows; for waterfowl such as ducks, mergansers, and great blue herons; and for mammals such as muskrats and otters. Even after beavers have moved on to other areas, the grassy meadows that result after the dams are abandoned and the ponds fill in become excellent habitats for deer, moose, and a variety of small mammals and birds.

Canoeists in Quetico are often quite pleased to encounter a beaver pond because it can provide relatively easy paddling across an area that may otherwise be difficult to get through or around. It is while beavers are carrying out their building tasks that canoeists are most apt to see them. Since they seem to start work early in the morning, take a long siesta at midday, and work again in the evening, the best time to see beavers is during their prime working hours. In late summer and fall, it is common

A beaver walks on its hind legs carrying mud for repairing a dam.

to see them swimming with the branches they are adding to their food cache. If you sit quietly in your canoe, well back from their lodge or dam in the early morning or evening, it is also possible to wacth them add wood to and plaster these structures with mud.

Beavers are very territorial and aggressively keep beavers that are not family members away from their territory. They have a pair of castor glands that store an oily liquid called castoreum that is secreted as a territorial scent marker, and they are able to distinguish their own castor scent from that of non-family members. Castoreum is deposited on the boundaries of their territory to create a "scent fence" to keep other beavers from trespassing on their territory.

261

Just as beavers have unusual physiological and metabolic adaptations that are especially advantageous in winter, they also have physical characteristics that are particularly useful in the seasons when they spend so much time in the water. There are numerous reports of beavers staying underwater for up to fifteen minutes. Factors that contribute to this ability to remain submerged for extended periods include: the capacity to exchange 75 percent of the air in their lungs as opposed to just 15 percent for humans, the ability to increase the flow of oxygen-rich blood to the brain while tolerating large amounts of carbon dioxide, and the lowering of their heart rate when they swim underwater.[4] They have valve-like flaps in their nostrils and ears that prevent water from entering when they are swimming. Thin, transparent membranes cover their eyes and act as goggles when they are in the water. They also have special lips that seal behind their teeth, allowing them to chew underwater and swim while holding branches in their teeth. Their large, webbed hind feet give them good propulsion in the water while their small and agile front paws are used much like we use our hands. Beavers can even walk upright in a bipedal fashion while carrying mud or sticks in their hands.

The unique beaver tail serves many purposes: for propulsion and as a rudder when it swims, as a prop as it is cutting down trees, as a support when it walks on its hind legs, and as a warning device on the water. When canoeing in bays or on creeks,

Photo by Jim Brandenburg/Minden Pictures.

A beaver feeds on a small branch in northern Minnesota and shows how adept it is at manipulating objects with its front feet.

canoeists frequently surprise beavers. They seem to have a zone of tolerance and, if you trespass within that zone, they warn other beavers of your presence. Slapping their tail against the water sends both an auditory and visual warning to other of their kin in the area. The tail is also an important reservoir for fat. In May, after a long winter when nutrient-rich plants are unavailable, the percent of fat in their tails is just 10 percent. During the summer and fall, beavers store excess energy as fat in their tails and the fat levels sky-rocket to between 50 and 60 percent by November. The fat is utilized during the winter when their food is primarily nutrient-poor bark.

CANOE TRIPS AND BEAVERS

Creeks are my favourite places to paddle. By building dams, beavers raise the water level enough that many creeks, such as McAlpine Creek between Kasakokwog Lake and Quetico Lake, are a pleasure to paddle even in low water conditions. The ease, or even the possibility, of a trip on Baptism Creek, on the creek between Blackstone Lake and Saganagons Lake, and on innumerable other creeks in Quetico, is dependent on water levels and the state of repair of beaver dams. Changing water levels, in part due to beaver activity, or the lack thereof, are constantly altering the length and difficulty of portages throughout Quetico Park and the BWCAW. Fortunately, the series of beaver dams between North Bay of Basswood Lake and Isabella Lake continue to make this a pleasant journey rather than a slog.

Paddling up a creek when the sun is coming up is a special joy. The sides of the mouth of the creek will be lit up with the sun shining on thousands of dew-covered spiderwebs, and birdsongs will fill the air. You paddle by fascinating plants, such as Arethusa orchids, pitcher plants, and cotton grass, and can see cattails at eye level. Ducks, great blue herons, painted turtles, and a variety of bird species are everywhere and a moose could always be around the next bend. As an added bonus, the animal very likely to be seen is the beaver, the creature responsible for creating conditions that make it easy to be up such an amazing creek — with a paddle.

AFTERWORDS

My ancestors lived for generations on homesteads and in small villages along the Sogne Fjord in Norway. During their long tenure on the land, they became an integral part of the fabric of Norway and developed beliefs and attitudes deeply rooted in the Norwegian soil. After just five generations of ancestors in the United States and having lived less than four decades in Canada, my North American roots are still shallow and I have only developed a tenuous appreciation of my environment and my place in it.

My attraction to archaeology is probably the result of my desire to obtain a better understanding of how people in the past adapted to the environment and lived without damaging it to the extent we do today. I had an anthropology professor at Trent University who loved repeating the old maxim "the past is a different country, they do things differently there."[1] We can undoubtedly learn from both the successes and the failures of these past cultures, especially from those who lived in the area we now call home. Obtaining a better understanding of our natural and cultural environment is an ongoing process for all of us and other cultures, both past and present, undoubtedly have solutions we have overlooked or discarded.

People with European ancestry, such as myself, are either recent arrivals in North America or descendents of relatively recent immigrants. After five hundred years, we still stubbornly persist in acting as though we are visitors rather than permanent residents who feel fully at home. As a result, we treat our adopted homeland as a collection of resources to be exploited with little thought given to the welfare of future generations.

We have also been slow in developing a spiritual connection, once common among Native Americans, to the land. The writer and poet Gary Snyder has stated that he has a deep hope that we might all, regardless of our country of origin, become *native* North Americans. He quoted a Crow Elder who noted: "You know, I think if people stay somewhere long enough — even white people — the spirits will begin to speak to them. It is the power of the spirits

Sunrise over the Quetico Lake entrance to McAlpine Creek.

coming from the land. The spirits and the old powers aren't lost, they just need people to be around long enough and the spirits will begin to influence them."[2]

With only Norwegian ancestors, not many people are whiter than I am, but there is still hope that the spirits of the land will start speaking to me more clearly. I hope that my children and their descendents will develop a deep appreciation for the Canadian landscape and the cultural mosaic they have inherited from the Canadians, Native and non-Native, who preceded them. Only then will they be able to experience the power of their surroundings and come to feel like *native* Canadians.

Ontario writer Jill Frayne describes a moment of connection between herself and the landscape, feeling as if she "was held in the land, not separate and apart but in it, just another sentient creature, another form of shrub or mountain."[3] There have been times in Quetico — snowshoeing at dusk along the French River, ambling along the ancient sand beach at The Pines on Pickerel Lake, paddling beneath the cliffs on Ottertrack Lake, walking beneath the giant pines on McNiece Lake, or simply sitting around the campfire in the evening — when I have profoundly felt as if I am *held in the land, not separate and apart from it.*

Time spent exploring Quetico is delightful. Writing about Quetico, on the other hand, is difficult for me — even painful at times. While working on this book, I have spent too many hours sitting in front of a computer and not enough time outside with friends investigating the world around me. After reading and writing so many words, I feel the need to engage in more explorations and excursions that fire both the body and the mind.

It is time for me to heed the words of Danish professor Peder Sorenson who in 1571 wrote:

> *Go my sons, burn your books,*
> *Buy yourselves stout shoes,*
> *Get away to the mountains, the deserts,*
> *And the deepest recesses of the earth.*
> *In this way and no other*
> *Will you gain a true knowledge of things*
> *And of their properties.*[4]

So long, I'm off to buy stout shoes.

NOTES

NEAR TO NATURE'S HEART: AN EXPLANATION

1. Jennie S.S. Richardson, "A Honeymoon in a Birch Bark Canoe: Being a Brief Account of the Wedding Journey of William H. and Jennie S.S. Richardson," *Millers Review* (1897).

INTRODUCTION

1. Norman Hallendy, *Inuksuit: Silent Messengers of the Arctic* (Vancouver: Douglas and McIntyre Ltd., 2000), 114.

PREFACE: QUETICO — ONE HUNDRED YEARS

1. Bruce Litteljohn, in an interview with Ernest Oberholtzer in October 1964. In John B. Ridley Research Library, Quetico Park Information Pavilion, at French Lake.
2. Gold was first dicovered at Eldorado, Ontario, in 1866. For information on this early gold rush, see Gerry Boyce, *Eldorado: Ontario's First Gold Rush*. Toronto: Natural Heritage Books, 1992.
3. Shan Walshe, "Saga of the Quetico–Superior Wilderness 1909–1984, Part I," information pamphlet put out by Ontario Parks for Quetico's 75th anniversary. Held in the John B. Ridley Research Library, French Lake (January 1984): 2.
4. Gerald Killan, *Protected Places: A History of Ontario's Provincial Park System* (Toronto: Dundurn Press, 1993), 22.
5. R. Newell Searle, *Saving Quetico-Superior: A Land Set Apart* (Minneapolis, MN: Minnesota Historical Society Press, 1977), 14.
6. Order-in-Council issued by the lieutenant-governor of Ontario, Sir John Morison Gibson, on April 1, 1909. From information compiled at the John B. Ridley Resource Library, French Lake, Quetico Provincial Park.
7. 1912 Report of Ontario Game and Fish Commission, "The Quetico Forest Reserve" in *Report of the Ontario Game and Fisheries Commission, 1911–1912*, published in 1912 by the Legislative Assembly of Canada, 79.
8. *Ibid.*
9. Algonquin Provincial Park was created in 1893 and Rondeau Provincial Park was created in 1894.
10. Aubrey White, "Memorandum for His Honourable, The Minister of Lands, Forests and Mines," Ontario Department of Lands, Forests and Mines (March 29, 1909). Ministry document, located at the John B. Ridley Library, Quetico Park Information Pavilion.
11. Leo Chosa, "Letter to Mr. George Watts, Crown Timber Agent, Fort Francis, Ontario," dated December 3, 1910. Located in Kawa Bay-24C file compiled by Shirley Peruniak and Andrea Allison, at John B. Ridley Resource Library.

12. Personal communication with Bruce Litteljohn, December 4, 2008.

13. George M. Warecki, *Protecting Ontario's Wilderness: A History of Changing Ideas and Preservation Politics, 1927–1973* (New York: Peter Lang, 2000), 296.

14. "Report of the Quetico Provincial Park Advisory Committee," May 26, 1972, Toronto, Ontario.

15. Statement in the Ontario Legislature attributed to Bud Wildman, Ontario Minister of Natural Resources, June 3, 1991.

16. "Governing Principles of the Lac La Croix Agreement of Co-Existence," Quetico Provincial Park Revised Park Policy (Toronto: Ontario Ministry of Natural Resources, 1995).

17. Portage Crews maintain portages, clean campsites, talk to canoeists about park policies, and aid those who require assistance. They also assist with other duties that are required by park staff and help fight forest fires if required. They get to spend a summer in Quetico and, as an added bonus, get paid for it.

18. Mike Barker, the district managet of the Atikokan District when the Advisory Committee Report was released, in an oral interview with Shirley Peruniak in May 1979.

19. Gerald Killan, *Protected Places: A History of Ontario's Provincial Park System* (Toronto: Dundurn Press, 1993), 51.

20. *Ely Miner*, July 21, 1916.

21. Miron L. Heinselman, "Fire in the Virgin Forests of the Boundary Waters Canoe Area," *Quaternary Research*, Vol. 3, No. 3 (1973): 379.

22. "Background Information" for the Quetico Park Master Plan (Toronto: Ontario Ministry of Natural Resources, July, 18, 2007): 2

PART ONE: ICE AGE LEGACY OF QUETICO PARK

CHAPTER 1: JOURNEY THROUGH THE ICE AGE

1. Philip Kor, senior conservation geologist for Ontario Parks; Brian Philips, retired geology professor, Lakehead University, Thunder Bay, Ontario; and Matthew Boyd, Department of Anthropology, Lakehead University, Thunder Bay, Ontario, were a valuable source of information and advice.

2. Grace Raynovich, "Extinct Bison Bones Dug Up Near Kenora," *Arch Notes, Ontario Archaeological Society Newsletter*, Vols. 80–83 (1980): 21.

3. Author's note: I first saw the antler in the mid-1970s when it was hanging in the entrance to the building that housed the Atikokan Library and Centennial Museum. The antler was mounted on a wooden plaque with an inscription indicating it came from the bottom of Steep Rock Lake. When I was a graduate student at Trent University in Peterborough, Ontario, in 1988, I became aware of the possible significance of this antler. I passed the information on to professors in the Anthropology Department who recognized the potential importance of this antler and obtained permission from the Atikokan Museum Board to have the antler carbon-dated.

4. Alfred Russel Wallace, *The Geographical Distribution of Animals*, Vol. 1 (London: Macmillan, 1876), 197.

CHAPTER 2: PALAEO-INDIANS — FIRST EXPLORERS OF THE QUETICO-SUPERIOR

1. William Ross, consulting archaeologist and former regional archaeologist for northern Ontario; Walt Okstad, historian/heritage program manager, Superior National Forest; Susan Mulholland, archaeology consultant in northern Minnesota; Tony Romano, archaeologist; Mike McCloud, archaeology consultant

in northwestern Ontario; Lee Johnson, archaeological technician, Superior National Forest; Bill Clayton, archaeological technician, Superior National Forest; all provided valuable background information and advice for this chapter.

2. James Adovasio and Jake Page, *The First Americans: In Pursuit of Archaeology's Greatest Mystery* (Chicago: Modern Library, 2003), 105.

3. Brian Fagan, *Ancient North America* (London: Thames and Hudson, 2005), 106.

4. Loren C. Eiseley, "The Paleo Indians: Their Survival and Diffusion," in *New Interpretations of Aboriginal American Cultural History* (Washington, D.C.: The Anthropological Society of Washington, 1971), 6.

5. "Woolly Mammoth Skeleton Wows Scientists," from http://www.cnn.com/2008/TECH/science/07/09/museum.mammoth.ap/ (accessed November 4, 2008).

6. Elaine Redepenning of Duluth, Minnesota, was a dedicated amateur archaeologist whose surface collection of artifacts from the Reservoir Lakes area north of Duluth became the primary source material for numerous articles and a book.

7. Mike McLeod, "The Paleo-Indian Tradition in the Thunder Bay Area, Earliest Evidence: Periglacial Peoples," in *The Deglaciation and Geoarchaeology of the Minnesota–Ontario Borderlands: A Fieldguide to the Excursions for the Midwest Friends of the Pleistocene, 47th Field Conference*, edited by B.A.M. Phillips and Mike McLeod (Thunder Bay: Department of Geology, Lakehead University, 2001).

8. Douglas Preston, "Clovis Hunters," foreword in *In Search of Ice Age Americans* by Kenneth Tankersley (Salt Lake City: Gibbs Smith, 2002), 9.

CHAPTER 3: THE FUTURE OF THE PAST IN QUETICO PARK — ARCHAEOLOGY AND ANISHINAABE SPIRITUAL BELIEFS

1. The chapter was written in collaboration with Andrew Hinshelwood, archaeological review officer, Ontario Ministry of Culture.

2. Luther Standing Bear, *Land of the Spotted Eagle* (Lincoln: University of Nebraska Press, 2006), 17.

3. Jane Jacobs, *Dark Age Ahead* (New York: Random House, 2004), 4.

4. Michael Budak, *Grand Mound* (St. Paul, MN: Minnesota Historical Society, 1995), 21.

5. N. Scott Momaday, "The Becoming of a Native" in *America in 1492*, edited by Alvin M. Josephy Jr. (New York: Vintage Press, 1993), 11.

6. Roger Anyon, T.J. Ferguson, Loretta Jackson, Lillie Lane, and Philipe Vicenti, "Native American Oral Tradition and Achaeology" in *Native Americans and Archaeologists: Stepping Stones to Common Ground*, edited by Nina Swidler (Lanham, MD: AltaMira Press, 1997), 78.

7. Ruth Gotthardt, archaeologist for the Yukon government, personal communication, July 17, 2008.

8. Doug Gilmore, park superintendant, Woodland Caribou Provincial Park, personal communication, August 24, 2008.

9. Richard K. Nelson. "Searching for the Lost Arrow: Physical and Spiritual Ecoogy in the Hunter's World" in *The Biophilia Hypothesis*, edited by Stephen Kellert and Edward O. Wison (Washington, D.C.: Island Press, 1997), 137.

10. Louise Erdrich, *Books and Islands in Ojibwa Country* (Washington, D.C.: National Geographic Society, 2003), 50.

11. Jon Nelson and Andrew Hinshelwood, "Understanding the Anishinawbe Landscape: Working with Lac La Croix Elders to Manage Quetico's Cultural Heritage," report submitted to the McLean Foundation, Sir Joseph Flavelle Foundation, and Friends of Quetico Park (August 2000): 14.

12. Doug Gilmore, park superintendent, Woodland Caribou Provincial Park, personal communication, August 22, 2008.

PART TWO: SPECIAL PLACES IN
QUETICO PARK

CHAPTER 4: "THE PINES" —
ANCIENT CAMPSITE ON PICKEREL LAKE

1. Sigurd Olson, "Young Ottertail" in *Listening Point* (Minneapolis: University of Minnesota Press, 1997), 89.
2. Sir George Simpson. *Narrative of a Journey Round the World, During the Years of 1841 and 1842*, Vol. 1 (London: H. Colborne, 1847), 39.
3. William Keating, *Narrative of an Expedition to the Source of St. Peter's River*, Vol. 2 (Minneapolis, MN: Ross & Haynes, Inc, 1959), 127.

CHAPTER 5: THE WAWIAG — RIVER WITH A PAST

1. Shan Walshe, "Wawiag River Community Complex," unpublished manuscript on file at the John B. Ridley Research Library, French Lake, Ontario, see page 16.
2. Jon Nelson, "Bill Muir: Quetico-Superior Botanist," *The Boundary Waters Journal,* Vol. 10, No. 4 (Spring 1997): 27.
3. E.J. Crossman, *Quetico Fishes* (Toronto: Royal Ontario Museum, 1976). 124.
4. Robert Readman, interviewed by Shan Walshe in March 1971. Interview on file at the John B. Ridley Library Research Library, Quetico Park Information Pavilion, French Lake, see page 1.
5. Bill Magie, *A Wonderful Country* (Ashland, WI: The Sigurd Olson Environmental Institute, Northland College, 1981), 30–32.

CHAPTER 6: KNIFE LAKE — VOLCANIC ROCKS AND REMARKABLE PEOPLE

1. Richard W. Ojakangas and Charles L. Matsch, *Minnesota's Geology* (Minneapolis, University of Minnesota Press, 1982), 184.
2. J.M. Clements, *The Vermillion Iron-Bearing District of Minnesota* (Washington D.C.: Monograph 45, United States Geological Survey, 1903), 135.
3. Personal communication with the council of Lac La Croix Elders in September 2000.
4. N.H. Winchell, *Eighth Annual Report for the Year 1879* (Minneapolis, MN: Minnesota Geological and Natural History Survey), 62.
5. J.M. Clements, *The Vermillion Iron-Bearing District of Minnesota* (Washington, D.C.: United States Geological Survey, 1903), 335 (Monograph 45).
6. For more information on Dorothy Molder, see Bob Cary, *Root Beer Lady* (Duluth, MN: Pfeifer-Hamilton, 1993).
7. James Wyatt, "Swimming Holes," in *Backpacker* vol.17, no. 5 (August 1989): 44.

CHAPTER 7: MCNIECE LAKE — HEART OF QUETICO PARK OLD-GROWTH

1. As quoted in Charles Wilkins, "The Mythic White Pine is in Trouble," in *Canadian Geographic*, Vol. 114, No. 5 (September/October 1994): 60.
2. Clifford Ahlgren, *Lob Trees in the Wilderness* (Minneapolis: University of Minnesota Press, 1984), 95.
3. Shan Walshe was the Quetico Park naturalist from 1970 until his death in 1991. An exceptional botanist and an outspoken advocate for wilderness, he was often referred to as the "conscience" of Quetico.
4. Willard Carmean, personal communication, March 2007.
5. For information on very old-growth trees elsewhere in Ontario, see Peter E. Kelly and Douglas W. Larson, *The Last Stand: A Journey Through the Ancient Cliff-Face Forest of the Niagara Escarpment* (Toronto: Natural Heritage/The Dundurn Group, 2007).
6. "Bear Hibernating in Bald Eagle's Nest," in *St. Paul Pioneer Press*, 17 March 2004.

7. Miron Heinselman, *The Boundary Waters Wilderness Ecosystem* (Minneapolis: University of Minnesota Press), 137.

8. Willard Carmean, "The Greenwood Lake Old-Growth White Pine Research and Education Reserve," background document written for the establishment and maintenance of a stand of old-growth white pine just east of Quetico Park, not dated.

CHAPTER 8: PRAIRIE PORTAGE — BOUNDARY WATERS CROSSROADS

1. Sigurd F. Olson, born in Chicago, Illinois, in 1899, was one of the most influential conservationists of the twentieth century. He died in 1982 after living much of his life in Ely, Minnesota. He wrote numerous books, including *Singing Wilderness* and *Reflections From the North Country* about the Quetico-Superior area.

2. Alexander Mackenzie, *The Journals and Letters of Sir Alexander Mackenzie*, edited by W. Kaye Lamb (Cambridge: Cambridge University Press, 1970), 103.

3. *Ibid*.

4. See Charles Gates, ed. *Five Fur Traders of the Northwest* (Minneapolis: University of Minnesota Press, 1933), 162.

5. Henry Longfellow excerpt, taken from J. McClatchy, compiler, *Henry Wadsworth Longfellow Poems And Other Writings* (New York: Library of America, 2000), 272.

6. Sigurd Olson, *Listening Point* (New York: Alfred A. Knopf, 1956), 142.

7. Shan Walshe, *Plants of Quetico and the Ontario Shield* (Toronto: University of Toronto Press, 1980), 118.

PART THREE: GLIMPSES INTO THE ECOLOGY OF QUETICO PARK

1. David Abram, *The Spell of the Sensuous* (New York: Knopf Publishing Group, 1997), 24.

2. John Muir, *My First Summer in the Sierra* (New York: Penguin, 1987), 114.

CHAPTER 9: SYMBIOSIS — REMARKABLE PARTNERS

1. Tom Wakeford, *Liaisons of Life* (New York: John Wiley and Sons, 2001), 40.

2. Berndt Heinrich, *The Mind of the Raven* (New York: HarperCollins, 1999), 194.

3. Richard K. Nelson, *Make Prayers to the Raven* (Chicago: University of Chicago Press, 1986), 212.

4. Lewis Thomas, "On the Uncertainty of Science," *Harvard Magazine*, Vol. 4, No.1 (September/October 1984): 22.

5. Lynn Margolis and Dorion Sagan, *Microcosmos: Four Billion Years of Evolution from Our Microbial Ancestors* (New York: Summit Press, 1986), 15.

CHAPTER 10: LICHENS — ENDURING, DELIGHTFUL, ORGANIC CRUD

1. H.G. Wells and Julian Huxley, *The Science of Life* (London, UK: The Literary Guild, 1934), 118.

2. Joe Walewski. *Lichens of the North Woods* (Duluth, MN: Kollath & Stensaas Publishing, 2007), 4.

3. Trevor Goward, quoted in http://www.lichen.com/biology.html (accessed on October 19, 2007).

4. Sir John Franklin led three expeditions to the Artic in attempts to discover and map the Northwest Passage. On his first expedition, they ran out of food and were on the verge of starvation. He recorded the following in his 1822 journal: "Previous to setting out, the whole party ate the remains of their old shoes, and whatever scraps of leather they had, to strengthen their stomachs for the fatigue of the day's journey.… The tripe-de-roche, even where we got enough, only serving to allay the pangs of hunger for a short time." For more information see, John Franklin, *The*

Journey to the Polar Sea (Westport, CT: Greenwood Press Reprint, 1969).

5. Sam Campbell, *A Tippy Canoe and Canada Too* (Indianapolis, IN: The Bobbs-Merrill Company, 1946), 224.

6. Henry David Thoreau, *Early Spring in Massachusetts: From the Journal of Henry David Thoreau* (Whitefish, MT: Kessinger Publishing Company, 2007): 64.

CHAPTER 11: THE ORCHID AND THE FUNGUS — SYMBIOTIC PARTNERS

1. Susan Orleans, *The Orchid Thief* (New York: Ballantine Books, 2000), 17.

2. Edward Culpeper, *Culpepers Complete Herbal Guide, 1653* (London, UK: Wordsworth Editions Ltd, 1995).

3. Information from Tom Wakeford, *Liaisons of Life* (New York: John Wiley and Sons, 2001), 40.

CHAPTER 12: ANTLER LOGIC — MOOSE RESEARCH IN QUETICO PARK

1. A. (Tony) B. Bubenik, foreword in *Moose Country: Saga of the Woodland Moose*, by Michael W.P. Runtz (Toronto: Stoddart Publishing Company Limited, 1991), xiii.

2. R. Gollat, H. R. Timmermann, J. McNicol, and M. Buss, *Moose Rut Dynamics Investigations, North Central Region* (Thunder Bay: Ontario Ministry of Natural Resources, 1981), 86.

3. George Bubenik and Peter Bubenik, "Palmated Antlers of Moose May Serve As a Parabolic Reflector of Sounds," *European Journal of Wildlife Research*, Vol. 54, No. 3 (August 2008): 94.

4. John Horton, "Moose Hearing Aids? CSU Professor Helps Show Antlers are Just That," in *The Cleveland Plain Dealer* (March 29, 2008): 17.

5. A. (Tony) B. Bubenik quoted in *Moose Country: Saga of the Woodland Moose*, by Michael W.P. Runtz (Toronto: Stoddart Publishing Company Limited, 1991): 78.

6. *Ibid.*, xiii.

CHAPTER 13: SNOWSHOES, BLACKFLIES, AND CARNIVOROUS PLANTS

1. Donald E. Schnell, *Carniverous Plants of the United States and Canada*, 2nd ed. (Portland, OR: Timber Press, 2002): 128.

2. Carl Zimmer, "The Processing Plant," *Discover Magazine* (September 1995): 94.

CHAPTER 14: A RAVEN'S KNOWLEDGE

1. Charles Wilkins, "The Bird the Haida Call the 'Trickster,'" *Canadian Geographic Magazine*, Vol. 114, No. 2 (March/April 1994): 74.

2. Fred Harrington, "Ravens Attracted to Wolf Howling," *Condor* (publication of the Cooper Ornithological Society), Vol. 80, No. 2 (1978): 837.

3. David Mech, *The Way of the Wolf* (Stillwater, MN: Voyageur Press, 1993): 4.

4. Richard K. Nelson, *Make Prayers to the Raven* (Chicago: University of Chicago Press, 1983), 17.

5. Bernd Heinrich, *Ravens in Winter* (New York: Summit Books, 1989), 64.

6. Sigurd Olson, "Birds of the Ski Trails" in *The Singing Wilderness* (New York: Alfred A. Knopf, 1957), 237.

7. Daniel A. Cristol and Paul V. Switzer, "Avian prey-dropping behavior. II. American crows and walnuts," *Behavioral Ecology*, Vol. 10, No. 3 (March 1999): 223.

8. Lawrence Kilham. *The American Crow and Common Raven* (College Station, TX: Texas A&M University Press, 1991), 241.

CHAPTER 15: FIERY INTERLUDES IN AN ENDLESS DANCE

1. Ted Williams, "Incineration of Yellowstone," in *Wildfire: A Reader*, edited by Alianor True (Washington D.C.: Island Press, 2001), 135.
2. Clifford Ahlgren and Isabelle Ahlgren, *Lob Trees in the Wilderness* (Minneapolis: University of Minnesota Press, 1984), 23.
3. Albert M. Swain, "A History of Fire and Vegetation in Northeastern Minnesota as Recorded in Lake Sediments," *Quaternary Research*, Vol. 3, No. 3 (1973): 395.
4. Miron L. Heinselman, "Fire in the Virgin Forests of the Boundary Waters Canoe Area," *Quaternary Research*, Vol. 3, No. 3 (1973): 343.
5. G.T. Woods and R.J. Day, *A Summary of the Fire Ecology Study of Quetico Provincial Park* (Toronto: Ontario Ministry of Natural Resources, 1977), 14.
6. Tim Lynham, personal communication, March 2008.
7. Miron L. Heinselman, "Fire in the Virgin Forests of the Boundary Waters Canoe Area," *Quaternary Research*, Vol. 3, No. 3 (1973): 329.
8. Richard Preston, *The Wild Trees: A Story of Passion and Daring* (New York: Random House, 2007), 12.

CHAPTER 16: TAILS BENEATH THE SNOW — LIFE IN THE PUKAK

1. Richard Conniff, "You Can Call Him Cute or You Can Call Him Hungry," *Smithsonian Magazine*, Vol. 28, No. 2 (February 1997): 53.
2. Carolyn M. King, "Weasel Roulette," *Natural History Magazine*, Vol. 100, No. 11 (November 1991): 37.
3. William O. Pruitt, "Life in the Snow," *Nature Canada*, Vol. 4, No. 4 (1975): 44.
4. *Ibid.*, 43.
5. Sigurd Olson, "Coming of the Snow" in *Singing Wilderness* (Minneapolis: University of Minnesota Press, 1997): 195.

CHAPTER 17: UNCOMMON SENSE — LIFE UNDER THE ICE

1. C.S. Wardle, "Effects of Temperature on the Maximum Swimming Speed of Fishes," in *Environmental Physiology of Fishes*, edited by M.A. Ali (New York: Plenum Press, 1980), 519–31.
2. Dwane Wilkin, Environmental News Network, "Half-frozen frogs have chilling tale to tell," posted October 26, 2000 (http://www.frogs.org/news/article.asp?CategoryID=1&InfoResourceID=518, accessed January 17, 2008).
3. Bernd Heinrich, *Winter World* (New York: HarperCollins, 2003), 175.
4. Richard Dawkins, *The Blind Watchmaker* (New York: W.W. Norton & Company, 1986), 140.

CHAPTER 18: FLOATERS, STILTERS, AND AGGRESSIVE PLANTS

1. Alaskan ecologists studying the interaction between vegetation and snowshoe hares came to some surprising conclusions that are summarized in the article found at http://www.wildlifenews.alaska.gov/index.cfm?adfg=wildlife_news.view_article&articles_id=339 (accessed March 3, 2008).
2. Henry David Thoreau, "A Winter Walk" in *Essays in Memory of Henry David Thoreau*, edited by Richard Dillman (Plymouth, UK: Rowman and Littlefield, 1990), 107.

CHAPTER 19: A COZY WINTER NEST
OF BEAVERS

1. Enos Mills, *In Beaver World* (Whitefish, MT: Kessinger
    Publishing, 1913), 123.
2. Peter Marchand, "Warm Welcome — Beaver Lodges,"
    Natural History, Vol. 100, No. 3 (March 2001): 22.
3. Peter C. Newman, "Canada's Fur-Trading Empire,"
    National Geographic, Vol. 173, No. 2 (August 1987): 367.
4. Dietland Muller-Schwarze and Lixing Sun, *The Beaver:
    Natural History of a Wetland Engineer* (Ithaca, NY:
    Cornell University Press, 2003): 18.

AFTERWORDS

1. Morgan Tamplin, personal communication, May 11,
    1988.
2. Gary Snyder, *Practice of the Wild* (New York: North Point
    Press, 1990), 39.
3. Jill Frayne, *Starting Out in the Afternoon* (Toronto:
    Vintage Press, 2002), 179.
4. Peder Sorenson, quoted in an address to Convocation
    at Memorial University of Newfoundland made by Dr.
    William O. Pruitt, Jr., on May 11, 2001, which was pub-
    lished on June 14, 2001, in *Gazette: A Memorial University
    of Newfoundland Publication*.

BIBLIOGRAPHY

PREFACE: QUETICO — ONE HUNDREDTH ANNIVERSARY OF A "MAGIC LAND"

Forester, Jeff. *The Forest For the Trees: How Humans Shaped the North Woods*. Minneapolis, Minnesota: Minnesota Historical Society Press, 2004.

Killan, Gerald. *Protected Places: History of Ontario's Provincial Park System*. Toronto: Dundurn Press, 1993.

Peruniak, Shirley. *Quetico Provincial Park: An Illustrated History*. Scarborough: Friends of Quetico Park, 2000.

Searle, R. Newell. *Saving Quetico-Superior: A Land Set Apart*. Minneapolis: Minnesota Historical Society Press, 1977.

Viita, Alan A. "Quetico-Atikokan: The Country Beyond." In *A History of Atikokan*. N.p., 1975.

Warecki, George M. *Protecting Ontario's Wilderness: A History of Changing Ideas and Preservation Politics, 1927–1973*. New York: Peter Lang, 2000.

PART ONE: ICE AGE LEGACY OF QUETICO PARK

CHAPTER 1: JOURNEY THROUGH THE ICE AGE

Flannery, Tim. *The Eternal Frontier: An Ecological History of North America and Its Peoples*. New York: Atlantic Monthly Press, 2001.

Goebel, Ted, Michael Waters, and Dennis O'Rourke. "The Late Pleistocenic Dispersal of Modern Humans in the Americas." *Science* No. 319 (March 14, 2008).

Jackson, Lawrence J. "Steep Rock and the Falls Bay Rangifer." *Arch Notes*, Vol. 88, No. 2 (March/April 1988).

Pielou, E. C. *After the Ice Age: The Return of Life to Glaciated North America*. Chicago: University of Chicago Press, 1991.

Teller, James T. and Harvey Thorleifsin. "The Lake Agassiz-Lake Superior Connection." In *Glacial Lake Agassiz*, edited by J.T. Teller and Lee Clayton. Geological Association of Canada Special Paper 26 (1983): 262–90.

Thorleifson, L.H., Geological Survey of Canada, 601 Booth Street, Ottawa, Ontario. http://www.geo.umn.edu/people/profs/thorleifson/review_lake_agassiz_history.pdf.

Ward, Peter D. *The Call of Distant Mammoths: Why The Ice Age Mammals Disappeared*. New York: Springer, 1998.

CHAPTER 2: PALAEO-INDIANS — FIRST EXPLORERS OF THE QUETICO-SUPERIOR

Adovasio, James and Jake Page, *The First Americans: In Pursuit of Archaeology's Greatest Mystery*. Chicago: Modern Library, 2003.

Fagan, Brian. *Ancient North America*. London: Thames and Hudson, 2005.

McLeod, Mike. "The Paleo-Indian Tradition in the Thunder Bay Area, Earliest Evidence: Periglacial Peoples." In *The Deglaciation and Geoarchaeology of the Minnesota–Ontario Borderlands: A Fieldguide to the Excursions for the Midwest Friends of the Pleistocene, 47th Field Conference*. Edited by B.A.M. Phillips and Mike McLeod. Thunder Bay: Department of Geology, Lakehead University, 2001.

Mulholland, Susan. "The Arrowhead Since the Glaciers: The Prehistory of Northeastern America." *Minnesota Archaeologist*, Vol. 59 (Fall 2000): 1–10.

Tankersley, Kenneth. *In Search of Ice Age Americans*. Salt Lake City: Gibbs Smith, Publisher, 2002.

CHAPTER 3: THE FUTURE OF THE PAST IN QUETICO PARK — ARCHAEOLOGY AND ANISHINAABE SPIRITUAL BELIEFS.

Berkes, Fikret. *Sacred Ecology: Traditional Ecological Knowledge and Resource Management*. Levittown, PA: Taylor & Francis, 1999.

Nelson, Jon and Andrew Hinshelwood. "Understanding the Anishinawbe Landscape: Working with Lac La Croix Elders to Manage Quetico's Cultural Heritage." Report submitted to the McLean Foundation, Sir Joseph Flavelle Foundation and Friends of Quetico Park, August 2000.

PART TWO: SPECIAL PLACES IN QUETICO PARK

CHAPTER 5: THE WAWIAG — RIVER WITH A PAST

Nelson, Jon. "Bill Muir: Quetico-Superior Botanist." *The Boundary Waters Journal*, Vol. 10, No. 4 (Spring 1997): 27.

CHAPTER 6: KNIFE LAKE — VOLCANIC ROCKS AND REMARKABLE PEOPLE

Cary, Bob. *Root Beer Lady*. Duluth: Pfeiffer-Hamilton Publishers, 1993.

Gruner, J.W. "Structural Geology of the Knife Lake Area of Northeastern Minnesota." Geological Society of America Bulletin, Vol. 52 (1941): 1577–1642.

Ojakangas, Richard W. and Charles L. Matsch. *Minnesota's Geology*. Minneapolis: University of Minnesota Press, 1982.

CHAPTER 7: MCNIECE LAKE — HEART OF QUETICO PARK OLD-GROWTH

Preston, Richard. *The Wild Trees: A Story of Passion and Daring*. New York: Random House, 2007.

CHAPTER 8: PRAIRIE PORTAGE — BOUNDARY WATERS CROSSROADS

Ahlgren, Clifford and Isabel Ahlgren. *Lob Trees in the Wilderness.* Minneapolis: University of Minnesota Press, 1984.

PART THREE: GLIMPSES INTO THE ECOLOGY OF QUETICO PARK

Abrams, David. *The Spell of the Sensuous.* New York: Knopf Publishing Group, 1997.

Heinselman, Miron L. *The Boundary Waters Wilderness Ecosystem.* Minneapolis: University of Minnesota Press, 1996.

CHAPTER 9: SYMBIOSIS — REMARKABLE PARTNERS

Douglas, Angela. *Symbiotic Associations.* Oxford: Oxford University Press, 1994.

Margulis, Lynn and Dorion Sagan. *Acquiring Genomes.* New York: Basic Books, 2002.

Margulis, Lynn. *Symbiosis As a Source of Evolutionary Innovation.* Boston: MIT Press, 1991.

Wakeford, Tom. *Liaisons of Life.* New York: John Wiley and Sons, 2001.

CHAPTER 10: LICHENS — ENDURING, DELIGHTFUL, ORGANIC CRUD

Brodo, Irwin M., Sylvia Duran Sharnoff, and Stephen Sharnoff. *Lichens of North America.* New Haven, CT: Yale University Press, 2001.

Campbell, Sam. *A Tippy Canoe and Canada Too.* New York: The Bobbs-Merrill Company, 1946.

Walewski, Joe. *Lichens of the North Woods.* Duluth, Kollath and Stensaas Publishing, 2007.

CHAPTER 11: THE ORCHID AND THE FUNGUS — SYMBIOTIC PARTNERS

Bernhardt, Peter. *Wiley Violets and Underground Orchids.* Chicago: University of Chicago Press, 2003.

Orleans, Susan. *The Orchid Thief.* New York: Ballantine Books, 2000.

Wakeford, Tom. *Liaisons of Life.* New York: John Wiley and Sons, 2001.

Walshe, Shan. *Plants of Quetico and the Ontario Shield.* Toronto: University of Toronto Press, 1980.

CHAPTER 12: ANTLER LOGIC — MOOSE RESEARCH IN QUETICO PARK

Brown, R.D., ed. *Antler Development in Cervidae.* A Proceedings of the First International Symposium of the Caesarkleberg Wildlife Research Institute. Kingsville, TX: College of Agriculture, Texas A&I University, 1989.

Bubenik, G.A. and A.B. Bubenik, eds. *Horns, Pronghorns, and Antlers: Evolution, Morphology, Physiology and Social Significance.* New York: Springer-Verlag, 1990.

Gollat, R., H.R. Timmermann, J. McNicol, M. Buss. *Moose Rut Dynamics Investigations, North Central Region.* Thunder Bay, ON: Ontario Ministry of Natural Resources, 1981.

Runtz, Michael W.P., *Moose Country: Saga of the Woodland Moose*. Toronto: Stoddard Company Limited, 1991.

CHAPTER 13: SNOWSHOES, BLACKFLIES, AND CARNIVOROUS PLANTS

Schnell, Donald E. *Carniverous Plants of the United States and Canada*, 2nd ed. Portland, OR: Timber Press, 1989.

Zimmer, Carl, "The Processing Plant." *Discover Magazine* (September 1995): 90–95.

CHAPTER 14: A RAVEN'S KNOWLEDGE

Elder, Dave. *Birds of Quetico Park and the Atikokan Area*. Atikokan, ON: Friends of Quetico Park, 1989.

Heinrich, Bernd. *Ravens in Winter*. New York: Summit Books, 1989.

Kilham, Lawrence. *The American Crow and Common Raven*. College Station, TX: Texas A&M University Press, 1991.

Mech, David. *The Wolf: The Ecology and Behavior of an Endangered Species*. Minneapolis: University of Minnesota Press, 1981.

Nelson, Richard K. *Make Prayers to the Raven*. Chicago: University of Chicago Press, 1983.

CHAPTER 15: FIERY INTERLUDES IN AN ENDLESS DANCE

Forester, Jeff. *The Forest for the Trees: How Humans Shaped the North Woods*. Minneapolis: Minnesota Historical Society Press, 2004.

Heinselman, Miron L. *The Boundary Waters Wilderness Ecosystem*. Minneapolis: University of Minnesota Press, 1996.

Heinselman, Miron L. "Fire in the Virgin Forests of the Boundary Waters Canoe Area." *Quaternary Research*, Vol. 3, No. 3 (1973).

Henry, J. David. *Canada's Boreal Forest*. Washington, D.C.: Smithsonian Institution Press, 2002.

Lynham, Timothy J. "Vegetation Recovery after Wildfire in Old-Growth Red and White Pine." *Frontline Express Bulletin*, No. 31, from http://cfs.nrcan.gc.ca/news/261.

Swain, Albert M. "A History of Fire and Vegetation in Northeastern Minnesota as Recorded in Lake Sediments." *Quaternary Research*, Vol. 3, No. 3, University of Washington (1973).

Whelan, Robert K. *The Ecology of Fire*. Cambridge, UK: Cambridge University Press, 1995.

Woods, G.T. and R.J. Day. *A Summary of the Fire Ecology Study of Quetico Provincial Park*. Toronto: Ontario Ministry of Natural Resources, 1977.

CHAPTER 16: TAILS BENEATH THE SNOW — LIFE IN THE PUKAK

Marchand, Peter. *Life in the Cold: An Introduction to Winter Ecology*. Hanover, NH: University Press of New England, 1991.

Pruitt, William O. *Wild Harmony: Animals of the North*. Vancouver: Douglas & McIntyre, 1990.

CHAPTER 17: UNCOMMON SENSE — LIFE UNDER THE ICE

Bronmark, Christer and Lard-Anders Hansson. *The Biology of Lakes and Ponds.* Oxford, UK: Oxford University Press, 1998.

CHAPTER 18: FLOATERS, STILTERS, AND AGGRESSIVE PLANTS

Halpenny, James, C. and Roy Douglas Ozanne. *Winter: An Ecological Handbook.* Boulder, CO: Johnson Publishing Company, 1989.

CHAPTER 19: A COZY WINTER NEST OF BEAVERS

Dugmore, A. Radcliff. *The Romance of the Beaver.* From http://www.kellscraft.com/RomanceoftheBeaver/ RomanceoftheBeaverContentPage.html.

Gould, James R. and Carol Grant Gould. *Animal Architects.* New York: Basic Books, 2007.

Muller-Schwarze, Dietland and Lixing Sun. *The Beaver: Natural History of a Wetland Engineer.* Ithaca, NY: Cornell University Press, 2003.

INDEX

ABOUT THE AUTHOR

After growing up in Minnesota, Jon Nelson and his wife Marie moved to Atikokan in northwestern Ontario to live in what seemed to be, and turned out to be, the ideal place for them. A few years later they were hired as Quetico Park rangers and spent twelve marvellous summers in the park. When the May-to-September work schedule became difficult with two school-age children to raise, Jon decided to go back to school. He was then able to spend six summers as an archaeologist in the park, trying to decipher a little of Quetico's past, while teaching at Confederation College in Thunder Bay during the winter. His involvement in the Native Studies program as well as his biology and chemistry teaching enabled Jon to apply much of what he had learned in Quetico.

This is Jon Nelson's first book, a work celebrating the Quetico Park he reveres and where he now spends as much time as possible. From Jon's perspective, the numerous people who have encouraged and assisted him in writing this book confirms that Quetico's magic is matched by the generosity of the people who love it.